MW01132245

Making the Whole Person Whole:

Papers and Presentations on Religion, Ethics, and Medicine

by Jack W. Provonsha

Making the Whole Person Whole:

Papers and Presentations on Religion, Ethics, and Medicine

by Jack W. Provonsha

Edited by

David R. Larson

Loma Linda University
Center for Christian Bioethics

 Unless otherwise indicated, all Scripture quotations are from the King James Version of the Bible.

For information contact:
Center for Christian Bioethics
Centennial Complex Suite 3227
24760 Stewart Street
Loma Linda, California 92354

First Edition: October 2018

Printed in the United States.

10 9 8 7 6 5 4 3 2 1

To Lorraine and Margaret

Table of Contents

Preface

"Let Jack be Jack!" This was our mantra as we prepared most of Doctor Provonsha's papers and presentations for publication. Although this was usually easy, sometimes it was a challenge. This was especially so with his insistence on using words like "man" when he meant "human" or "humanity." Several of us remonstrated with him about this over the years with no success.

Provonsha was fond of Loma Linda University's motto, "To Make Man Whole," and this contributed to his reluctance to make the change. University leaders now talk more about "continuing the teaching and healing ministry of Jesus." This would have pleased him as well because he believed that Jesus, not Hippocrates, was the true father of the "spirit," albeit not the methods, of contemporary medicine. Yet he would have been nostalgic about the theme of "Making the Whole Man Whole," as he often put it.

Before he died, he left with me some papers and presentations that he asked me to turn into a book. I agreed to do so. However, instead of working with the ones he gave me, which weren't his best work because of his age and increasing consequences of Parkinsonism, I went back to a larger collection of his somewhat earlier efforts which were already in my possession. The result is a larger and more representative collection.

My goal was to shorten each paper or presentation by at least thirty percent, which is every editor's hope, and I reached it. I did not change what Provonsha had to say or how he said it. I am confident of this because he was pleased with earlier things edited for him. "You understand me," he said.

"Let Jack be Jack!" meant including some things I would have preferred to leave out. That in this book he says some things he himself probably would not put the same way today is not the problem. It is that for years we openly disagreed on some issues and about them I still think he was mistaken. Yet I remain convinced of the value of his overall point of view and how he typically related it to practical issues.

This is a long way of saying something which is too important to be passed over without much thought. Although this book is published by the Center for Christian Bioethics at Loma Linda University Health, it does not necessarily reflect the views of any of the University's units, administration, Board of Trustees, or any person who is affiliated with any of them. Because I disagreed with Provonsha on some things, I am certain that others will too, even though they probably won't be the same ones. This is how it should be.

I do not recommend reading this book "straight through." Reading the first biographical chapters by James Walters and me, and then the last autobiographical ones by Provonsha, provides a good overview of his life and thought. Having done this, it might be best to read those chapters here and there which seem most interesting.

There is much repetition in these chapters. This is because their purpose is to display the different ways he employed Ellen White's statement that human beings are created in the Image of God "with the power to think and to do." Educators often put the whole of the paragraph to which this belongs to good pedagogical use. Provonsha made it his primary ethical resource as well. This is worked out theoretically in his *Christian Ethics in a Situation of Change* that the Center for Christian Bioethics also plans to publish.

David R. Larson
October, 2018

Acknowledgments

Many gifted and giving people helped make this book possible. Those whose generosity established the Loma Linda University Center for Christian Bioethics come first to mind. Many contributed in order to establish the Jack and Margaret Provonsha Endowment which will support the Center in perpetuity. The Cafferky Endowment will long help the Center in the same way. The name of the Center's Ralph and Carolyn Thompson Library honors two people whose financial and other types of support was amazingly strong and steady from when the Center was only an idea until now. Many bioethics institutes and centers have come and gone over the years. This one has thrived, and this is only because of the continuing support of generous friends.

Each of the Center's Directors or Co-Directors from the Loma Linda University School of Religion have made major contributions. Mark Carr, who succeeded me in leading the Center, arranged for all the typed manuscripts to be digitalized. He also began editing some of the papers. Roy Branson followed Mark

Carr. He and his Assistants, John Lou and Alice Ing, helped me think through different ways of selecting and arranging the material. They also gave me various production schedules which I experienced as easier for them to make than for me to keep. James Walters, who with me and Doctor Provonsha were the Center's three Co-Founders, succeeded Roy Branson. In addition to consulting his own memory, he did important research that recovered much of the Center's history. He also wrote the only analysis and appraisal of Provonsha's published books that I know of. Walters is one of the persons without whom there would be no Center. Gerald Winslow is the Center's current Director. In addition to "proofing" the manuscript at least twice, he allocated the financial resources and applied the administrative skill, which finally brought the project to a conclusion. His Administrative Liaison, MaryJane Rasnic, and his Graduate Assistant, Adam Borecky, who earned a MA degree in bioethics at LLU between his third and fourth years of medical school, helped tie things up. In addition to proofreading the whole manuscript more than once, Borecky swiftly mastered the computer program InDesign in order to format it. He also created the index, remaining his typical cheerful self—ebullient, actually—even though our last minute changes were many.

Others worked even more directly on the text. Early on, Gayle Foster inched her way through the manuscripts, some of which were then still mimeographed, and made some initial recommendations. Beverly Rumble, an accomplished editor in Maryland, did much of the heavy lifting in the middle of the project. Her contribution was huge. Bronwen Fae Watts Larson, to whom I am fortunately married, worked her way through the entire manuscript several times, chapter-by-chapter, as I completed each draft. She had been very attentive to Provonsha in the last portion of his life and working on this book after he died was one more of her many gifts to him. He was grateful for her generosity and said so. Under the circumstances, what she did for him amazed many and me most of all.

Linda Sorter, a teacher, who is Provonsha's daughter with his first wife Lorraine, was a much needed source of information and joyfulness at critical junctures. She also worked through an early draft and made beneficial recommendations. That James Sorter, her husband and true companion, died unexpectedly not long before this book was published is most unfortunate.

This anthology is dedicated to Provonsha's two wives who preceded him in death. Lorraine was his companion in his younger years and Margaret was the same throughout most of his adult life. He truly loved them both and they did him.

Part I

Introductions

1
Perspectives

James W. Walters

Jack W. Provonsha was one of the most significant theologians in the Seventh-day Adventist church in the last century.[1] He filled various roles—religion professor, consultant to church administrators for over a quarter century, author of scores of essays and five books, and teacher of a popular Sabbath School class whose tapes were distributed worldwide.[2]

His impact on his church transcended individual roles; his spiritual ethos was an intellectual integrity that allowed the next generation of Adventist theologians to stand on his shoulders. He saw himself, as he put it, standing on the "giant shoulders" of the Adventist pioneers[3] as others did on his.

---

[1]Raymond F. Cottrell, keen observer of Adventism, lists the three most influential theologians of the 20th century church as M.L. Andreasen, Edward Heppenstall, and Gerhard Hasel. He'd put Provonsha in the top five.

[2]The Sabbath School class was perhaps Provonsha's most influential platform because it advanced progressive Adventist theology at a time when many well-read Adventists needed a charismatic and credible mentor.

[3]Jack W. Provonsha, *A Remnant in Crisis* (Washington, D.C.: Review and Herald Publishing Association, 1993), 21.

This anthology of some of Provonsha's most outstanding lectures is highly appropriate, debuting a third of a century after he, Dave Larson and I began dreaming of an ethics center at Loma Linda University, one which Provonsha would come to direct for its first two years just before his retirement. Beyond his immeasurable influence on perhaps nine thousand students at Loma LindaUniversity, at least three aspects of his work at the university endure: The Center for Christian Bioethics, which he founded, his lectures (as represented in this volume), and his books. In this reflective essay, I'll first address the Center and then focus on his most significant book publications.

Provonsha's Center

The LLU Center for Christian Bioethics' roots go back to at least 1982. Provonsha had been at LLU for twenty-four years at that time, Dave Larson had been teaching at LLU for eight years, and I had only been at LLU for two. Provonsha was the "Big Ethicist" on campus—and rightfully so. He was a physician, having received his MD from LLU in 1953. He was a theological ethicist, having attended Harvard for graduate study, finishing his PhD at Claremont Graduate School in 1967. Sixty-two years of age when the Center began, he was a mature and popular Adventist thinker whose students packed into the School of Religion amphitheater on the second floor of Griggs Hall. Further, his Sabbath School class, meeting in Randall Visitors Center, was well attended. Both Larson and I coveted the opportunities when we would be asked to teach that class in his absence.

He had a special mystique. He would appear at his well-attended Sabbath School classes just before it was time to begin and swiftly after the session was over, he largely disappeared from campus to his rural home in Yucaipa. He was essentially above the give-and-take of campus life; his lack of familiarity contributed to his image of reverence, even awe, at the University.

He was a scholar and intellectual path-maker in Adventism who sometimes ruffled church administration's feathers. For example, I recall that once he was summoned to an out-of-town meeting with church administrators and Andrews University Seminary professor Gerhard Hasel for a "discussion" of his recently published 1982 book, *You Can Go Home Again* (Review and Herald, 1982). Regardless, he was a godsend to LLU faculty and students who were attempting to reconcile traditional Adventist views of inspiration and revelation with the science they were teaching and learning in their classes.

Despite his great strengths, Provonsha was more of a dreamer than an organizer. Enter Dave and Jim, a couple of "thirty-somethings." We saw the need for an Adventist ethics institution—given that the pioneering Hastings Center in New York had been founded over a decade earlier, followed shortly by the Kennedy Institute of Ethics Center at Georgetown University. Given Provonsha's pioneering of bioethics at LLU since 1958 (natural for him, with both a PhD and MD, but still avant-garde), it just seemed appropriate that Loma Linda University, as the leading Adventist health-related institution of higher learning, should establish a special bioethics focus.

Dave and I initially brainstormed about a plan that we'd pitch to him, at first debating whether we should recommend a center or a lectureship. Either choice would be established in close collaboration with Provonsha and incorporate him as Director, if he'd desire. It didn't take long for the two young guys to agree on the need for a Center, and we broached this to Doctor Provonsha, who readily agreed, stating that LLU needed a *Christian* Bioethics Center. Later he would say that "The Center is like a 3-piece suit: Dave and Jim are the trousers and coat; I'm the vest that gets all the gravy."

Dave and I, working with him, came up with the original proposal—a 4-page concept paper that won approval by what is now the School of Religion and University leadership, and finally went to the LLU Board of Trustees. We made the proposal as persuasive as possible, beginning by quoting then General Conference president, Neal C. Wilson, who a couple of years earlier had called for Adventist leadership in all things medical, including bioethics.

Even so, the proposal was not initially voted by the Board

because ethics was still a questionable discipline in Adventism. General Conference leaders, who dominated Board proceedings, warned the Center staff that the Center would not speak on ethical matters for the church! In August 1983, the Board approved the Center, with the stipulation that $100,000 must be raised before its doors could be opened. That amount was raised by January 1, 1984, and the Center was officially in business.

Provonsha was the Center's Director, and he served in that capacity until he retired in 1985. I vividly recall his retirement announcement at one of our weekly religion faculty meetings. Without fanfare he calmly announced that he'd be retiring, giving a couple of reasons: (1) he wanted to give more attention to writing and publishing, and (2) his forebears were not long lived.

Provonsha was a very private person and perhaps the religion Dean knew of his impending retirement. I, along with most other faculty members, were stunned that this theological-ethical giant would be stepping down from his academic post at the height of his intellectual powers.

Having served as Associate Director for two years, upon Provonsha's retirement in 1985, Dave became the Director, and then Theological Co-Director with Doctor Robert Orr as Clinical Co-Director, for a total of 17 years until 2002. He then passed on leadership to Mark Carr, a former pastor in Alaska (like Provonsha before him), who had recently completed a PhD in religious ethics at the University of Virginia. Mark led the Center for eight years, followed by the late Roy Branson who served as Director, as well as the School of Religion Academic Dean, until his untimely death in 2015. I was happy to serve as Interim Director for a year, but always was more interested in the practice of ethics in policy formation, establishing other institutions, programs and scholarship. In July, 2016 Gerald Winslow, the former School of Religion Dean, assumed the directorship.

Although Provonsha served as Director of the Center for only a couple of years, what he set into motion has not only endured, but thrived. Yes, it began with an idea—really a vision—but in part it has been money that has, by design, ensured that it would continue.

In the first couple of years, the Center's founders raised well over a half million dollars. Provonsha and I visited centers of Adventist medical excellence (e.g., Hinsdale, Illinois and Orlando, Florida), speaking to gatherings of physicians about what the Center for Christian Bioethics could become. Most funds went into a general endowment, but others went into special endowments, such as the Ladd Endowment, set up by Dr. Ronald and Mrs. Anita Cafferky, in the name of Anita's parents.

Among the Center's accomplishments are:

- The Ralph and Carolyn Thomson Library, housed in the School of Religion, and overseen by the Center's director. For years, Dave liked to report that our library was "the best bioethics library in the West." Carolyn took an early interest in the Center, not only serving on its board, but with her husband funding this fine library.
- *Update*, a quarterly publication featuring news about the Center along with academic and clinical ethics articles produced by ethics faculty and visiting lecturers. For years, at ethics professional meetings, we LLU ethicists would get positive comments on *Update*, sent gratis to over a thousand bioethicists across the nation.
- The case of Baby Fae, in which Doctor Leonard Bailey transplanted a baboon heart into the chest of a human infant, put Loma Linda University Medical Center on the international map. It also gave Provonsha and us academic ethicists the opportunity to address the related bioethical issues. In this connection, I published a protocol for appropriate use of anencephalic infants as organ sources.
- Bioethics Grand Rounds began as monthly noon sessions in the A-Level Amphitheater in the Loma Linda University Medical Center in 1985, and it continues as a periodic focus on pressing issues of the day in bioethics. It has always been produced for the larger academic and clinical community—all LLU students, all LLUMC staff, as well as community guests.
- The Jack W. Provonsha Lectureship was begun in 1988,

and this annual event—open to the public—has featured such guests as geriatric-researcher Joanne Lynn, and prolific bioethics author Tristram Engelhardt, Jr.

- The Clinical Ethics Service provides bioethics consultations for challenging cases that constantly occur in the LLUMC. The service began with the Center's Clinical Co-Director Robert Orr, MD. Now, five physicians, most of whom took a two-year fellowship with Orr, continue the service under the leadership of Dr. Grace Oei.
- Loma Linda's Center joined with the nation's leading bioethics think-tank, the Hastings Center (New York), in co-sponsoring a conference at Loma Linda, "Biomedical Ethics Today: Old Models and New," in 1985. I edited the conference papers and published them with the title, *Bioethics Today: A New Ethical Vision* (Loma Linda University Press, 1988).
- The Center convened a conference on nuclear ethics in the Loma Linda University Church in 1986, with cosponsors such as the Interfaith Center to Reverse the Arms Race (Pasadena) and Physicians for Social Responsibility (Riverside/San Bernardino chapter). I edited the resulting anthology *War No More? Options in Nuclear Ethics* (Fortress Press, 1989).
- In 1988, the Center convened an international conference at Loma Linda deliberately featuring the varied and sometimes conflicting views on abortion in the Seventh-day Adventist church. This conference resulted in the book, *Abortion: Ethical Issues and Options* (Center for Christian Bioethics, 1992), which Dave edited. The conference and book helped lead the church's General Conference to give further study to the topic and issue updated guidelines.
- Funded by the National Endowment for the Humanities, the Center convened a conference on ethics and aging that fostered discussions of health care allocation in times of increasing scarcity. The conference associated with this project resulted in two books. Gerald Winslow and I ed-

ited *Facing Limits: Ethics and Health Care for the Elderly* (Westview, 1993). I edited *Choosing Who's to Live: Ethics and Aging* (University of Illinois, 1996).

- Charles Teel, Jr. convened a conference which explored the ethical implications of a number of Seventh-day Adventist doctrines. He edited *Remnant and Republic: Adventist Themes for Personal and Social Ethics* (Center for Christian Bioethics, 1995).
- The Center convened a conference on "Eschatology and Bioethics" with papers which are still to become chapters in a book.
- In January 2006, Dave collaborated with the Association of Adventist Forums and Seventh-day Adventist Kinship International in convening an interdisciplinary conference on homosexuality. He, David Ferguson, and Fritz Guy edited its papers for a book, *Christianity and Homosexuality: Some Seventh-day Adventist Perspectives* (Adventist Forum, 2008).
- At least twice, Mark Carr expanded the Jack W. Provonsha Lecture into a year-long series of presentations by people with a variety of perspectives from all over the nation which he connected to a seminar he was leading for graduate students in ethics. The first collection of essays is titled *Physician Assisted Suicide: Religious Perspectives on Death with Dignity* (Wheatmark, 2010). The second series will soon be published with the title of *On the Moral Status of the Human Embryo*.

In addition to these books, the LLU professors who participated in the Center's life made many public presentations, appeared in many media events, and published many articles.

Provonsha's Books

The first thing to be said about Provonsha's doctoral dissertation and his published books is that they are more about philosophy of religion and theology than ethics, and when he wrote about ethics he wrote about Christian ethics. This is because he was foremost a theological ethicist. Good ethics flows from good theology, and the latter was Provonsha's emphasis. A second aspect of his books is their distinctively Adventist thrust.

An analysis of Provonsha's major books portrays him as increasingly espousing his Adventist roots. He used his considerable talents to elaborate—for the contemporary, professionally educated person—a more intellectually palatable version of Adventism. Interestingly, his only book written and published after his retirement was *A Remnant in Crisis* (Review and Herald Publishing Association, 1983), and it is about contemporary Adventism.

Perhaps the greatest slight to a theologian is for his or her writings to be ignored. In the publication of this volume, we will honor Provonsha, in part, by not only recognizing his significant publications, but by hazarding an overall interpretation.

I will focus on his four major books because these represent his opportunity to develop most fully his settled convictions, as opposed to his essays and many important oral presentations which are more informal and may represent more experimental or rhetorical interests. These four books span twenty-six of his most productive years.

Christian Ethics in a Situation of Change, which was drawn from his dissertation, is a manuscript on Christian ethical theory.[4] *God is with Us* (Review and Herald, 1974) articulates a Christian understanding of deity. *You Can Go Home Again* (Review and Herald, 1982) is a volume on the atonement. *A Remnant in Crisis* (Review and Herald, 1993), is on Adventist "specialness."

An analysis of his major works suggests an Adventist who helpfully imbibed of mainstream, even liberal ethical and theological thinking, but who was increasingly drawn to his own religious roots.

Two concerns that were central to his writing—love and epistemology—were vital to the mainline theological ethicists and thinkers whom he had read and studied in graduate school.

---

[4]Jack Provonsha, *Christian Ethics in a Situation of Change* (Published by the author, 1967).

How We Love

Christian love remained the central, unchanging constant for Provonsha. In *Christian Ethics in a Situation of Change,*[5] he concluded that every decision must be made on the basis of "whether it is *ultimately* for or against love."[6] Near the conclusion of *Remnant*, 26 years later, he claimed that the "finishing of the work" will come when "all can see the difference between self-service and sacrificial love."[7]

In using the New Testament motif of love, more specifically *agape*, as the fundamental principle in his work, he was in keeping with a key theme of long standing. He drew on a variety of works: Anders Nygren had published his influential *Agape and Eros* in 1953.[8] Love was the touchstone of Paul Ramsey's 1950 *Basic Christian Ethics.*[9] Love was a significant theme of Paul Lehmann.[10] Provonsha completed his dissertation in 1967, the same year that Gene Outka completed his work on the same topic—*agape.*[11] The previous year Joseph Fletcher's popular *Situation Ethics*[12] was published, and this work was widely and appreciatively cited by Provonsha.

---

[5]This manuscript is the theological heart of Provonsha's doctoral dissertation, "An Appraisal of the Hallucinogenic Drugs from the Standpoint of a Christian Person-Agapeic Ethic" PhD diss. (Claremont Graduate School, 1967). The manuscript consists of the introduction and final three chapters (14, 15, and 16) of the dissertation. Provonsha excluded many pages that dealt with the drug problem itself. Provonsha's curriculum vitae indicates that this manuscript was the core of a planned, larger project. The text of Provonsha's that I am using is essentially a re-numbered photocopy of key sections of the 1967 dissertation. Henceforth, I will refer to this manuscript as *Ethics.*

[6]*Ethics,* 6.

[7]*Remnant,* 147.

[8]Anders Nygren, *Agape and Eros* (Chicago: University of Chicago Press, 1982).

[9]Paul Ramsey, *Basic Christian Ethics.* Library of Theological Ethics (Philadelphia: Westminster/John Knox Press, 1993).

[10]Paul Lehmann, *Ethics in a Christian Context.* Library of Theological Ethics (Philadelphia: Westminster/John Knox Press, 2006).

[11]Gene Outka, *Agape, An Ethical Analysis* (New Haven and London: Yale University Press, 1972).

[12]Joseph Fletcher, *Situation Ethics: The New Morality,* 2nd edition. (Philadelphia: Westminster/John Knox Press, 1997).

Using Paul Tillich's four terms rather than Nygren's two, and siding with Tillich[13] against Nygren[14] in emphasizing their continuity rather than their discontinuity, Provonsha defined *agape* (as distinguished from *eros, philia* and *epithymia*) as "spontaneous and underived" love of the other, and wholly of divine origin. However, the crucial human role is in providing the occasion or situation for *agape's* reign. Only "the right action, the loving action, will be the one rendering agape possible."[15] Whether a person opts for this loving action is totally up to the person; more specifically, it involves a person's freedom to choose.

Provonsha was emphatic and extensive in his treatment of human freedom. He declared that *agape* "presupposes" human freedom, and here he doesn't mean some carefully nuanced philosophical category, but the "old-fashioned" kind.[16] He saw freedom as a natural part of the human being, as "something inherent in man qua man."[17]

The importance of freedom to him can hardly be over-emphasized.[18] The essential notion is that human beings, created in God's image, are innately endowed with a freedom to choose good or evil, right or wrong. The very idea of self-less love for God and others is dependent on a person being able to consciously and freely choose such love. If freedom is an illusion, the idea of a loving action is meaningless.

He held that one's capacity for moral choice is nothing less than that of divine agency, a capacity given in human creation by God. Here he followed Reinhold Niebuhr who emphasized the

[13]Paul Tillich, *Love, Power and Justice: Ontological Analyses and Ethical Applications* (Oxford: Oxford University Press, 1960).

[14]Nygren, Ibid.

[15]*Ethics,* 6.

[16]*Ethics,* 25.

[17]*Ethics,* 28. Provonsha rejected freedom as absence of coercion, supposedly held to by Hobbes, Edwards. Russell; and Sidgwick. He also questioned freedom as an acquired quality, as coming from human achievement or divine grace.

[18]In chapter two of the 1967 manuscript, entitled "The Agape Premise—the Free Agent," seven of eight subsections deal with freedom, e.g. freedom and determinism, freedom as 'creative self', freedom and destiny, freedom and agape. Discussion of freedom and its implications take up fully half of this manuscript.

human capacity for self-transcendence.[19]

Humans, like lower animals, are often driven by instincts and natural proclivities. But only human beings can deliberate and responsibly decide. He cited Paul Tillich who wrote that humans have such freedom that "'man is free even from his freedom; that is, he can surrender his humanity.'"[20] He nevertheless personally told me that the writings of Ellen G. White, Adventism's most influential author, had profoundly informed his substantive thought.[21]

How We Know

Doctor Provonsha was particularly indebted to contemporary thought for a key element of his epistemology, the study of how we know. Here he unapologetically invoked metaphor and symbol as the only means we have for talking of God and also for understanding the significance of Christ's salvific death.

Following Tillich,[22] he distinguished sign from symbol. Whereas a sign is arbitrarily chosen to designate its subject, a symbol partakes in the reality toward which it points. He frequently cited the Sabbath as possessing important symbolic qualities.[23] But in regard to God, "all" that man can say is symbolic.

His modesty about what can be said about God went further. He recognized that we humans read into our ideas of God our own

---

[19]Reinhold Niebuhr, *The Nature and Destiny of Man: A Christian Interpretation* (Philadelphia: Westminster/John Knox Press, 1996), vol I, 3-56.
[20]Tillich as quoted by Provonsha, *Ethics,* 43; cf. 49.
[21]Often in Provonsha's writing there is a reference to conscious thought and action as distinctive of humans. For example, he speaks of love as constituting "the highest function of human reason and action—a unique quality of man as man. It is this capacity in man which dignifies him as man, as a person—the bearer of the divine image." *An Appraisal of the Hallucinogenic Drugs, 293-4.* One is reminded of Ellen White's often-repeated definition of what it means to be created in the image of God: "Every human being...is endowed with a power akin to that of the Creator—individuality, power to think and to do." *Education* (Mountain View, CA: Pacific Press, 1903, 1952), 17.
[22]Paul Tillich, *Dynamics of Faith* (San Francisco: HarperOne, 2009), 47-62.
[23]*God is with Us,* 34-38.

"need and wish fulfillment." This notion was expressed elsewhere by his view that our "creative memories" are often at work in our re-creation of the past. We humans adapt things as they once were to "the deeper needs of the present. We do not see things as they *are* or even as they *were*. We see them as *we* are."[24] He confessed that some of the old ideas are more "emotionally and intellectually satisfying."[25]

Another word for symbol is "event-window."[26] He saw various Hebrew rituals as such windows—the ancient Day of Atonement, the heavenly sanctuary, and particularly the Sabbath.[27]

Significantly, at times, Provonsha embraced socio-historical criticism to expose deficient ways we sometimes come to knowledge. In his treatment of various atonement theories, he more than once explained how a thinker came to a particular emphasis by showing the dominant form of government that was then in place. For instance, he explained Anselm's theory of the "satisfaction" of God, as a result of the socio-political milieu in which sin was analogous to a serf dishonoring his feudal lord and either accepting punishment or providing an alternate satisfaction.[28] He contended that we can learn about God, at least provisionally, "by beholding man."[29] We learn such things as God's unity, his personhood, and his goodness.

He saw the New Testament writers using a variety of metaphors to describe the significance of Christ's death and resurrection. None of them are satisfactory to the event; they are all symbols or event-windows that illuminate but do not fully disclose. The problem is that theologians have taken them literally and drawn too much from the mere symbols. They didn't realize that the New Testament writers were using, as we all use, "ant language."

[24]*God is with Us,* 68 (Provonsha's emphasis). Eight years later nearly identical words were used: We see things "not as they are, but in terms of what we are." *Home Again,* 21 (again, Provonsha's emphasis).
[25]*God is with Us,* 7.
[26]*Home Again,* 103.
[27]Ibid.
[28]*Home Again,* 28.
[29]*God is with Us,* 46.

Jack Provonsha: Adventist Thinker

Some professional theologians are personal atheists. Others are personal believers and active churchmen. Provonsha was a professional theologian who believed not only as a Christian but also as an unapologetic Adventist.

He grappled with the human craving for certainty and the natural sciences' ability to provide it, albeit about the mundane matters of existence. The further we get from quantifiable processes, the less certain we are. Thus, as he said, the behavioral sciences and even more so theology do not provide such certainty.[30] We can know nothing with absolute certainty in philosophy. The best knowledge is more or less probable. "Rational certainty is an impossibility," he declared. "Only faith knows for sure!"[31]

Accordingly, Provonsha wrote his final three books from within his faith experience. He hadn't forgotten or forsaken his former theological insights and convictions, but they were increasingly secondary to his lived Adventist faith. And it is "God" whom Provonsha experienced as an Adventist believer; it is "god" whom he knows as a mainline theologian. It's not that these are two separate beings.

Provonsha saw them as complementary; "god" is an idea, albeit a grand idea, that emerges from one's study of nature—a god of wisdom, design, order, power, and existence. These are important general concepts, but they fall far short of the God of the Bible, a God of revelation who acts as a person, and does not exist as a mere concept.[32] "Behind the what is a who."[33]

An Evolving Focus

Provonsha was explicitly confessional in *God is With Us* and *You Can Go Home Again*. He called the latter an "un-theology." Here he avoided hair-splitting "conceptual clarity" in his passion to confess his faith in God's mysterious saving act. If he needed to engage in

---

[30]*Ethics,* 30; *Home Again,* 22.
[31]*Home Again,* 22.
[32]*God is with Us,* 40.
[33]*God is with Us,* 64.

some "shortfall theologizing" along the way, it was merely "to create the setting for the confession."[34]

In turning toward more specifically Adventist issues in his books, the progression is gradual. For instance, in *Christian Ethics in a Situation of Change,* there are no explicit references to Ellen White, whereas in *Remnant,* he referred to Ellen White as his "spiritual mother," and several times gave two or three pages to a series of Ellen White quotations. In the papers and presentations in this volume he repeatedly drew on her account of the image of God as the "power to think and to do." Elsewhere he referred to White's exposition of a point he made, or he cited her as an authoritative commentary on more obscure biblical texts.

For instance, in reference to Lucifer's rebellion in heaven prior to the Genesis story of creation, he cited Ellen White's special, extra-biblical knowledge: "We shall have to depend on Spirit of Prophecy sources...since the Bible is largely silent regarding this period, except by way of inference. There are, of course, corroborating texts for most of Mrs. White's key positions if we will but search for them."[35] He continued to appreciate his sophisticated theological, philosophical education; it is just superseded by more vital, higher concerns. And at times those earlier insights are transformed into specifically Adventist ends.

For instance, take Paul Tillich's notion of the "multidimensional unity" of the human person—a concept that Provonsha often cited. In his first manuscript, this Tillichian insight aided Provonsha in countering Nygren's bifurcation of love: *agape* vs. *eros.*[36] The theme of unity became a constant with him. In the name of unity he rejected the notion that the Hebrew people's God is different from the New Testament God—God is one.[37] Elsewhere, he rejected the forensic view of the atonement because it implies a demigod who is placated by sacrificial blood. This is a "divine outrage," he said,

[34]*Home Again,* 7, 8.
[35]*Remnant,* 138.
[36]*Ethics,* 16.
[37]*Home Again,* 48.

and it contradicts the dominant biblical theme of a loving God.[38] And with similar unitarian reasoning he largely discounted evolutionary theory because a Darwinian god so differs from the God of Abraham, Isaac and Jacob.[39] His unitarian commitment was broad.

A Prophetic Movement

In *God is With Us* he adopted "the theologians" notion of the "invisible church." It is comprised of all of God's people, regardless of label. This idea was quite refreshing to many Adventists who were chaffing under traditional Adventist exclusivity.

He depicted the "visible church" and the smaller "prophetic movement" as comprised of people who are both inside and outside of the "invisible church."[40] He held that as we neared the Second Coming of Christ a growing polarization would increasingly gather all those who are members of the "invisible church" in one direction and all those who are not members of it in another direction.

Like the prophets of old, the "prophetic movement," which is comprised of people who are and are not members of the "invisible church," has a distinctive contribution to make to the wider world

---

[38]*Home Again,* 17.

[39]In his most venturesome reconciliation of scientific evidence for very old organic material and a recent special creation, Provonsha speculates that Lucifer's defection in heaven could have occurred many years before the Genesis story (he cites several Ellen White passages). Thus, perhaps eons ago, Satan, "a universe-class contender" may have used genetic experiments that "look very much like what we see in the natural record that is attributed by the secular scientist to the autonomous working of nature in its process of evolution." Satanic life-forms could have evolved "even to the level of hominids"—but not to *Homo Sapiens,* who, with our higher brain capacities, were created, as the Bible recounts, in the image of God. "The evolutionists' picture looks more like a painting of the devil than it does a portrait of God." Provonsha readily admits that his speculation is just a model, but it gives believers time to "carefully examine the evidence." And "it leaves the Genesis story largely intact. It also allows us to take seriously the messages of the rocks and fossils. You see, both accounts could contain truth." Jack W. Provonsha, "The Creation/Evolution Debate in the Light of the Great Controversy between Christ and Satan," (unpublished paper), 19-21, an edited version of which is found in chapter 23 of this book.

[40]*Remnant*, 46.

which fits with the special needs of specific circumstances.

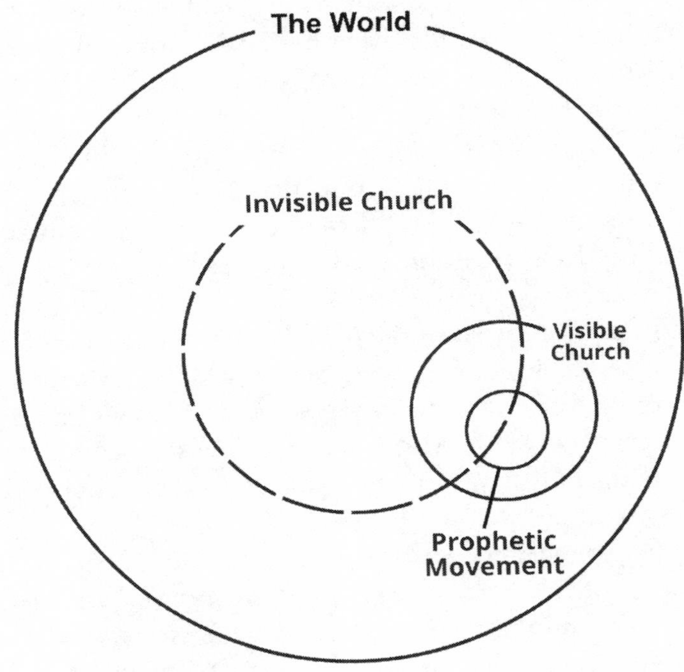

Although others thought there could be several simultaneous "prophetic movements," he held that there is only one and that it is the Advent Movement. He questioned whether the Adventist church as an *institution* will survive the end time,[41] but he appeared exclusive in terms of the essential *doctrinal claims* of earth's final survivors:

> On that "day of judgment" the prophetic movement may, like that small nidus of ice [dropped into super-cooled water], function as a social "catalyst" in an unstable world, where perhaps even large numbers of God's true church, visible and invisible, reacting to and resisting the formation of Babylon,

[41] *Remnant,* 163.

will "come out of her" to stand and be counted.[42]

Interestingly, Provonsha used the subjective mood in expressing his ideas, as though God could choose to conclude human history in a rather different fashion. The whole tenor of *A Remnant in Crisis* supports the literalness of Adventist eschatology, but here his subjunctive mood raises the possibility of question. Elsewhere, he cited unique eschatological statements by Ellen White, and then offered a most creative interpretation. For example:

> Christ is waiting with longing desire for the manifestation of Himself in His church. When the character of Christ shall be perfectly reproduced in His people, then He will come to claim them as His own.[43]

After asserting that "Surely the foregoing statement....does not mean what it seems to say," he creatively reasoned that the real question is not how good we *have* to be, but how good we *get* to be. "'Have to be' implies the imposition of an unwanted burden, whereas 'get to be' suggests opportunity, freedom to become something valued."[44] Those who truly want to be saved will be, for "Grace is the way to goodness!"[45] Just why we should take Ellen White literally in regard to the remnant being of correct belief, but not take her literally in regard to their perfect character, is not explained.

Specialness

In *Remnant,* Provonsha put a premium on Adventism's "special" role. It is not specialness for its own sake, but because of the unique role God has called Adventism to perform in earth's final days. He asserted that Adventists were previously naive about our-

---

[42]*Remnant,* 165.

[43]Ellen G. White, *Christ's Object Lessons* (Mt. View, CA: Pacific Press Publishing Association, 1993), 69.

[44]*Remnant,* 108.

[45]*Remnant,* 109.

selves being the only "true church," God's special "treasure," that we could finish God's work solo. The church has matured, but he "worries" that we have lost our sense of being a special "mouthpiece," of having a special "message," a unique "mission." We are facing in the First World the biggest crisis since the Great Disappointment, he held; then it concerned *arrival*; today it is "*survival* as a force in the world."[46]

Five Key Adventist Themes

When a patient is experiencing cardiac arrest, the physician does not give much attention to that patient's bedsores. Likewise, Provonsha's books concern grander, weightier matters than the specific Adventist issues that often get our attention. But there are five key themes that get at least tangential treatment:

The Investigative Judgment. The original Adventist idea of the investigative judgment is "simple nonsense." That God learns something by "poring over some books" is "naive" in its "anthropomorphic literalism." He simply rejected "out-of-hand" any need for a "pre-Advent judgment," but he retained what he called the "essence of the idea" in redefining investigative judgment as the redeemed examining records to verify God's justice. He cited such passages as I Corinthians 6: 2, 32: "Do you not know that the saints will judge the world?[47]

---

[46]*Remnant,* 166-69, the concluding pages of the book (Provonsha's emphasis). His concern for specialness is further illustrated in his concluding paragraphs in chapters 3 and 4 in the book, in which he laments that without our special message, "we are just another part of the visible church, in which case it makes little difference whether we are Adventists, Baptists, Methodists, Presbyterians, Roman Catholics...." p. 60. A similar conclusion is found on p. 48. The special message of which Provonsha speaks is well known to Adventists, centered in the "Three Angels' Messages" of Revelation 14, especially the call to worship God as Creator. Here, according to Provonsha, is crystallized the "Adventist synthesis" of timely truths: respect of God's Creation, including the world and our own bodies, and respect for His Sabbath as creation in time. Further, it includes a message of grace and renewal—a new creation. It is a message for every tribe and nation, a message of good news and judgment, a judgment beginning with the initiation of God's prophetic movement.

[47]*Remnant,* 120.

Great Disappointment of 1844. He found the traditional Millerite Adventist interpretations of Daniel's prophecies ambiguous. But this is not of "great importance." "[T]he point is that our Millerite ancestors and their heirs were convinced from their study that 1843-1844 was the time, and it is more important *what they believed and what they did about it* than what Daniel had in mind."[48]

A Final Great Controversy. The "mid-nineteenth century literally marked the occasion of the beginning of the final separation of the two kingdoms. Of first order importance was the fact that a movement was being born to carry the Three Angels' Message about God to the world and the foundation was being laid for the final struggle of the kingdom of light with the kingdom of darkness."[49]

Creation/Evolution. Provonsha equivocated. In *God Is with Us* he referred to the "Creation-event" as a symbol that has importance in itself, but "it simply is not all that important, especially in its details."[50] Further, as "natural history" the actual events of a distant Creation cannot be precisely known today, and besides, any attempt would be "distorted" by the "presuppositions" of the seekers. But twenty years later in *Remnant* he cited the "Sabbath problem" as a concern for Adventists. Then he adds that "to attribute the salient features of the theory of evolution to God is to come up with the wrong kind of God! The God of the evolutionary hypothesis... would be Nietzsche's god, not the Father of Jesus Christ."[51]

Ellen White's literary indebtedness. He only parenthetically suggested that Ellen White "apparently often 'heard' the voice of God" speaking to her as she read her library books. She evidently had an "unusual sensitivity to such intuitions" and she "quite understandably" used "the very words of the authors through which (the intuitions) were presented to her mind—with or without quotation marks."[52]

---

[48]*Remnant,* 133-35 (Provonsha's emphasis).
[49]*Remnant,* 135.
[50]*God is with Us,* 60.
[51]*Remnant,* 74, 75.
[52]*Remnant,* 57, 58.

A Loma Linda physician, who studied under Provonsha when he was in medical school, shared with me that he saw Provonsha retaining the traditional "Adventist Narrative,"—a 6,000-year drama, with a great controversy plot, and Adventists featured in the climax. This is essentially accurate.

Provonsha kept the basic plot, but he creatively revised the script for contemporary society. There are certain "givens" that one must adhere to as a "believer." For him, one such given is God's goodness. He applied this abstract virtue of the divine to origins—and advances some unique ideas, as we have seen; however, his adoption of "unity" and "continuity" as methodological constants logically force him to reject the *implications* of biological evolution, and consequently evolution itself.

However, the most significant tension I see in Provonsha's work as a whole is between his "givens" or faith claims, on the one hand, and his revisions or reasoned positions, on the other. For example, given what he has said about our subjectivity in knowing anything, how can we know that God's character must rule out evolutionary development? For some Adventist scientists, it is as much "nonsense" to believe in a literal Genesis story as it is to believe in God needing a hundred plus years to pore over record books in the heavenly sanctuary.

This epistemological tension was never resolved in Provonsha's writing. He lived with it. Though he could have, he didn't ratchet up his metaphorical understanding of reality to a higher level, which would have allowed him to be less committed to certain Adventist claims on origins and eschatology. Or he could have changed from Adventism's commitment to propositional truth to one of confessional community. He was philosophically open to such new conceptualizations, as he cautioned against making "any particular concept normative for all time."[53] If a new concept of Adventism catches on, it would be an old story: crisis yields to opportunity.

---

[53] *Home Again*, 22.

2
Glimpses

David R. Larson

Like a composer who turns a simple tune into a symphony, Jack W. Provonsha transformed aspects of his Seventh-day Adventist heritage into a powerful philosophical orientation which those with other backgrounds and points of view can evaluate from their own standpoints. From start to finish, and at every point in between, his views were *from* his Adventism and *for* the larger world by which he was more than willing to have those ideas judged.[1]

The simple tune with which he began is the statement by Adventist pioneer and visionary Ellen G. White that "*Every human being, created in the image of God, is endowed with a power akin to that of the Creator—individuality, power to think and to do.*"[2] The symphony is the yet-to-be published *Christian Ethics in a Situation of Change,*[3] which consists of selected portions of his 1967 Claremont PhD dissertation. Its title is "An Appraisal of the Hallucino-

[1]See Chapters 24, 25, and 26.
[2]Ellen G. White, *Education* (Mt.View, CA: Pacific Press, 1903) 16, 17.
[3]Jack W. Provonsha, *Christian Ethics in a Situation of Change* (Loma Linda: By Author, 1967).

genic Drugs from the Standpoint of a Christian Person-Agapeic Ethic."[4] How in Doctor Provonsha's life and thought the tune became a symphony is a dramatic Adventist odyssey.[5]

Peter, Ellen, and "Archie."

Doctor Provonsha's Seventh-day Adventist heritage began when a young man who had been born on July 26, 1835 as the eleventh child (six girls and five boys) of Francois Provencher and his wife Angelique Bourbeau dit Carignan, made three big changes. He changed his location from Quebec to Wisconsin, his last name from Provencher to Provonsha and his Christian denomination from Roman Catholicism to Seventh-day Adventism.[6]

I do not know why Peter changed his name to "Provonsha." The most likely answer is that this is the name many Provenchers took when they migrated to the United States from Canada and perhaps Europe or even elsewhere. There are many Provenchers in the United States today and some of them think of themselves as Peter's distant relatives. There are also quite a few Provonshas who may be related to Peter in some way even though they do not descend from him. In addition, there are any number of Provonchas,

---

[4]Jack W. Provonsha, *An Appraisal of the Hallucinogenic Drugs from the Standpoint of a Christian Person-Agapic Ethic,* PhD dissertation (Claremont Graduate School, 1967).

[5]Provonsha's thought was like every type of postmodernism because he agreed that we all begin with some non-neutral point of view and that, insofar as it is possible, it is best to acknowledge it to oneself and announce it to others. His was not like those forms of postmodernism which hold that only criticisms from those who speak from the same point-of view count. Pregnant women know something which we all should: everybody starts somewhere but nobody gets to stay there.

[6]These "glimpses" are partly based on my contacts with Provonsha when we both taught at what is now Loma Linda University Health. The introductory chapter by Jim Walters in this book chronicles how all three of us collaborated in the establishment of the LLU Center for Christian Bioethics. Linda Provonsha Sorter, Provonsha's first daughter, was especially helpful. Much information is scattered here and there on the Internet. Kathie Provonsha Sterling Anderson, his second daughter, has made several helpful contributions there. Yet everyone agrees that the record in Clyde Provonsha's family Bible is the most reliable primary source. I have not seen it; however, I have learned from those who have.

Provanchas, Pravanchas and so forth. One way or another, many of these are probably related to the great number of Provenchers well beyond Peter's family of origin because they can be traced back at least as far as seventeenth century France.

Elder H. S. Case brought the Great Advent Movement to Wisconsin in 1851 when Peter was sixteen years old. This was seven years after the Great Disappointment of October 22, 1844 when thousands had waited in vain for the Second Coming of Jesus. Two of Case's first "converts," Waterman Phelps and J. H. Waggoner, swiftly multiplied his evangelistic successes.

Phelps faded from view after he lost his campaign to have the new denomination called "Church of God" to Adventist pioneer James White, his visionary wife Ellen and their supporters which included J. H. Waggoner. Phelps died in Wisconsin in 1874 when he was sixty years old. Waggoner died in Switzerland in 1889 when he was sixty-nine years old. He was there to continue in Europe his major denominational contributions as an author and editor.

Unlike Phelps, who eventually fell out of favor and expressed doubts about Ellen White's visions (or perhaps the other way around), Waggoner became close enough to the Whites to travel with them to California to establish a denominational stronghold in the West. He was the father of E. J. Waggoner who, along with A. T. Jones and the encouragement of Ellen White, sparked a decisive theological reorientation from divine law to divine grace during a historic meeting of the denomination's leaders at Minneapolis, Minnesota in 1888.

The records show that Peter Provonsha once gave fifty cents to the Maintenance Fund of John Harvey Kellogg's Medical Missionary and Benevolent Association. His gift was probably put to good use because the organization established 30 sanitariums, 12 vegetarian restaurants and many other urban clinics to aid the poor.

As evidenced by U. S. Patent 5131701A, which was published on February 20, 1894, Peter was an inventor. This patent was for a better "door securer." Peter wrote that it was needed because "security of an individual at home or while traveling has become a major concern due to the increasing incidence of breaking and entering."

I don't know if Peter and Ellen Sophia Lane were both Adventists when they married on Christmas, December 25, 1862. This was eleven years after Elder H. S. Case brought Adventism to Wisconsin. It was three months *after* the [regional] Illinois Conference was organized in Avon, Wisconsin on October 27, 1862. It was five months *before* the [international] General Conference was established on May 20 and 21, 1863 in Battle Creek, Michigan with thirty-five hundred members in 125 churches. It was about five years *before* the first Wisconsin Camp meeting began on September 20, 1867, in Johntown Center. These camp meetings continue to this day with about 5,000 Adventists now lodging each year in tents, cabins and recreational vehicles at Camp Wakonda near Westfield for a nine day conference.

Peter and Ellen returned home from one of these camp meetings with a little boy because the ministers had announced that his parents, Charles Shepard and Miranda Hopkins Shepard, could not provide for him. They gave the boy a home for good, in both senses of the term, and they added their name to the ones he already had.

Although this made him Archiel Edward Shepard Provonsha, everyone knew him as "Archie" and this is how he is remembered today. Because it is still frequent among the Shepards, the name Archiel has apparently descended among them from someone other than the Archiel who also became a Provonsha because so far none of his descendants have this name.

The records of Peter and Ellen Provonsha list this Archiel as their only child. The records of Charles and Miranda Shepard show that they had two children: this Archiel and Charles Deystine Shepard. Even if they continued to claim him only biologically, the Shepards never gave this Archiel completely away. This coincides with a story Provonsha sometimes told about Miranda Jane Shepard once or twice frightening Archie when he was a youngster by showing up only to him and introducing herself as his "real mother."

Archie married Mary Hermann in what some say was a double wedding with Mary's sister as the other bride. They spent most of their lives in the Rocky Mountain region of the United States when parts of it were still a bit like the "Wild West." They lived in Colorado and then in Utah where they helped to establish Adventism in the home of Mormonism. Mary, who had been born in 1871 in Sheboygan County, Wisconsin died in 1921 in Maricopa County, Arizona even though they had moved there in hopes that its drier weather would improve her health. Born in 1869 or 1870 in Outagamie, Wisconsin, Archie died in 1932 in Lane County, Oregon.

Archie and Mary had five surviving children: Edd, Arwin, Alice, Gordon and Clyde. Edd turned out to be a rancher and sometime sheriff. Alice married Union Pacific Railroad machinist Haskel Bates. Gordon and Clyde were commercial and fine artists. They had a successful studio in Los Angeles until Gordon's untimely death at which time Clyde moved to Northern California and did well on his own.

For a while when they were young, Gordon and Clyde, and perhaps others, traveled with Archie from town to town painting everything that could be painted—houses, cars, shops, anything which stood still long enough to be painted—and then moved on. Gordon and Clyde painted landscapes in store front windows while many watched and quite a few purchased. A number of these early paintings are treasured by people today and sometimes they are bought and sold on the Internet. In time, Archie and the family were able to settle down. He ran his own automobile paint shop and they lived much more comfortably.

From Moab to Mountain View

Arwin R. Provonsha, one of Archie and Mary's sons, married Maud Voss, and they had three children, one of whom was Jack W. Provonsha. Jack's younger sister Wanda taught nursing on the Portland, Oregon campus of Walla Walla University, which is in the southeastern portion of the state of Washington. His older brother Merrill lived in Northern California, Washington and Oregon.

Arwin V. Provonsha, who recently retired from a renowned career as an entomologist and scientific artist at Purdue University, is Provonsha's much younger half-brother from his father's second marriage to Laura Ethel McPhail, who was usually known as "Ethel." A second species of North American Mayflies which he and his Purdue University Colleague, William P. McCafferty discovered in larvae along the Black and Pee Dee Rivers in North Carolina and the Savannah River in Georgia has been known as *Amercaenis Provonsha and McCafferty* at least since 2006.[7] For decades, separately and together, they published many scientific books and papers.

The frequent emergence of unusual creativity among all of Peter and Ellen's descendants, including Jack Provonsha, poses interesting questions about "nature and nurture" because none of them is related to either Peter or Ellen genetically. Insofar as it is genetic, it would seem that this talent flowed *through* Archie *from* his biological parents *Charles and Miranda Jane Hopkins Shepard* and *with* his wife Mary Hermann Provonsha. Yet genes as such aren't everything because it is increasingly evident that different environments prompt some of them to be more expressive than others. Peter and Ellen Provonsha must have provided a context in which the Shepard genetic artistic and inventive talent was decidedly expressive—and Archie and Mary even more. That this unusual creativity is the result of a fortunate mix of "nature and nurture" is another way to say this.

In any case, Jack Provonsha was born in Moab, Utah in 1920. Because his father's nickname was "Stub," it isn't surprising that Provonsha was short, strong, and smart with a quiet sense of humor. He became a shepherd on a Utah ranch run by his Uncle Edd after his parents divorced when he was about 14 years old. Primarily because the writings of Ellen White (1827–1915), a visionary Adventist pioneer, inspired him to make the most of his talents, he decided to complete his education. Hitchhiking some of the

---

[7]A. V. Provonsha and W. P. McCafferty, "A Second Species of North American mayfly genus Amercaenis Provonsha and McCafferty (Ephemeroptera: Caenidae," *Journal of Insect Science*, vol. 6, issue 1 (2006): 10.

distance, he traveled from Utah to Walla Walla College, where he inquired if he could live on campus and work his way through high school and then college.

Two young women behind a counter burst into laughter at his appearance. Thoroughly humiliated, he fled to Palo Alto, California. There he found a family near Stanford University who gave him room and board, plus access to their library, in exchange for household and yard work. He also worked at the Pacific Press Publishing Association and, like his sister Wanda, he studied at Mountain View Academy.

Although he and his mother and sister did not live together, for a while they were all in the same general area south of San Francisco. He met Lorraine Scharff while they were teenagers at Mountain View Academy. They fell in love, and in time they married.

His years in the Mountain View area were decisive. He lived within driving distance of his mother and sister. He met Graham Maxwell with whom he would later teach at Loma Linda. He fell in love with Lorraine and she with him. He first tasted the academic life which would be his life's work. Once when he and I were about to land at the San Jose airport in a commercial airliner, he commented on how many "ghosts" he had in the area.

Love, Loss, and New Love

It wasn't long before he and Lorraine married and established a home in Angwin, California, where he attended Pacific Union College (PUC). It took him five, rather than the customary four, years to earn his degree because he paid his own way by working primarily in the school's printing shop as he had at the Pacific Press Publishing Association in Mountain View.

While at PUC, he painted at least two portraits of lasting value. One was of Guy Wolfkill, a popular professor of education with only one arm but many provocative ideas. The other was of Jesus as a muscular young man in a carpenter shop. At his request, this large painting of a youthful and well-built Carpenter in Nazareth was among the very few things that were with him in the little bedroom in Loma Linda where he died at the age of 84 in 2004. Both paintings show that already in his college days he was an independent thinker.

After he graduated from PUC, he and Lorraine moved to Utah where they served briefly in pastoral and evangelistic ministry. Among many other things, a bit reminiscent of what Gordon and Clyde had done many years earlier, he created a three dimensional depiction of the Battle of Armageddon in a Salt Lake City storefront window. He and Lorraine also sang duets for evangelistic meetings.

They then transferred to Fairbanks, Alaska where they are credited with founding a congregation with nine initial members and a cabin made out of railroad ties in which to worship. These happy days ended when Lorraine, who was pregnant, suddenly fell ill. She died from toxemia before he could return from one of his travels for the church. The first of his two daughters, Linda, was successfully delivered and she subsequently did well.

After Lorraine's death, he attended to his recurring dream of becoming both a doctor and a minister like his hero Albert Schweitzer. Returning to Pacific Union College, he completed the necessary prerequisites and then entered the School of Medicine at what we now call Loma Linda University Health. For several summers, he returned to Alaska to work in the construction and fishing industries. His mother, Maud, looked after Linda much of the time.

He and Margaret Anderson met each other at Loma Linda. An excellent student and clinician a year ahead of him in medical school, she was the daughter of Swedish immigrants. He proposed, she accepted, and for the next half-century they were true companions.

After completing their medical studies, he and Margaret traveled with Linda to Takoma Park, Maryland, for their internships. This is where their daughter Kathie was born. Upon completing their studies in the Washington, D.C., area, they moved their family to California's Central Valley, a region that was plagued by huge differences between those who owned large acreages and those who worked the fields. They both practiced family medicine in Riverdale, a hot and dusty town twenty-three miles south of Fresno. As recently as 2010, Riverdale had a population of only 3,150, a number that fluxuates as the migrant workers come and go.

He and Margaret soon moved to Seldovia, Alaska. Reachable even today only by boat, ferry or airplane, it is about 14 miles "as the crow flies" southwest of Homer on the shores of Kachemak Bay in the Kenai Peninsula Borough. Although many tourists enjoy its three hotels, scenery and sport fishing each year, today only 226 people permanently reside there. In previous years, when the herring cannery was flourishing, ten times that many—about 2,000—called it home. Gerald Winslow reports that the building that was their medical clinic still stood ten years ago, albeit with a sign that says "closed." He and Margaret were "medical missionaries" who brought physical and spiritual healing to many in that region, some of whom Provonsha reached by an airplane that he piloted.

Arthur Bietz, a minister and psychologist who had earned a doctorate at the University of Southern California, a rare achievement among Adventist ministers of the time, was pastoring the large White Memorial Seventh-day Adventist Church in Los Angeles and teaching religion in the College of Medical Evangelists (CME), now Loma Linda University Health. Keeping in touch with Provonsha by mail, Bietz encouraged him to continue his education and, while still in Alaska, to read the works of the best religious thinkers of all time.

The eventual result of these exchanges was that he and Margaret and their daughters found themselves in the Boston area with the encouragement of Bietz and the CME. He studied ethics and religion at Harvard University where he enjoyed classes from Paul Tillich, Joseph Fletcher, and others, and earned an MA degree. It is difficult to imagine greater differences than those between Alaska's remote villages and Boston which some of its citizens call "the hub of the universe!"

Los Angeles and Loma Linda

Once they were back in Southern California, Margaret plunged into the practice of medicine. He also practiced medicine while becoming a member of Bietz's team of religion teachers in Los Angeles. In subsequent years, he often described the time he worked with Bietz as the happiest of his professional life. I think that this is because Bietz, who was only seven years older, was the kind of thinker Provonsha wanted to be—not a linguist or historian who specializes in details but an integrator of broad themes of religious studies with other disciplines, especially psychology and psychiatry.

Provonsha entered a doctoral program at Claremont Graduate School, slightly east of Los Angeles. He earned a PhD with the guidance of Joseph C. Hough, Jr., who subsequently became Dean of Vanderbilt Divinity School and then president of Union Theological Seminary in New York City.

When the College of Medical Evangelists consolidated in Loma Linda and became Loma Linda University, so that its medical students no longer spent their first two years there (on "the farm") and their second two years in Los Angeles ("the city"), Provonsha and A. Graham Maxwell entered the most productive stage of their careers.

From their teenage years at Mountain View Academy until they both died in Loma Linda, his life intersected with Maxwell's. A New Testament scholar who had earned his doctorate at the University of Chicago Divinity School, Maxwell was the Dean of what is now the Loma Linda University Health School of Religion for almost all of the years Provonsha taught there.

They were different but complementary in their positive impact upon others. He was from Utah and Maxwell was from England. He came from modest financial circumstances. Maxwell's were more than financially comfortable. He was an almost pensive introvert. Maxwell was an extrovert even though his style of lecturing, which became less formal over the years, was that of a restrained and polished English gentlemen. When they were both at Mountain View Academy, Maxwell was the son of the most prolific author and editor of the Pacific Press Publishing Association. He helped to run the machines that printed the books and magazines. On the other hand, at that time Provonsha and Lorraine had each other's affection, and that more than made up for everything else.

The two theologians also differed in some of their views. Provonsha denied complete divine foreknowledge. Maxwell affirmed it. No matter what the announced topic was, in his public presentations Maxwell always, without exception, returned to what he called "the larger view" and "the truth about God." Although he never used the expression, Provonsha frequently, but not always, returned to "the truth about humanity." Maxwell typically reasoned from God to humanity, and Provonsha from humanity to God. Together they pretty much covered the entire theological landscape.

Their huge influence began with the religion courses which they taught in the University. It expanded from there to their Sabbath School classes each Saturday morning. For a while, nearly two hundred people attended Maxwell's weekly sessions and twice that many attended Doctor Provonsha's two sections.

Some people attended three sessions each Sabbath: Provonsha's early class, then Maxwell's class and, finally, the church service at the six thousand member church on the Loma Linda campus to hear the provocative sermons of senior pastor William A. Loveless.

Thanks to the tireless efforts of Dr. and Mrs. Gerald Kirk of Redlands, California, and many unpaid recruits, the influence of Maxwell and Provonsha stretched still farther as people in many nations listened to and discussed audio recordings of these sessions.

Both theologians were in constant demand as speakers throughout the entire nation. Provonsha was invited more than once to speak at Walla Walla College, the campus from which he had fled in shame not so many years before. Both he and Maxwell published several books. He also duplicated many of his presentations so that they could be read as well as heard. This present volume consists of a representative and edited selection of these previously unpublished manuscripts.

Provonsha's LLU title as "Professor of Philosophy of Religion and Christian Ethics" was unusual and revealing. To be a specialist in philosophy of religion and philosophic ethics, or just plain ethics, would have made immediate sense because they both function *outside* the circle of any community of faith's convictions. To be one in both "Christian theology" and "Christian ethics" would have also been swiftly plausible because they both do their work *within* the Christian circle. Provonsha combined the secular concerns of one area of study with the religious ones of the other in a crisscross of academic thinking.

Because they display the flow of his thinking, these otherwise tedious distinctions are worth noticing. They show that as a philosopher of religion he made his case for Christianity without usually appealing to distinctively religious authorities or experiences. Having established the viability of Christianity on these general terms, he then went on to explore its specific ethical opportunities and obligations. This is why he taught a course in philosophy of religion for freshman medical school students and a course in Christian ethics for the sophomore ones.

That he did all of his work in ethics from a specifically Christian point of view is evident even in his most technical and seemingly secular writing. This includes his PhD dissertation which he titled "An Appraisal of the Hallucinogenic Drugs from the Standpoint of a Christian Person-Agapeic Ethic"[8] and the chapters he excerpted from it in *Christian Ethics in a Situation of Change.*

Patmos on the Puget Sound

Provonsha was a minister, doctor, philosopher of religion, Christian ethicist, artist, musician, sculptor, pilot, scuba diver, horseback rider, hiker, rock climber, and more. Perhaps surprisingly, given all this, he was also a quiet and private person who often recharged his physical and emotional batteries in the wilderness areas of the "American West." For him, being alone or with a small group of relatives or friends in remote regions was often soothing and renewing. These excursions must have reminded him of his earlier years on his Uncle Edd's ranch in Utah.

All through the years that he taught at LLUH, Doctor Mar-

[8]Jack W. Provonsha, *An Appraisal of the Hallucinogenic Drugs From the Standpoint of a Christian Person-Agapic Ethic.* PhD diss (Claremont Graduate School, 1967).

garet Provonsha practiced medicine on campus and in nearby towns. When they reached retirement age, they moved to a beautiful house he had built at the water's edge near the opening to the Puget Sound, west of Seattle, by which virtually every boat passed. In time, it became too solitary even for him, so much so that he sometimes referred to it as his "Isle of Patmos" experience.

When Provonsha's Parkinson's disease progressed to the point that he and his wife could no longer live alone in the state of Washington, they moved to a semi-rural area near Arcata, in northern California, across the street and a few houses down from his daughter, Linda. At the time, she was a public school teacher, and her husband, Jim, was a public school administrator. Not long after they moved to northern California, Doctor Margaret Provonsha died in a nearby convalescent facility, in the arms of Linda, her stepdaughter.

Provonsha was now a widower for the second time. When caring for him became too much for his daughter Linda and his aid Hosanna, my wife Bronwen and I moved him and a few of his things back to Loma Linda. Although it was difficult for him to leave his dog, many books, fine home, daughter and son-in-law behind, he was characteristically stoical about it. We tried to make him comfortable in our Subaru; however, he rightly described the journey as seven hundred miles in a "medieval torture chamber." Except for those who were paid to be his caregivers, Bronwen spent more time helping him in the final chapter of his life at Loma Linda than anyone else.

Parkinsonism is a merciless disease and thus it was with him. He didn't tremble; however, his muscles and mind gradually faded. This was a very distressing process for him and all the rest of us. Yet no chapter in his life had been easy. The unknown shepherd had become a famous and much appreciated professor despite many continuing challenges. Thousands all over the world who mourned his death will be grateful to him for the rest of their lives.

Hypnosis at Hobergs

I encountered Provonsha for the first time about 1961 when he was entering his forties and I was approaching my middle teens. This happened at Hobergs Resort, a vacation destination in northern California where Adventist ministers and doctors in that part of the Golden State met for a conference one weekend each winter. I was there with the rest of my family because my father was a minister.

One snowy Sabbath afternoon, I observed from a chair on the back wall a discussion among the adults about "Current Issues in Religion and Medicine" or something similar. It wasn't long before the conversation officially turned to hypnosis, a topic that was more interesting in the late 1950s and early 1960s than it is now. Two of the responses were predictable. Some condemned it simply because Ellen White had done so generations earlier in connection with her objections to spiritualism. Others were uncomfortable with the heavy-handed use of her writings as an unquestionable authority so many years after her death. When Provonsha finally had a chance to speak, I found what he said different and refreshing.

Our task, he said, was to develop a way to assess the morality of all medical interventions and not merely hypnosis. He made it clear that we would not find a "ready-made" standard. Using all the resources within our reach, we would have to compose it ourselves and take responsibility for doing so. We were to study Scripture and the writings of Ellen White and as many other helpful sources as we could find; however, we were to grant none of them absolute extrinsic authority. The intrinsic merit of ideas, no matter their source, should carry the day.

Although I don't recall if he actually quoted all of these lines by Ellen White, I do know that he made excellent use of some of them. I have italicized six of the passage's words because they were his emphasis.

> Every human being, created in the image of God, is endowed with a power akin to that of the Creator—*individuality, power to think and to do.* The men in whom this power is developed are the men who bear responsibilities, who are leaders in enterprise, and who influence character. It is the

> work of true education to develop this power, to train the youth to be thinkers, and not mere reflectors of other men's thought. Instead of confining their study to that which men have said or written, let students be directed to the sources of truth, to the vast fields opened for research in nature and revelation. Let them contemplate the great facts of duty and destiny, and the mind will expand and strengthen. Instead of educated weaklings, institutions of learning may send forth men strong to think and to act, men who are masters and not slaves of circumstances, men who possess breadth of mind, clearness of thought, and the courage of their convictions.[9]

He reviewed a considerable amount of scientific research that demonstrated hypnosis often decreases "individuality" and "the power to think and to do," making one more suggestible and vulnerable. Although he had quoted Ellen White, he had used what she said as *evidence* rather than *authority*. Therapeutic efficacy with the "Image of God" in mind, not extrinsic religious authority, was to have the final say.

As I listened to him back then, and as I have thought about it since, it has seemed to me that, even if he wasn't intentional about it, the case he developed against hypnosis at Hobergs and elsewhere was not absolute, but conditional. In my mind, there isn't much difference between claiming that hypnosis is wrong *because* it makes one more vulnerable and suggestible and saying that it is wrong *if it does this* but that it is not wrong *if it doesn't.*

Many years later I asked Provonsha if my thinking about this was accurate and his answer was "yes." His agreement is important to me even though it didn't mean much to him because I think that we all have become more aware that the word "hypnosis" is used by many different people with many different meanings. We should stick to his main point. It is that any medical intervention is ethically right to the degree that it strengthens the "power to think and to do" and wrong to the degree that it weakens it.

---

[9]Ellen White, *Education* (Mt. View, CA: Pacific Press, 1903), 17-18.

Person Centered Agape

It was my good fortune to hear Provonsha address the ethics of hypnosis when he was early in his career because it is the way he addressed all the other issues throughout the subsequent years. He returned to it regularly in his work as an ethicist, as his colleague Maxwell continued to emphasize "the larger view" and "the truth about God."

In each case, Provonsha wondered if, in the long run, the option under consideration would increase or decrease what Ellen White had called the "Image of God—individuality and the power to think and to do." Although he translated her religious language into secular terms like "agency" and "self-determination," his meaning was consistent.

His treatment of hypnosis was a circle on which, over time, he added additional concentric ones as he addressed other issues such as abortion, euthanasia, organ transplantation, artificial insemination and, beyond them, self-defense, war, pornography and gambling.

For Provonsha, agency and self-determination were not as important in and of themselves as they were the necessary preconditions for the capacity to love in a distinctively human way. For Aristotle and many others in the natural law tradition, the *ability to think* is what made human life distinctive. For him it was the *capacity to love*. His was an *agapeic* ethic.

He titled his Claremont PhD dissertation "An Appraisal of the Hallucinogenic Drugs from the Standpoint of a Christian Person-Agapeic Ethic." The hyphenated word "Person-Agapeic" signals that his *agapeic* ethical theory differed from most of the others at the time. In a word, their theories focused straightforwardly on the *norm* of love but, somewhat more subtly and closer to his Adventist heritage, his concentrated upon the distinctively human *capacity* to love as that norm's purpose.

Agapeic ethical theories typically flow straightforwardly in three steps. They begin by arguing that love is the supreme standard with which to distinguish right and wrong. Their second move is to clarify what they mean by "love." Their third one is to apply this standard to deeds, policies and persons to see if they measure up. Although they may do so on either an act-by-act or rule-by-rule basis, they always ask what the norm of love requires us to do.

This is not how Provonsha's theory flows. On the one hand, his is not an *agapeic* theory, as such, but *a person-agapeic theory* because it has more in common with the natural law tradition in ethics than it does either with the utilitarianism or Kantianism that are the most frequent philosophical articulations of *agape*. Instead of beginning with an abstract norm like love, justice, or the sanctity of life and then applying it to specific issues or cases, he begins with an account of what is uniquely human and then asks what we can do to make it possible.

On the other hand, his theory was unlike many versions of the natural law tradition because he did not make the capacity to think the distinctive feature of human life but the capacity to love in a certain way. As he saw it, as we move up the scale of life, animals can increasingly practice love as *epithymia* or *libido* (sexual), *philia* (emotional) and perhaps even some elements of *eros* (aesthetic); however, they cannot practice *agape* (ethical). As he often put it, inanimate objects can be *acted upon*, living things can *react*, but only adult, normal and healthy human beings can *act*.

Although he did not belabor the point, he basically accepted the view of Anders Nygren[10] and others that, as the term has come to be used, *agape* is other-regarding, self-sacrificial, proactive, spontaneous, unmotivated by anything but itself, without regard to how much its recipients deserve it. Thus, *agape* is creative of value and not merely aware of it, and it is directed toward the person instead of through him or her to some ideal exemplification of humankind. As God treats all humans, *agape* relates to others not according to what they deserve but in harmony with what it decides.

Yet, he repeatedly emphasized his agreement with Paul Tillich[11] in rejecting the idea that *agape*, on the one hand, and the other types of love, on the other, are necessarily contrary to one

---

[10]Anders Nygren, *Agape and Eros* (Chicago: University of Chicago Press, 1982).
[11]Paul Tillich, *Love, Power, and Justice: Ontological Analyses and Ethical Applications* (Oxford: Oxford University Press, 1954), 27-34.

another. Illustrating this point, he frequently drew a cluster of concentric circles with *agape* as the innermost one, and *eros, philia,* and *epithymia* circling it as planets do around a sun. Each one is an acceptable and even necessary type of love as long as it stays in its proper orbit and its circumference is controlled by *agape*. Trouble begins when any of them breaks away from its true path and speeds away in its own irresponsible direction. Every other type of love—*epithyima* or *libido*, *philia* and even *eros*—is destructive in its own way when its orbit is not centered and controlled by *agap*e.

As one can anticipate before being told, he was not a determinist who believed that all human decisions are wholly decided by factors over which those who make them have absolutely no influence. Not even certain that determinism made sense on its own terms, he was not a compatibilist either. This is the position that there are ways—just what they are being a matter of continuing conversation—to say of the same decision that it is both determined and free. The idea of freedom he had in mind is what many call libertarianism. This is the view that, adult, normal and healthy human beings who are not experiencing overwhelming outside pressure can (1) decide things which they do not have to decide and (2) each of these decisions actually does alter what will happen in the future, even if only slightly.

What is the source of libertarian freedom? Doctor Provonsha's response to this question is that, in principle, there can be no answer, at least none like the questioner probably seeks. This is because libertarian freedom is basic and any other answer would mistakenly present itself as more basic than it. From a secular point of view, libertarian freedom is *sui generis*. It is because it is. The only thing else that one can say about it is that it is impossible for human beings to live their lives over any length of time without presupposing it. From a Christian point of view, libertarian freedom is the divine gift which distinguishes human beings from other living things. It is part of the Image of God.

Although he did not use the distinction, he used the word "freedom" in its formal rather than its material sense. According to Christian theology, the first is the ability to decide between right and wrong. The second is actually choosing that which is right.

He made a mantra out of Paul Lehmann's thesis that the purpose of Christian ethics is to make and keep human life human.[12] Yet it served him as a conceptually empty vessel into which he poured his own understanding of what it means to "be human."

Rightsizing Situations

Provonsha bristled at criticisms of "situation ethics" or "contextualism" and their parallels for at least two reasons. One of these is that, personally knowing a number of its advocates, he thought that *ad hominem* attacks on them were ignorant at best and malevolent at worst. The other is that he actually did believe that *agape* is properly more concerned with the needs of people than the obligations of norms.

He gave commandments, principles, rules, and policies much presumptive weight because they decrease the time it takes to make a decision and because they lessen the dangers of thinking about an ethical issue as though one were the first person to do so. They also serve a pedagogical purpose by encouraging us to rehearse what we ought to do before we face difficult dilemmas in real life. Yet they are presumptive and not absolute. For him, situationism avoided the errors of legalism, on the one hand, and antinomianism, on the other.

His criticism of some theories of situationism was that the situations or contexts they discussed were too small and short-sighted. Surprisingly, perhaps, this is one of the places where Provonsha's Adventism is most evident. We can see this if we review the enlarging and lengthening of the various situations he considered, even though he never laid them out this explicitly.

There is the situation that consists of one person's own life. Here is where mood altering experiences—pharmaceutical, psychological and religious—are to be considered.

There is the situation that consists of two people. This is where he makes his few but cautionary comments to the effect that peo-

[12]Paul Lehmann, *Ethics in a Christian Context,* Library of Theological Ethics, (Louisville: Westminster/John Knox Press, 2006).

ple who are sexually intimate ought to take into account the long range consequences of their actions and, presumably, the wider circle of relatives and friends who might be affected, positively or negatively, by their actions.

There is the situation of the family. This is the context in which many difficult bioethical questions are often asked. When it comes to ethical perplexities at the beginning and end of life, some might be surprised by how many members of the family should be considered in his view. When it comes to abortion, not only the interests of the pregnant woman and the embryo are to be considered. Likewise, at the other end of life, not only the interests of the dying patient should be taken into account.

As he did elsewhere, at both the beginning and ending of life, Provonsha employed Tillich's distinction between a "sign" and "symbol."[13] Like a simple street marker, a sign points to something other than itself. More like the emblems of the Eucharist or Lord's Supper, a "symbol" also participates in that to which it points. How we treat that which is symbolized is very much affected by how we treat the symbol. Although a fetus might not yet be a person who enjoys individuality, rationality, and liberty, and perhaps never will, his or her fragile life is a symbol of our own contingency. Likewise, at the other end of life, an individual who no longer enjoys these personal traits still symbolizes our mortality. How we treat these symbols of human life shapes how we treat our own humanity.

There is the situation of culture. This is the one that seems to have preoccupied Provonsha the most. As exhibited in the title of *Christian Ethics in a Situation of Change*, he was very concerned about rapid social transitions. He attributed much contemporary ethical disintegration not to the perversity of individuals but to the ethical disorientation caused by too much change in all directions too swiftly.

Long before the use of personal computers and smart telephones of various kinds became widespread, he often expressed worries about the long range cultural impact of advances in transportation and communications. Today he would be joining many

[13]Paul Tillich, *Dynamics of Faith* (San Francisco: HarperOne, 2009), 47-62.

of those who have created these devices in warning against the dangers of overusing or misusing them.

Many of those who traveled with him through these widening and lengthening situations or contexts, were startled when he expanded these to include the universe as a whole in the cosmic "Great Controversy." This is a universe-wide conflict between right and wrong, and whether God is worthy of our respect and trust. Although he did not say as much about it as Maxwell did, Provonsha's entire outlook from his childhood to his death was permeated with this narrative or metanarrative.

I believe that this is what he had in mind when he wrote, in *Christian Ethics in Situation of Change,* that "every decision must ultimately be made in terms of the total situation including the long-range consequences, that is, whether it is *ultimately* for or against love."[14] Not for nothing did he use the word "ultimately" twice in one sentence.

Blurry Eyes

Provonsha knew that we all have faulty vision. He repeatedly expressed his belief that we all live in particular times and places and these help us to see some things clearly and blind us to others. Perhaps because he himself had lived in so many very different "spots," he was very much aware that our cultural conditioning prevents each of us from seeing things precisely as they are. Thus, if we are to learn, somewhere along the way there must be those who will "talk down" to all of us.

He held that science can help us clear our blurry eyes. On the one hand, the dedication of the best scientists to follow the evidence wherever it leads is wholly laudable and exemplary from a Christian point of view. So is their emphasis upon observation, verification, repeatability, and predictability.

This is where the limitations of the scientific method begin to be evident. Not only in religion, but in many other realms of life as well, important things happen only once. As it is practiced today, science often has difficulty handling such singularities. Another

---

[14]*Christian Ethics in a Situation of Change*, 6 (Provonsha's emphasis).

big challenge is that the deterministic tendencies of much contemporary science make it difficult for science to make room for libertarian freedom.

One way to deal with these problems is to limit the scope of the scientific method to that which is repeatable and predictable. Another is to rethink the scientific method so that it can more comfortably deal with singularities and liberty. He preferred the second "solution."

Provonsha would have been horrified at those types of postmodernism that dismiss science as irrelevant or even destructive. Despite science's limitations and frequent pretenses, he would not have been willing to trade the scientific method for the unending and unruly dance of fundamentally contrary understandings that many now celebrate. He lived in an integrated universe and was unalterably persuaded that God does exist and he believed that others should be as well.

He tried to decrease the confidence among some pre-modern Adventists that they are "in the truth" because they have interpreted Scripture correctly. He also tried to decrease a similar confidence among some modern Adventists that they are superior to their predecessors because they use the scientific method. This is why he said that "we see things as we are and not as they are." I am confident that if he were alive today he would think that some postmodern Adventists have learned this lesson only too well. He would invite them not to give the impression that all assertions are wholly perspectival. Beauty might be entirely in the eye of the beholder but truth isn't, and truth really did matter to him. After all, he was an Adventist!

That we are all culturally conditioned is only part of the problem. Another is that we are all caught in the wrongness that the Bible calls sin. As sinners, not merely as finite human beings, we see some things and do not see others. As this passage from Ellen White to which Provonsha frequently returned suggests, sin and salvation affect knowing:

The perception and appreciation of truth, He [Jesus] said,

> depends less upon the mind than upon the heart. Truth must be received into the soul; it claims the homage of the will. If truth could be submitted to the reason alone, pride would be no hindrance in the way of its reception. But it is to be received through the work of grace in the heart; and its reception depends upon the renunciation of every sin that the Spirit of God reveals. Man's advantages for obtaining a knowledge of the truth, however great these may be, will prove of no benefit to him unless the heart is open to receive the truth.[15]

He did not understand these lines and others like them to mean that only genuine Christians can distinguish truth and error; however, he did believe that the ability of a person to learn the truth about anything significantly depends upon a humble willingness to make the evidence the center of attention. The more self-centered we are, the less we are able to understand. "Excessive self-centeredness" is a secular expression for "sin." No matter what we call it, in addition to cultural conditioning, sin blurs our moral vision.

Provonsha believed that God attempts through usual and unusual ways to liberate us, at least in part, from the limitations caused by our cultural conditioning and excessive self-centeredness. This was the role of the prophets in biblical times and it is their role in ours. Yet some of the things prophets say and do in order to attract attention and convey their messages are so culturally specific, and so aimed at local issues, that they make little or no sense to those who live elsewhere. Transferring their messages to other circumstances requires skilled interpretation.

"Prophetic movements" have similar roles. Like individual prophets, they have things to say which are not broad generalities but specific messages that a particular society needs to hear at that time. This is how he described Adventism.

Of all the questions which occur to persons of faith who are

[15]Ellen G. White, *The Desire of Ages* (Mountain View, CA.: Pacific Press, 1898), 445.

scientifically inclined, those posed by the predatory nature of the entire ecological order perplexed him the most. This is why he once put forward as a "thought experiment" the possibility that it is of demonic origin. Perhaps the world in which we live is what God allowed Satan to bring about in order to demonstrate what Satan would do everywhere if he could. Quite a few scientists and theologians understandably thought this proposal was bizarre. For this reason, I initially thought that I would not include it in this collection.

I changed my mind and included it. This is because, at the very least, this essay demonstrates that he unblinkingly faced the seriousness of the challenge predation poses to Christian convictions. The problem of theodicy is not merely that people hurt one another by misusing their freedom (moral evil). It is not only that misfortunes like earthquakes and tsunamis routinely kill thousands of innocent people (natural evil). It is also that predation permeates the entire natural world and it is difficult to see how any other system could be as effective, efficient and frequently beautiful (ecological evil). This makes mockery of every theodicy which *easily* integrates Neo-Darwinism and Christianity. This is not a good place to be facile.

His hypothesis, which jolted him as much as it did anyone else, was that (1) Lucifer rebelled against God before the creation of life on our world and that (2) God permitted Lucifer to create it basically the way it is in order to demonstrate the evilness of Lucifer's ways. After all, can one actually picture the principle of predation which permeates all of life, and apart from which it is difficult to imagine life, as the handiwork of a loving God?

The first of these two claims is conventional Christianity but the second most definitely isn't. He knew this and it troubled him. This is why he rarely mentioned it. When he did, he explicitly described it as a hypothetical conjecture. Although he did not expect that the idea would catch on, he did hope that it would help keep the conversation going and that someone would eventually propose something better.

As I've indicated, I honor him for asking the right question even though his speculative and tentative answer was almost certainly wrong. I am confident that, were he still with us, he would accept this verdict as a compliment.

God: Unity of Unities

When Provonsha was in his early eighties, my wife, Bronwen, and I lived with him in his home near Arcata, California for several weeks one summer. We temporarily substituted for his daughter, Linda, and his son-in-law, Jim, who were at Puerto Vallarta, Mexico, on their annual trek, which he applauded, to help save the eggs of sea turtles from gatherers who would otherwise make the magnificent animals extinct.

One afternoon, as we drove past the Humboldt Unitarian Universalist Fellowship in Bayside, California, about three miles south and east of town, he interrupted the long silence with "If I had not been an Adventist, I would like to have been a Unitarian." He said nothing more, and neither did I because we both knew what he meant.

Although he was a thoroughgoing Trinitarian, Provonsha respected the Unitarian tradition of open inquiry and social activism. He appreciated its rejection of extrinsic and absolute religious authority. That it is a small community of faith with a positive influence which exceeds all expectations for a group its size was a plus for him. So was its desire to learn from every source of genuine wisdom.

Most importantly, he shared with the Unitarians a basic intuition, something much more powerful and pervasive than an inference, that the whole of reality is fundamentally integrated. It has been said that some see all things in their togetherness, while others see them in their apartness. With the Unitarians, he saw everything in its togetherness.

He was deeply committed to a synthesis of faith and reason, religion and science. and natural and supernatural. Statements by Ellen White like this one kept him allergic to driving wedges between these and other conceptual couplets:

> In dwelling upon the laws of matter and the laws of nature, many lose sight of, if they do not deny, the continual and direct agency of God. They convey the idea that nature acts independently of God, having in and of itself its own limits and its own powers wherewith to work. In their minds there is a marked distinction between the natural and the supernatural. The natural is ascribed to ordinary causes, unconnected with the power of God. Vital power is attributed to matter, and nature is made a deity. It is supposed that matter is placed in certain relations and left to act from fixed laws with which God Himself cannot interfere; that nature is endowed with certain properties and placed subject to laws, and is then left to itself to obey these laws and perform the work originally commanded.
>
> This is false science; there is nothing in the word of God to sustain it. God does not annul His laws, but He is continually working through them, using them as His instruments. They are not self-working. God is perpetually at work in nature. She is His servant, directed as He pleases. Nature in her work testifies of the intelligent presence and active agency of a Being who moves in all His works according to His will. It is not by an original power inherent in nature that year by year the earth yields its bounties and continues its march around the sun. The hand of infinite power is perpetually at work guiding this planet. It is God's power momentarily exercised that keeps it in position in its rotation.[16]

Because he was a Seventh-day Adventist both chance and by choice, long before he studied with Paul Tillich, he had rejected all dualistic attempts to separate body and soul.[17] Yet he thought that Tillich's description of human nature as a "multi-dimensional

[16]Ellen G. White, *Testimonies for the Church, vol. 8* (Mountain View, CA: Pacific Press, 1948), 259.

[17]"Human beings are *not aggregations but integrations* of body, soul, and spirit" is one way some earlier Adventists had put it.

unity"[18] was especially helpful, and he used it often.

He seemed never to tire of establishing the implausibility of Plato's view that the physical and the spiritual are so different that the soul survives the death of the body. He held that this view of human nature, in addition to being philosophically and scientifically mistaken, was the source of many other theoretical and practical problems as well.

Provonsha used a word that increasing numbers of others today are also using: *wholism*. For many of them, the term refers to the positive way people in clinical contexts ought to treat one another and their patients. Although he was a doctor, this was not his emphasis. For him, *wholism* was a philosophical theory, a compelling alternative to the dualism of Plato and Rene Descartes.

Although wholism permeated all the positions he took on ethical issues, it was most evident in his discussions of abortion and euthanasia. He saw no special moment in human gestation at which the new life receives or becomes a soul. He saw the entire movement from conception to birth as a gradual movement of a body/soul ("psychosomatic") unity toward the individuality, rationality, and liberty that is the distinctive feature of human life. In addition to "Image of God," he often spoke of this as "personhood."

Just as a human being can become more and more of a person, in this special sense of the word, he or she can become less and less of one. This can happen toward the end of life; however, it can also happen along life's way because of deformity, disease, trauma, stress, and wasteful living. We have very real ethical obligations to human beings who are not yet, never will be, or who are no longer persons. This is partly because they are symbols of our own vulnerability. These obligations differ from the ones we have for actual persons and, in times of inevitable and inescapable conflict, they must defer.

Provonsha often spoke of the unity of God, particularly when he was discussing differing interpretations of the crucifixion of Jesus. He used diverse analogies drawn from human experience

---

[18]Paul Tillich, *Systematic Theology, Vol.3, Life in the Spirit* (Chicago: University of Chicago Press, 1976), 11-30.

to interpret what happened at the cross. He was very uncomfortable with interpretations that picture the agonizing death of Jesus as necessary to satisfy the wrath of God. For one thing, he held in harmony with some passages of Scripture, that we experience divine wrath when we suffer the negative consequences of misusing our own individuality, rationality, and liberty. For another, he sensed that picturing Jesus satisfying the Father implies very real tension between them. He also denied that the First Member of the Trinity does not suffer but that the Second one does. In his view, they both do because in the end there is only one God.

Although the expression is my own, Provonsha would have been comfortable with describing God as the Unity of Unities. On occasion, he did speak approvingly about some features of pantheism. His disagreement with it was not about the idea that God permeates everything. He rightly thought that traditional doctrines of divine omnipresence say the same thing.

His reservations about pantheism were twofold: (1) Pantheism, in the most precise meaning of the term, holds that the words *God* and *universe* mean exactly the same thing. He held, with standard Christian theology, that God is more than the universe and that the universe depends on God for its very being. (2) Pantheism denies in God's own experience the very individuality, rationality, and liberty that is the Image of God in human life.

While he explicitly rejected *pantheism*, without a doubt, his understanding of God was one type of *panentheism*. Far from thinking that God and universe are the same thing, or that they differ and each has its own power to be, this type of panentheism highlights the declaration of the Apostle Paul, quoting some Greek poets, that "in" and "by" God "we live, and move and have our own being."[19]

Provonsha most emphatically did not believe that there are some events in the future that God does not know. His point is that there is nothing there to be known because the event has not oc-

[19]Acts 17:28. Although most translations say "in" God, some say "by" God. My suggestion that Provonsha had both in mind is an assertion about him and not the text. Even if the Greek poets meant one or the other of these, he meant both.

curred. God knows everything about the future that can be known; however, some things have not happened and, because of human freedom, they might never occur. God cannot unconditionally know that something will take place when, because of libertarian freedom its occurrence is conditional. This limits God in no way.

The Finale

Although he read widely and learned from many, Provonsha made primary use of the writings of three authors. From Paul Lehmann he took "contextualism" and the theme of "making and keeping human life human." From Joseph Fletcher, he took the importance of *agape* and a willingness to accept responsibility for the ethical decisions we make. From Paul Tillich, he took the term but not the concept of "multidimensional unity," the distinction between "sign" and "symbol," and the continuity between the different forms of love.

He *adopted* none of these. He *adapted* all of them for his own purposes in light of what Ellen White had said about "the power to think and to do; knowing with the heart," the ultimate unity of religion and science at their best, the "Great Controversy," the inexplicability of evil and the dependence of distinctively human love upon libertarian freedom.

He integrated these with his own experiences of, and not merely knowledge about, unsettling rapid personal and social change. Adventism is a "prophetic movement" with a unique but vulnerable mission, and God is the Interactive Ground and Unity of Unities.[20] This is the symphony which started off as a simple tune. Here is its finale:

> To those who worship the Creator, all of man's vocations, providing that they are in harmony with the Creator's intentions, are sacred.

---

[20]He never strung together these words for God as I have; however, they are scattered throughout his writings and I am confident that he would approve of what I have done. He would have one proviso. It is that we should use more traditional language when we are preaching or otherwise ministering.

The laboratory is as holy as the chancel, the market place as holy as the sanctuary, and there is holiness in housework, being a mother, or the construction of a fine piece of furniture or a home. There are no intrinsically sacred or profane professions. There are only sacred or profane people.[21]

[21]In chapter 27 of this book, *The Road Ahead*.

Part II

Medical Ethics

3
A Christian Appraisal of Therapeutic Abortion

It may be useful to frame the abortion issue as a question regarding the value of an intrauterine tumor. There are other tumors in that location, of course, and they form a useful contrast in a study of relative value. Some of these, such as an ordinary leiomyoma or fibroid, if they are small and produce no discomfort or dysfunction, have little if any value either positive or negative. At least their negative value may be so insignificant as not to warrant risking the higher values of life and health through surgical removal.

Other tumors may have only negative value. For example, even minute leiomyosarcomas or adenocarcinomas possess such strong negative value as to demand the taking of considerable risk to eliminate them, including relatively permanent impairment of health.

The pregnancy "tumor" differs from these in that, although it may possess a similar disvalue in the sense of jeopardizing the life and health of the maternal host, or even a different disvalue relating to the disruption of social relationships, it may also possess positive values so strong as to warrant subjecting the mother to considerable danger in order to preserve it.

The positive value we place on the pregnancy tumor, as over against the others, is based on its potential for becoming a human life and thus in the fact that it shares in the worth that we ascribe to human existence.

A number of medical voices have been suggesting that the issue be entirely removed from the moral arena, that it is solely a medical or technical problem and should be so treated. That is to say that the pregnancy tumor has precisely the same kind of amoral value as any other tumor.

These same voices, however, would be unwilling to assign to the newborn child a similar status. They would not, for example, grant the mother an equal right to dispose of her newborn at will. It is evident, then, that there is thought to be a morally significant difference between the two, the former being considered as "tissue" and the latter as "human."

This throws into focus one of the chief points at issue in the abortion problem. When exactly does such a metamorphosis from tissue to human being take place? Without detailing the arguments, it may be useful to notice some of the traditional "moments of transition" from tissue to human that have been proposed in the past.

According to the chronology of the developing organism, the earliest "moment" has traditionally been the "instant" of conception. No one that I know of has ever granted "human" status to prefertilized germ cells. Nature's prodigality in its treatment of such cells provides a kind of value-index. It is manifestly impossible for any but a very small fraction of them to become anything more than just what they are—cells—useless and short lived at that. By contrast the fertilized cell, to use a simplistic metaphor, rallies the resources of the whole parent body around it for its nurture and protection.

Theological dogma relating to the infusion of the soul into the body largely conditioned the value of a newly fertilized ovum throughout much of Christian history. In earlier times this followed Aristotle's belief that the male embryo received its soul at forty days and the female at eighty. More recently this view was supplanted by the above earlier point of infusion.

According to such a view, the fertilized ovum possesses the rights of a human being from the beginning, and its willful destruction constitutes a crime. In a situation of competition between this life and the life of the mother, the issue is resolved on other grounds—for instance, on which has had opportunity to prepare for the hereafter.

In a logical sequence the next "moment" would probably be that of transition from embryo to fetus, that is, the time when all the features of the future organism are finally present, even if in a small and underdeveloped form. Practical reasons prevented this from being considered seriously by our forefathers but it does have some relevance to present considerations of possible injury to the embryonic organism from chemical, viral, or other agents, and whether this justifies abortion.

Other "moments" such as "quickening" have been suggested. This proposal possesses a certain inner logic since it is at this time that the "tumor" may assume a new kind of "human" meaning to the people in its life. Even the physician as he checks the fetal position and heart tones is likely to find the term "tumor" increasingly inappropriate. To the parent fetal movements often produce a new relationship characterized by a heightened feeling of identification with that little "somebody in there."

The commonest modern proposal is the "moment" of viability when the fetus has achieved sufficient maturity to be able to "go it alone" if necessary, when it is potentially independent from the maternal organism. The issue has not yet been legally clarified but there is a tendency to consider willful death of the fetus after this time to be a crime other than abortion.

The term "independence" is crucial here and raises several questions, among them whether the newborn who is nutritionally bound to its mother's breast or artificial equivalent is really so different from the fetus bound by an umbilical cord and placenta? How independent is the newborn, even for years afterward? Even in adulthood our independence is relative. Probably none of us could survive for long without somebody else somewhere along the line.

The independence of the newborn from his mother's oxygen supply is obvious but even this is not absolute. Air must be kept available and free of obstruction—that is, from blankets and the like—and the infant may not be able to do this for himself. Incidentally, a "moment" sometimes suggested as the time the fetus becomes human is that first breath of air. It has some biblical support going for it. After all, the Bible does describe the creation of the first human as God breathing "into his nostrils the breath of life."[1] This definition may, however, seem a bit arbitrary since breathing is not an exclusively human activity and what we are after is the moment when the organism becomes human. Similar to this moment in its arbitrariness is the rabbinical notion that the infant becomes human when the greater part of his body is delivered—whether it makes any difference which end comes first I am unable to discover.

To be sure, the fetus or newborn at viability can be related to in new ways. Never before did it "mean" human to quite this extent. But the question remains, is it in fact human? Can it perform a single exclusively human action? Most of its activities are performed by lower animals at least as effectively.

This question leads us to the last "moment" that is being seriously proposed. It is difficult to locate this point with precision since it depends on an elusive function which is itself difficult to define.

Moral theorists and others sometimes contrast man with lower members of the animal kingdom in terms of his freedom—his capacity to create, to initiate, to do novel things he did not have to do. Lesser animals are assumed to behave within the general pattern of causality where every effect has a previous cause however devious and remote. Most animals merely respond in reflex ways to stimuli. Man, however, may be the initiating cause of at least some of his actions, that is, actions can take place in which the causes are traceable back no further than the man who acted.

This possibility in man can, of course, neither be absolutely confirmed nor disconfirmed and some reject the notion out of hand. But it is a theoretical necessity if we use such terms as responsibil-

[1]Genesis 2:7.

ity seriously. A man cannot be held responsible for doing what he could not help doing. Our whole normative structure is illusory if such freedom is not a reality. We can describe how people in fact behave (descriptive ethics) but we cannot say how they "ought" to behave (normative ethics) unless they can choose so to behave.

The Christian commandment to love is posited on such a reality. The biblical command to love has to do with love as a principle related to will, commitment, and choice, rather than to mere sentimentality. Such a command makes no sense if man cannot will an act with his private label on it, if he cannot do something about which he can say, "I did it; it is mine." It is this freedom that defines a human being in a biblical or Judeo-Christian context.

If this is so, we may define man as becoming human at the instant he becomes responsible. But when is that? Can we know? Probably no one but an omniscient being would know the exact moment, although it probably occurs somewhere in early childhood depending upon individual precocity and other variables.

But of what possible use can so imprecise a definition be to the problem at hand? Or worse, how actually disturbing such a definition might be since it would extend our "tissue" definition far beyond anything currently proposed—even into infancy and early childhood. On such a ground it would be as morally defensible to practice infanticide as to carry out an early abortion—a horrible thought. Which is precisely the point this paper wishes to make and the reason for extending its discussion of "moments" thus far.

The morality of abortion concerns other levels of value than the "momentary human value" for which we have been searching. One of these is the potentiality for becoming human. The "human" value conditions the quest to be sure. When we speak of the value of one tumor over another in terms of the potentiality of one to become a human being—we are obviously influenced by our regard for the essentially human.

Potentiality for becoming human begins at the moment a normal fertilized ovum is implanted. This point is chosen because, at least at present, it is not possible for an *in vitro* conception, that is, one in an extracorporeal "test tube" environment, to go on to maturation. Perhaps one day Huxley's *Brave New World* will be upon us, perish the thought, but not yet. Nor is it usually possible for an embryo to mature in a fallopian tube or some other extra uterine location in the mother's body. Potentiality implies the "possibility of becoming." We can also speak of an ascending scale of potentiality. The more nearly the embryo or fetus approaches the conditions of being human the higher its level of potentiality. The phrase "normal fertilized ovum" is employed because a "blighted" or abnormal ovum may also never be able to become a human by our functional definition and if recognized may be assigned nonhuman value.

Another basis for considering abortion as a moral matter goes beyond such human potentiality, however, and is based on that quality in man that makes him a moral being, his capacity for experiencing value and meaning.

Man is by definition a symbol-using animal. He is *homo faber*, man the maker (of tools that is), *home sapiens*, man the thinker, but he is also the man the symbol user. By symbol is meant an entity that "means," refers to or points to, another entity and which may in some cases be treated as if it were in fact this other entity.

The capacity for doing this is possibly derived from, certainly involved in, both his *faber* and *sapiens* qualities. It is the basis for his speech. Words are such symbols. It is also the major basis for his intellection. Try thinking a thought without using words. Certainly it is the essential foundation of his capacity to communicate and thus of his whole social structure.

The value of meaning, of symbols, even if they are only word symbols, to religion, for example, should be obvious. This is also true in the realm of morals. It is the meaning of the act not the act per se that gives it its moral quality. It is killing with intent that constitutes the crime, not the mere fact of killing—as in an accident where no culpable neglect was involved. This is a fact of great importance to the whole of morals and numerous examples could be given in its support.

Another fact regarding symbols is of importance to our present consideration. Symbols point to, or refer to something beyond themselves. Thus they are vehicles of communication. But they may also be "taken for" that to which they point. In other words, the attitudes toward the symbols will deeply condition the attitudes toward that which they point. Religious people have always known this when they have demanded respect for the sacred symbols—the Holy Bible for example. Disrespect for the sacred book negatively conditions one's respect for the God of the book. How one treats his symbols will influence, reinforce, or diminish his valuing attitudes toward that to which the symbol points. That's the way it is because that's the way man is.

Let us now relate this to our subject at hand. It is perfectly possible to bring "thing" meanings to an embryo and even to a fetus, to think of them in "tumor" terms and thus as objects of medical technique rather than morals. It is also, however, possible to think of babies, children, and brown men and women in these same terms, as Dachau and My Lai have violently told us.

The question is, ought we to do this? Do we really want to endanger human existence by rejecting what keeps it human? This may happen if we do not use and preserve all of the reinforcing resources and techniques available to us. Nuremberg taught us at least this. I ought to view the miracle developing in my wife's body with the compassionate respect that it deserves as a gift from God. To the extent that I am able to do this will my eager anticipation of the miracle condition the nest into which it is brought into the world. And this has all kinds of implications for the future of the child and its society as every depth study has amply shown. At least a part of the world's ills have descended upon us because we have lost the capacity to celebrate life, and especially at its beginnings.

Unfortunately, it cannot always be like that—there are babies conceived by accident, by lust, by incest, rape, unwanted and often foredoomed to the worst that society can do to them. And there are already too many mouths to feed and there is a sick society and there are mothers that are ill—and therefore there must be abortions, not because it is good but because it is necessary. The question remains, when?

A symbol's value is derived from that to which it points. The symbol possesses, therefore, a lesser, secondary kind of value. This means that when it seriously competes with, rather than serves, that to which it points, we must be prepared to sacrifice the symbol.

In the terms of our present problem, the increasingly potential human organism developing in its mother's body is not yet human—but it "means" human and can serve human values by crystallizing and conditioning respect for human life. But if for some reason it should come to threaten human existence unduly, it cannot be permitted to survive.

Notice that I have referred to human existence and not merely to life itself. "Human" existence can cease even while the organism lives on whenever that quality we spoke of earlier, separating man from the brutes, is lost. It is a tenuous quality at best, easily diminished or destroyed by a variety of functional disturbances—physical, mental, emotional, social. A threat in any or all of these areas may seriously jeopardize what makes life human and if such a threat is posed by a secondary symbolic value the symbol must go.

To express this in more traditional terms, whenever the developing embryo or fetus places in jeopardy the mother's physical, mental, or emotional health, and that jeopardy is judged to be of sufficiently serious nature, the potential human symbol, the embryo or fetus, may be sacrificed. It is the judgment of jeopardy, however, that is difficult and society must not thrust such a decision upon a potential mother unassisted.

If all men were ethically sensitive and informed, and all possessed a high level of sound judgment, we would require very little regulation in these matters. But since all men are not so gifted, they ought to assist each other and protect the weak and the inept both from themselves and from others. Undoubtedly it will be important for some time to come for good men to place their heads together and share the burden of deciding what is ultimately best for everyone involved, share it with each other, with hospital administrators, and with the troubled potential mothers on whom the burden chiefly falls. It is also incumbent on a society as it protects its collective moral sensitivities, that it be prepared to "pick up the tab" for such protection.

A few specifics remain. What of the chemical (e.g. thalidomide), viral (e.g. Rubella) or other damaged embryo or fetus? On a Christian scale of values such as suggested by the following diagram, where the actual human takes priority over a potential human, what cannot ever be human because of genetic or developmental defect must find its place farther down the scale. The subhuman, even if it has certain symbolic value, cannot take priority over the potential human. It would, therefore, not be right to also sacrifice normal, potential humans in the process of eradicating abnormal individuals estimated on a purely statistical basis. This is particularly true if we have no way of predetermining the extent of congenital defects. Ordinarily, the abnormality must be cared for after delivery, and again with society being prepared to pay the price for preserving the human values involved. Abortion might be performed, however, if the mother's mental health were sufficiently threatened by the possibility of abnormality. When the day arrives that serious dehumanizing defects can with certainty be diagnosed in utero, then it will be possible to routinely abort certain of these.

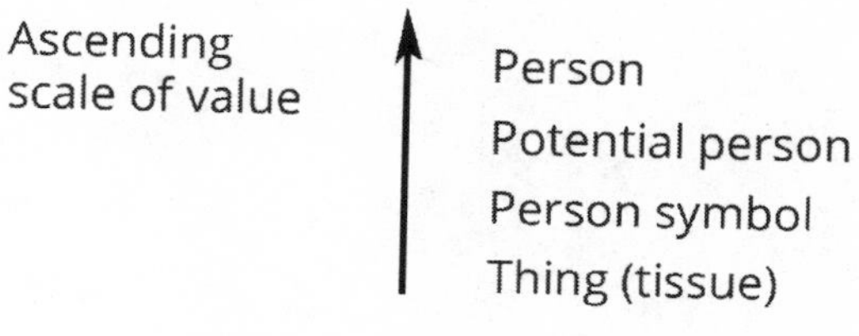

Ascending scale of value ↑

Person
Potential person
Person symbol
Thing (tissue)

The time of performing a legitimate abortion is on the above terms a largely technical matter, but for symbolic reasons it should be done as early as possible especially, since we are dealing with an ascending scale of potentiality and thus increasing symbolic meaning and value.

To summarize, what is presently subhuman, or what merely "means" human though actually is not, may possess a value that warrants reasonable efforts at its preservation. We must not usually, however, allow such to enter into serious competition with actual human existence either directly or indirectly. Its value is largely a supporting reinforcing value and when the threat exceeds the value of this support, morally it becomes expendable. An abortion may be performed whenever it threatens not just life, but what makes life human. It can never be right to interfere with so important a value for trivial or casual reasons. Because this involves judgment and a certain expertise, it is probable that the decision making should be shared by a community of sensitive and informed persons in addition to the persons subjectively involved.

4
Mind Manipulation: A Christian Ethical Analysis

An ethician is one who is concerned with those patterns of behavior and social interaction that serve to keep human life human. A Christian ethician is one who does so from a Christian perspective.

The nature of humanness is crucial to any systematic treatment of the many new questions our technology has thrust upon us. It is the obvious key, for example, to any attempt to deal with the question of abortion. It also hovers over the controversy regarding the maintenance of life-support systems at the other end of life. And it is essential to every ethical analysis of mind manipulation.

Humanness and the Image of God

A biblically based Christian ethic is likely to derive its definition of what it is to be human from the Genesis account of creation.[1] There, at the end of a series of creation events involving an ascending scale of biologic complexity, the ultimate creation was achieved in man. In him, God placed His own Image, and it was this feature that separated him from all of the lesser creation.

---

[1]Genesis 1-3.

Although the Image of God is not easy to define, it is not an empty expression. It means all the characteristics of God that He created in man, in a limited measure to be sure. Among these was that which most resembles God—creativity.

A statement in the book *Education* by Ellen G. White points to this quality.

> Every human being, created in the image of God, is endowed with a power akin to that of the Creator—individuality, power to think and to do. The men in whom this power is developed are the men who bear responsibilities, who are leaders in enterprise, and who influence character. It is the work of true education to develop this power, to train the youth to be thinkers, and not mere reflectors of other men's thought. . . Instead of educated weaklings, institutions of learning may send forth men strong to think and to act, men who are masters and not slaves of circumstances.[2]

This power in man set him apart from all the other objects and biologic forms in that vast creation, even though they also shared a great deal in other respects.

In that creation, objects, mere inanimate things, *could be acted upon*. Living, organic creatures shared that quality with objects. They could also be acted upon. But living creatures *could also react* in various ways. Man shared with inanimate objects the ability to be acted upon, and with other living creatures the ability to react, but man transcended both in his *ability to act*, that is, to do something that was not merely the effect of some prior cause.

He could do something he did not have to do. Ellen White refers to this potential in connection with the origin of sin when she states that sin was "uncaused."[3] But it is also the basis for *agape* or responsible love—the moral love of the commandment whose essence is volition rather than sentiment.

---

[2]Ellen G. White, *Education* (Pacific Press Publishing Association, 1903), 17, 18.
[3]Ellen G. White, *Great Controversy* (Mt. View, CA: Pacific Press, 1911), 493, 503.

The Image of God and Creative Freedom

It is difficult to conceive of anything as mysterious as man's capacity to do something that he did not have to do in a universe where everything else at the macroscopic level seems to be locked into the principle of causal determination. Current reductions of thought and memory to psychochemical processes, themselves causal in nature, make it tempting to revive dualism—a doctrine in which the soul uses the body without being affected by it, as in Descartes' ghost within the machine. But this will not do because we are aware that the so-called activities of the soul are very much at the mercy of body structures and processes. This is the meaning of *psychosomatic*. Thus, the creative act may be the only essential mystery in the universe, and perhaps it can never be defined by or reduced to anything else. It is essentially unique—*sui generis.*

Because an orderly universe is one in which causes consistently and predictably produce their effects, to introduce a quality so different as the mystery of freedom, or the creative act, has seemed irrational and unscientific to every determinist. Voltaire gave this view a classic expression:

> It would be very comic that one part of the world was arranged, and the other were not; that one part of what happens did not have to happen. If one looks closely at it, one sees that the doctrine contrary to destiny is absurd.[4]

Baron d'Holbach, also a prominent person in the French Enlightenment, wrote in this spirit:

> Man, whom thinks himself free, is a fly, whom imagines he has power to move the universe, while he is himself unknowingly carried along by it.[5]

---

[4]Paul Edwards, "Hard and Soft Determinism," *Determinism and Freedom in the Age of Modern Science,* Sidney Hook, ed., (New York: New York University Press, 1958), 108.

[5]Ibid.

Equally familiar, if less picturesque, is this statement by Arthur Schopenhauer:

> Every man, being what he is and placed in the circumstances which for the moment obtain, but which on their part also arise by strict necessity, can absolutely never do anything else than just what at that moment he does do.[6]

According to the great Pierre-Simon Laplace:

> An intelligence knowing, at any given instant of time, all forces acting in nature, as well as the momentary positions of all things of which the universe consists, would be able to comprehend the motions of the largest bodies of the world and those of the smallest atoms in a single formula, provided it were sufficiently powerful to subject all data to analysis. To it, nothing would be uncertain, both future and past would be present before its eyes.[7]

Sigmund Freud once asked these questions about a person who doubted thoroughgoing determinism:

> What does the man mean by this? He means to maintain that there are any occurrences so small that they fail to come within the causal sequence of things, that they might well be other than they are? Anyone thus breaking away from the determination of natural phenomena, at any single point, has thrown over the whole scientific outlook on the world.[8]

Psychoanalysts and behaviorists are aware, of course, that some fairly radical changes have occurred in physical science

---

[6]Ibid.

[7]Ibid., 148.

[8]Sigmund Freud, *A General Introduction to Psychoanalysis* (New York: Liveright, 1935), p. 27.

theory since Freud's day. However, even though they may have adjusted to these changes in many cases, the basic position often remains unaltered in practice.

Creative Freedom and Love

From a Christian point of view, a major reason for rejecting so inclusive a notion of determinism is that, if what Schopenhauer and other determinists say is correct, God, who is the First Cause, is ultimately responsible for everything good and bad that has ever happened in the entire universe. This is difficult to reconcile with the Christian idea of divine love. It is actually impossible.

Contrary to this, Ellen White wrote that "In the final execution of the judgment it will be seen that no cause for sin exists."[9] By this, she meant no reason more basic than the freedom of those who used it to turn against God. This is a major element in the final vindication of God.

In addition, if there is no self-determination, that is, a self that can partly choose its own destiny by an exercise of its own volition, there can be no such thing as responsible human love. This is because this kind of love, *agape*, is an act of creative freedom.

It is possible on these terms to set forth the essential truth of Christian morality. It is that anything that lessens man's capacity for creative freedom, for freely choosing to do something that did not have to be done, and for being responsible for this, is a violation of the moral law.

In the language of the earlier quotation from the book *Education* by Ellen White, whatever lessens man's ability "to think and to do," whatever reduces him to a "mere reflector of other men's thoughts" is not only bad education; it is a violation of the Creator's intention expressed in His having made man in His Image. On Christian biblical grounds, whatever enhances the Image of God in man is morally right, and whatever diminishes it is morally wrong.

Creative Freedom and Psychotropic Drugs

Some agents such as alcohol and marijuana are ethically threat-

[9]White, *Great Controversy,* 503.

ening primarily for this reason. Yet, although the facts are not yet all in, I predict that prolonged exposure to marijuana will result in changes not unlike, if less dramatic, than those of the far more potent lysergic acid diethylamide or LSD.

Note some of its observed effects, particularly as they concern an ethic of self-determination. Keith Killam says:

> One of the most striking characteristics of subjects under the effects of LSD is the suggestibility that can be imposed by the environment, including the therapists or associates. Single phrases or trivial changes in the surroundings can produce exaggerated shifts in mood.[10]

Timothy Leary, the so-called "priest" of LSD, and his associates noted this fact and valued it as a means of modifying behavior and value systems:

> The attitude and behavior of the guide [a person not under the drug who is provided to shape the experience] are critical factors. He possesses enormous power to shape the experience. With the cognitive mind suspended, the subject is in a heightened state of suggestibility. The guide can move consciousness with the slightest gesture or reaction.[11]

Sidney Cohen considered "exquisite suggestibility" to be the major feature of LSD back in the days when it was used therapeutically:

> The LSD state is, in essence, of greatly heightened suggestibility, with environmental cues sensed most exquisitely.[12]

Some authorities see LSD as providing:

[10]Keith Killam, "Background Considerations," in *Utopiates, The Use and Users of LSD 25,* Richard H. Blum, et al., eds. (New York: Atherton Press, 1964), 119.
[11]Timothy Leary, et al., *The Psychedelic Experience* (New York: University Books, 1964), 108.
[12]Sidney Cohen, *The Beyond Within; The LSD Story* (New York: Atheneum, 1964), 190.

> A mental state in which thoughts and feelings assume an exaggerated sense of meaning, importance, and significance. While under the influence of the drug, patients seem to have a prolonged form of 'eureka' or 'aha' experience whereby old ideas may be seen in an entirely new light and new ideas are more readily accepted."[13]

In one out of ten persons, this can result in radical, value-system changes lasting for prolonged periods of time from only one LSD session.[14]

There are numerous other psychotropic substances, of course, although perhaps none as thoroughly studied or that produce such dramatic effects as this potent chemical. Still, to the degree that they are similar in their potential for increasing hetero-control through increased suggestibility—thus lessening self-determination—these other drugs are also relatively subject to the same ethical criticism.

Creative Freedom and Brainwashing

Psychotropic drugs have been investigated by totalitarian governments as possible means of modifying the behavior and belief systems of subjugated aliens as well as dissident citizens. Such governments have generally taken recourse, however, to the radical form of behavior modification that has come to be known as brainwashing.

Robert Jay Lifton, who has studied brainwashing extensively, notes that

> Any ideology—that is, any set of emotionally-charged convictions about man and his relationship to the natural or supernatural world—may be carried by its adherents in a to-

[13]A. M. Ludwig, et al., "A Controlled Comparison of Five Brief Treatment Techniques Employing LSD, Hypnosis, and Psychotherapy," *American Journal of Psychotherapy* 19:432 (July 1965).

[14]J. N. Sherwood, et al., "The Psychedelic Experience—A New Concept in Psychotherapy," *Journal of Neuropsychiatry* 4:71, Nov-Dec, 1962.

> talistic direction. But this is most likely to occur with those ideologies which are most sweeping in their content and most ambitious—or messianic—in their claims, whether religious, political, or scientific. And where totalism exists, a religion, a political movement, or even a scientific organization becomes little more than an exclusive cult.[15]

Brainwashing takes its theoretical point of departure from the work of the Russian psychologist, Pavlov, who discovered in his work on conditioning, among other things, that the replacement of one conditioned response with another could be greatly facilitated by the presence of anxiety or other strong emotions. The totalitarian governments of the Soviet Union, Nazi Germany, and the People's Republic of China quickly saw the implications of Pavlov's work to their own attempts to control their masses.

Brainwashing, as an example of mind manipulation, illustrates the common denominator of practically all states involving vulnerability to suggestion: disinhibition derived from ego uncertainty, bewilderment about who one is.

In brainwashed subjects, uncertainty about the self was created by fatigue, sleep deprivation, isolation from customary activities and familiar persons. Uncertainty was also deepened by onslaughts on their sense of personal worth. As a result of an unrelenting pressure to confess, feelings of guilt began to stalk their every waking moment and much of their sleep as well.

Feelings of self-disesteem that become internalized as guilt can create undermined identity. As Robert Jay Lifton says in his classic book about brainwashed prisoners:

> Each was reduced to something not fully human and yet not quite animal, no longer the adult and yet not quite the child; instead, an adult human was placed in the position of an infant or a sub-human animal, helplessly being manipulated by larger and stronger "adults" or "trainers." In this state

[15] Robert Jay Lifton, *Thought Reform and the Psychology of Totalism: A Study of "Brainwashing" in China* (New York: W. W. Norton, 1961), 419.

> they were not only more readily influenced, but they were also susceptible to destructive and aggressive influences arising within themselves.[16]

Those who successfully resisted their brainwashers did so largely because they discovered techniques for maintaining identity and autonomy.

Creative Freedom and Charismatic Experiences

Another dissociative state stands out against the backdrop of an ethics of self-determination. This is the so-called charismatic religious experience. The following description is by a sympathetic clinical psychologist named Harry Goldsmith:

> When the believer "prays in tongues" the ego is circumvented and bypassed. Since the spiritual message cannot be rationally understood, there can be nothing in it to offend or threaten the self-protective and self-enhancing roles of the ego. Thus the person can be made to come to grips spiritually with aspects of himself that might be too shameful, novel, or unacceptable otherwise. . . . The ego, or self, is denied by allowing it no rational understanding of the experience, while the once-dormant spirit of man through union with the Holy Spirit now feels infinitely enhanced. Moreover, the superego has no cause for alarm or censure. Thus, for the moment the carnal man is subdued or bypassed and the spiritual man is in full control.[17]

Lowered inhibitions and increased suggestibility were also noted from a less favorable point of view by psychiatrist William Sargant among snake-handling Christians:

> The descent of the Holy Ghost on these meetings, which was reserved for whites, was supposedly shown by the occur-

[16]Ibid., 67, 68.

[17]Harry Goldsmith, *View,* No 2, 1965, 31, 32.

> rence of wild excitement, bodily jerkings, and the final exhaustion and collapse, in the more susceptible participants. Such hysterical states were induced by means of rhythmic singing and hand clapping, and the handling of genuinely poisonous snakes. . . . When protective inhibition causes a breakdown and leaves the mind highly suggestible to new behavior patterns, the conversion may be non-specific. If the preacher arrives in time to preach chastity and sobriety, well and good; but the "murderer" [the devil] had learned that on the night that followed a sudden emotional disruption, a sanctified girl might be as easily persuaded to erotic abandon as to the acceptance of the Gospel message.[18]

Such religious charismatic religious experiences are of concern to an ethic of self-determination.

Creative Freedom and Hypnosis

Ellen White, while unfamiliar with most of the psychotropic substances now available to us, expressed an attitude toward alcohol that was consistent with an ethic of self-determination. The same can be said about her many critical references to what she called "mind control." Here are but three typical examples:

> No man or woman should exercise his or her will to control the senses or reason of another, so that the mind of the person is rendered passively subject to the will of the one who is exercising the control.[19]
>
> God has not given one ray of light or encouragement for our physicians to take up the work of having one mind completely control the mind of another, so that one acts out the will of another. Let us learn the ways and purposes of God. Let not the enemy gain the least advantage over

[18]William Sargant, *Battle for the Mind: A Physiology of Conversion and Brain-Washing* (Baltimore: Penguin Books, 1961), 222, 223.

[19]Ellen G. White, *Medical Ministry* (Mt. View, CA: Pacific Press Publishing 1932), 111.

> you. Let him not lead you to dare to endeavor to control another mind until it becomes a machine in your hands.[20] It is not God's purpose that any human being should yield his mind and will to the control of another, becoming a passive instrument in his hands. No one is to merge his individuality in that of another.[21]

She was equally forceful in her rejection of hypnosis; however, support for her apprehension in the ordinary literature on hypnosis is hard to come by. This is so partly because few of the authorities appear to share her definition of humanness.

Following, however, are three statements about hypnosis that suggest something that would be of concern to an ethic that emphasizes as a norm enhancing or diminishing the Image of God:

> There is nothing mysterious about hypnosis; it is simply a highly suggestible state into which the willing subject is induced by a skilled operator.[22]

> [The subject] does not use his critical faculties, or is rendered unable to use them with respect to the suggestions, at least at the time the suggestion takes its initial effect. This is probably one reason why it is not uncommon to prepare the subject for this beforehand, by instructing him to make his mind blank, to be completely passive, not to think or to analyze what he is being told, what he feels or what he does. . . . One must ask whether inhibition or abolition of the critical faculties may not be the main character and condition for suggestibility and hypnosis.[23]

Sigmund Freud once remarked that hypnosis endows the hyp-

---

[20]Ibid., 114.

[21]Ellen G. White, *The Ministry of Healing* (Mt. View, CA: Pacific Press, 1909), 242, 243.

[22]Floyd L. Ruch, *Psychology and Life* (Chicago: Scott, Foresman, 1948), p. 139.

[23]Ibid., 23.

notist with an authority which was probably never possessed by even a priest or miracle man. Referring to this statement, one specialist wrote that:

> Hypnosis requires co-operation to an unusual degree. The subject who submits to hypnosis is seemingly being asked to relinquish his capacities for reality testing, his ability to control the real and mental world and, in essence, much of his adult individuality.[24]

The development of dependency on the part of subjects undergoing repeated hypnosis is fairly well recognized.

> There is inherent in the hypnotic situation great potential for the rapid development, by the subject, of strong positive feelings toward the hypnotist which further complicates the situation. It is this mechanism which seems to bring about and intensify the subject's extreme cooperation. These feelings not only render the subject extremely receptive to suggestions but often give him an extraordinarily forceful, even overpowering, affectively-toned motivation to carry them out.[25]

> Hypnosis, as a two-person interaction, is anything but a casual relationship. It places the subject in an especially vulnerable position. This fact puts hypnosis in a special category, and puts the hypnotist in a position of great responsibility during and following hypnosis.[26]

All of which serves to make Ellen White's point and mine.

Conclusion

Whether one objects on ethical grounds to the use of anything that decreases inhibitions and increases suggestibility depends

---

[24]Ibid.
[25]Ibid.
[26]Ibid.

upon one's presuppositions. On the one hand, from the standpoint of any of the determinisms, manipulative techniques are simply amoral methods for modifying behavior and attitudes. On the other hand, because the essence of morality lies in man's capacity for exercising freedom, self-determination, or creative love, these all present profound ethical threats. No human being has the right to exercise such authority over the mind and will of another. Doing this is to sin against the Image of God.

5
Euthanasia: Love, Life, and Death

There is a rabbinical story of a famous Jewish elder who lay at the point of death. A large number of rabbis came to his house to pray for him and since there were so many praying it was impossible for him to die. Meanwhile, he was suffering dreadful agony. This went on for hours. Finally a woman in the house went to the roof top and dropped a heavy jar to the pavement below. It made such a loud crash that all the rabbis stopped to listen—and the man died.

There are many physicians, clergymen, nurses, and hospital administrators who wonder at times if it wouldn't be useful to add a new department to the hospital called the department of "dropped pots." But would we really want to add such a service to the others offered in our hospitals and nursing homes?

It is ironic that man is confronted with his most complex moral issues at a time when a breakdown of his decision making mechanisms has rendered him least able to deal with them. Technological developments, especially as they effect modern medicine, have made it possible for him to do things he could never do before. But a simultaneous erosion of religious belief has thrown his usual methods of deciding whether in fact he ought to do them into radical disarray.

Modern man can often no longer with assurance appeal to the divine will of God out of a prevailing skepticism whether that "ancient superstition" bears any relation to what is really real and if God is dead, as Nietzsche said, then everything is permitted. He may not be able to appeal to institutions like the church for guidance, for the church has too often buried its voice along with its own interment of God.

We cannot even depend upon custom. It is a commonplace in ethical discourse to note that the folkways or customs of a people may continue to be passed on from generation to generation long after the circumstances that originally gave rise to them cease to exist. Their genesis may even be entirely forgotten so that when asked why such and such is done later generations can only reply with some kind of rationalization or a simple "that's the way things are done." But enduring custom may offer little help to modern man for many of his problems are too novel. No one has ever faced them before in precisely this fashion. Answers to some of these moral questions cannot be simply read off the literal codes and traditions of the past, even if they were respected.

It would appear that the structure of morality itself is in question. As Jews or Christians, we are challenged as never before in honoring a biblically based code of morality, to demonstrate the relevance and healthiness of our way of life. What we perceive to be the law of God, whether at Mount Sinai or as it is elaborated in the New Testament love ethic, is on trial. Whether it is the timeless and universal expression of the good and the right that we have claimed it to be depends on whether it is adequate to the present task.

Was the Judeo-Christian ethic only applicable to a prescientific, largely agrarian, rural culture that never dreamed of our resuscitation gadgets and surgical and other wizardry? Or does it still make some kind of sense when we discover the principles behind their mode of expression and learn to state them in current ethical metaphors?

Some years ago on a California highway, a driver of a loaded gasoline truck swerved to avoid hitting a passing motorist and lost control of his rig which subsequently piled into a bridge abutment. The truck overturned but miraculously did not, for the moment, go up in flames. The driver was pinned in his cab but was otherwise not seriously hurt. As he struggled to free himself he became aware of an odor of burning oil and gasoline coming from the region of his motor and realized to his horror that it was on fire and that is was only a question of time until the whole rig would go. The flames from the engine quickly spread to the cab.

About this time a California highway patrolman happened by and rushed over to offer assistance. He tried desperately to free the truck driver but without the necessary tools his attempts proved unsuccessful. Moreover, since they were some distance from the nearest town, it was obvious that there was little chance of obtaining such equipment in time.

At this time the driver also realized the hopelessness of his situation and, as the flames licked closer to him, he began to plead with the officer to take his revolver and shoot him to prevent his burning to death.

What should the officer have done? There wasn't much time. Already the danger of a violent gasoline explosion was imminent.

True to "custom" or "training" (or something) the officer did not comply with the request and was forced to flee the flames with the screams of the dying man ringing in his ears. Was his usual pattern of behavior adequate to this situation?

How does this situation essentially differ from the following more familiar one, at least to doctors? My wife, and partner in the practice of medicine, had as a patient an elderly female with extensive and inoperable carcinoma of the rectum who in spite of liberal use of analgesics was suffering considerable discomfort. The outcome was not in doubt. Morning after morning as my doctor-wife made her hospital rounds the woman would look at her disdainfully and say, "You call yourself a doctor and yet you allow me to lie here and suffer. Why do you not give me something to put me out of my misery?" How do the two situations differ—except in the matter of time?

The various euthanasia societies here and abroad have had just such situations in mind when they have proposed that incurably suffering persons should have the right to request a merciful death. They have had material aplenty to support their proposals. Their propaganda literature is rife with accounts like that of the famed English satirist and Irish clergyman, Jonathan Swift, who after a life of highly creative letters, ended it all in a horrible demeaning death. According to Joseph Fletcher,

> It was a death degrading to himself and to those close to him. His mind crumbled to pieces. It took him eight years to die while his brain rotted.
>
> The pain in Swift's eye was so acute that it took five men to hold him down, to keep him from tearing out his eye with his own hands. For the last three years he sat and drooled. Knives had to be kept entirely out of his reach. When the end came finally, his fits and convulsion lasted thirty-six hours.[1]

This matter has been enormously complicated by the technical advances modern medicine has made in the art of resuscitation and artificial life support, and this is what has most changed about the situation. The older question was, "Shall I or shall I not do anything to hasten death?" The newer question is more likely to be, "How long shall I continue to prevent death?" "How long shall I keep the patient alive?"

Not long ago I was called to give a consultation in the medicine service of a nearby hospital. The patient was a man in his eighties who had developed a chronic but fairly rare pseudomonas infection of his middle ear. This had persisted for many months and had only recently been complicated by a meningitis which was cleared with

---

[1]Joseph Fletcher, *Morals and Medicine: The Moral Problems of the Patient's Right to Know the Truth, Contraception, Artificial Insemination, Sterilization and Euthanasia* (New Jersey: Princeton University Press, 1954), 174-75.

great difficulty. Gradually the organism had developed resistance to almost all the available antibiotics except one, a somewhat toxic but extremely expensive medication. To keep his infection under control the residents on the service estimated that it would cost in the neighborhood of three hundred dollars a day just for the medication.

They wanted to know "if it is right to spend that kind of money on a senile old man who cannot be cured in any case, while depriving others of resources that might be more usefully spent." With limited public funds available, how shall they be allocated?

It is not an easy thing to decide to discontinue a procedure with the certain knowledge that the moment we have signed that order we have doomed the patient to imminent death. At least it ought not to be easy and pray God that it never will be.

Religious leaders of various persuasions have made things a little softer on our consciences by stating that we do not need to use extraordinary means. But what exactly is an "extraordinary means?" Some things are listed by these spokesmen, but what is extraordinary today may be quite ordinary tomorrow. Or what is ordinary in one place might be extraordinary in a different one. There is also the difficulty of knowing when a patient's condition is hopeless from a medical point of view.

No ethical system or method, biblical or otherwise, can be expected to obviate the necessity of making decisions. Life is too complex to allow for an elaborate set of rules from which to simply read off the answer to every possible moral question. This is manifestly the case with an ethic based on the Bible. Rather, we may look for a general guidance framework within which to make up our own minds about moral issues. We can ask the Bible that it provide a pattern of general principles of action which make our wrestling meaningful.

Every ethics method must contain at least two elements to be complete: (1) a norm of highest value with reference to which it becomes possible to use terms like "right" and "wrong" with meaning, and (2) a system or method for applying the norm to the specific situation. No ethic can offer practical assistance if either of these is missing. If one doesn't know where one is going or how to get there, there is little point in even beginning.

A biblically based ethic sets forth love as its highest norm. Both Testaments attest to this. According to the Bible, one is expected to answer the question, "What am I to do?" by saying, "I am to do the loving thing."

Unfortunately, if we leave it all to that we have really fulfilled neither of the requirements of an adequate ethic. Because of how the term "love" is commonly understood, at times it might not help us to discover what the right action is.

The norm of love may be ambiguous because of the protean ways the word can be employed. Love is how a small child feels about her new dress, a boy about playing football, or strawberry ice cream, a lover about his new girl and how she feels about accepting his invitation to an evening on the town. It describes how a mother feels about her infant. It also describes how brothers, companions and friends feel toward each other. The believer loves God, but two people in the back seat of a car at a drive-in movie may also "make love not war." How can one word suffice for all of the emotions these various situations suggest?

If love were considered the highest norm in some of these cases, it could be destructive of other values and thus not the basis for the right or ethical decision. It might not always do to act in terms of how you feel about each other. How can so transitory a thing as sentiment be the basis for a consistent religious experience with God, or even a consistent marriage?

Few Christian ethicists would hold love to be the highest moral norm when it is understood in such a broad and inclusive sense; however, the supreme norm of Christian ethics is a certain kind of love. The biblical Greek term for this peculiar love is *agape.* [2]

Agape differs from other kinds of love in that it is more related to action than to emotion or sentiment. Jesus did not ask His fol-

---

[2]Joseph Fletcher, *Situation Ethics: The New Morality,* Library of Theological Ethics, 2nd edition, (Louisville: Westminster/John Knox Press, 1997) and Paul Tillich, *Love, Power and Justice: Ontological Analyses and Ethical Applications* (Oxford: Oxford University Press, 1954).

lowers to feel a certain emotion for the enemy—one cannot turn feelings of this sort off or on like a faucet—but to behave in a certain way toward Him. All of the other loves are effects of certain cause: sexual feelings are aroused in a conditioned fashion by certain well known stimuli; brotherly, comradely love is the consequence of shared experience. *Agape* love is not caused to happen like a conditioned response. To love at this level is to act on principle out of responsible choice. It does not have to happen. It involves decision and will.

This brings us to the second aspect of an adequate ethic. This is a method by which the norm may be applied to specific situations. Now the question is about how we discover what the loving act is.

Some contemporary expressions of the love ethic seem to avoid answering this question, and thus bring such an ethic into disrepute. I have in mind the several kinds of "situationism" which vary in their validity. To say as Augustine did, "Love, then do what you will," and to say no more, is not to offer much help in facing the issues of everyday living.

The Bible did not leave love without content. It gives us general and numerous fairly specific examples of how one behaves lovingly, and thus responsibly, toward the neighbor. Such examples, call them laws or whatever, are descriptions of how love operates and thus are in the direction of fulfilling the second requirement of an adequate ethic.

Unhappily, the nature of the complex struggle is such that specific examples would have to be extended almost indefinitely to deal with every possible moral situation. It would undoubtedly be reassuring to possess such an encyclopedic compendium of all possible moral questions with their appropriate answers. Good decision making could then be reduced to good reading which would greatly simplify matters, providing of course, one always had access to such a library. This might prove fairly cumbersome at times, however.

God did not create merely good readers. For His own good reasons, He created deciders. *Agape* love being what it is, God could not create it like He could a stone or even an electronic computer.

He could only create its precondition—choosing, deciding, intelligent beings—and let them decide to love.

The second part of an adequate ethic, the method for applying the norm to the specific situation, may in this case be derived from an analysis of the norm itself. It comes out I think like this: the right action is related to God's own action which is the one that creates the precondition of *agape* love.

Right is whatever enhances personhood for the sake of the possibility of practicing *agape* love. Wrong is whatever diminishes personhood and thus reduces the possibility of love again at the agape level. Whatever has as its ultimate effect the depersonalization of human beings, which is their ability to practice *agape* love, is morally wrong.

The implications of this are far reaching and we cannot explore all of them. But those who practice medicine, particularly with the technical tools now available, need to discover this ethical truth as people have never needed to know it before.

According to such an ethic, not life itself, but a certain quality of life, is of primary importance, namely the personal. Whenever personal life, which is possessing the ability for responsible behavior by practicing *agape*, is actually or potentially present, it holds the highest order of claim upon us. When, however, this capacity is irretrievably lost, the level of the claim shifts on the value scale and we no longer are faced with the same degree of obligation. At that same moment of loss, those persons—physicians included—who make up the social environment of such an individual begin to take priority.

It makes no moral sense to deprive actual persons in order to minister to the needs of what was once a person but is such no longer. This fact should help us determine the amount of effort and expense to put into maintaining its survival.

The difficulty of deciding when personhood is lost is not easily overcome. We shall probably always have to depend on indirect indicators, ever granting a large benefit of doubt in the presence of uncertainty. The present attempts at a new definition of death are movements in this direction and we should continue them. It is important to recognize, however, that personhood may be diminished or lost long before the fact is demonstrated on the electroencephalogram or in abolished reflexes.

Pain itself, even severe anxiety, can be relatively depersonalizing in the sense of our definition. Rarely may a patient in severe agony be able to make his usual considered and responsible decisions.

Medications may also have depersonalizing outcomes when we use them to counter the effects of suffering in patients. The ethical practitioner must therefore always make clinical judgments regarding their use in maximizing whatever potential for practicing *agape* is present. This may call for weighing the depersonalizing effects of pain and anxiety over and against those of the countering drugs. Medicating terminal patients into insensibility until their bodies finally give out exhibits a fair degree of ethical insensitivity.

When the human person under treatment becomes an "object," the physician's responsibility changes. If there is something to be gained by keeping the organism functional—experimental information perhaps, or for the purpose of organ donation, or whatever—it may be done, but not to the point of unduly depriving others—patients, family, community—of their quality of life.

When I stated earlier that "when the personal capacity is irretrievably lost the level shifts on the value scale," I did not mean that the organism immediately became of no value. It possesses a lower and perhaps slightly different kind of value. It still may have what, for want of a better term, I shall call "symbolic" value.

One hears occasionally around places like geriatric medical institutions the term "vegetable." Yet an elderly cerebrovascular accident patient in a deep coma still means somebody's grandmother, or still means, or should mean, human being, and must be treated with the respect that her face indicates unless we are all to suffer immeasurable human loss.

While symbols have the function of pointing beyond themselves to something else, they also tend to enhance, reinforce, and preserve the values to which they point. How we relate to what symbolizes humanity will condition very greatly our sensitivities toward what is in fact human.

6
Perceptions of Death as a Factor in Bioethical Decision Making

The New Jersey Supreme Court in 1976 granted Karen Quinlan's parents the freedom to order that the ventilator sustaining her life be discontinued. In 1985 the same Court allowed Claire Conroy's nephew the power to mandate the discontinuation in certain circumstances other life-sustaining measures such as feeding tubes. Although these decisions clarified much for other subsequent patients, they accomplished nothing for these two. Surprisingly, breathing on her own, Quinlan lived for another nine years after her ventilator was discontinued. Conroy died before all the legal issues were settled.[1]

The Court's decision in the Conroy case[2] must have come as something of a shock to those who had kept Karen alive for almost a decade using technologies it then made legally discretionary. Her parents fortunately made it known that they would not have requested that the feeding tube be removed even if it had

---

[1] *In Re Quinlan,* 355 A. 2d 647 (1976).
[2] *Matter of Conroy,* 486 A. 2d 1209 (1985).

been legally permissible. Their daughter died, after the Court's ruling in the Conroy case, from pneumonia for which they declined antibiotics.

One can only conjecture what went through the New Jersey Supreme Court's collective mind as it made the Conroy decision. Did it feel a tinge of regret for all of those years of meaningless existence for what remained of Karen Quinlan? Was it trying to be helpful in preventing further such cases?

Whatever their motives, the decision comes in a package that doesn't really help anyone very much, least of all the care-providers who are so frequently saddled with such moral dilemmas. Indeed, it may have even made matters worse, actually decreasing the willingness of physicians to withhold treatment from the terminally ill.

The restrictions surrounding the option are precise and burdensome. If the decision was handed down with the intention of setting legal precedent, as we are told it was, it effectively illustrates that such matters should almost never fall into the hands of the courts. One of the reasons why such issues end up in the courts is that there are some major defects in our ethical decision making process. One such defect has to do with who makes the decisions and another with how they are made. Directly related to the second issue, we need a new and better definition of "death."

For most of medical history, for two or so thousand years, who made the decisions was not in doubt. It was the doctor, and he was to keep such matters to himself except, perhaps, to inform the family. The patient was not to be told.

The change began to occur in the middle of the twentieth century. Obviously, "autonomy" and "self-determination" are not twentieth-century innovations. It is just that they were not often formally applied in the past to the physician-patient relationship. There were many exceptions, of course, in actual practice.

Autonomy and self-determination are expressions of patient competence. Their minimum prerequisite is conscious volition in the presence of adequate information. But what of the incompetent subject, the severely brain-damaged, those with Alzheimer's disease? Who will decide for them?

That pattern, too, is now fairly well established. We not only have the final rights over our bodies, we have a right to a proxy, a right to have someone speak for us if we are unable to speak for ourselves, the proxy being a person who decides as though he were the patient.

How can we be sure what the patient would want? This is difficult unless, as in the case of incompetent adults who have told us in advance in such devices as a living will, in which case the document serves as proxy. At the very least, it may be safely assumed that the incompetent patient would want to be "better off" because of the procedure, with a resulting improved quantity and quality of life.

The first step in the decision-making process is asking competent patients what they prefer. The second step is decision by proxy, with the carefully-guarded proviso that the proxy truly have the subject's interest at heart, choosing what the subject would choose were he able.

But what if the subject is incompetent and there is no clearly appropriate proxy? Here is where there is a missing piece. Usually the next step has been to turn to the courts for assistance, as symbolic representatives of the larger society. Our legal authorities are thus presumably also the guardians of the interests of our most vulnerable citizens.

In a representative democracy, this arrangement has a lot going for it. All of us look out for each one of us through our representative institutions. Unfortunately, there is some question about whether calling up a designated judge at 2:00 AM to get him to order what appears to us to be a life-saving blood transfusion on the child of a member of the Jehovah's Witness faith, is the clearest expression of that ideal.

How can we be sure that such an official, clothed as he may be in the hallowed robes of legal authority, is in a position to really have the best interest of that small subject at heart, more than the parents, more than the doctors? He may have the power but does he always have the right or the wisdom?

A better way to achieve our idea in this third step is patterned after our jury system. In this alternative an attempt is made to bring together a representative cross section of peers to pool their collective judgment. We can improve on the jury model as presently instituted, by training such a group, both formally and in the classroom of experience, and giving it continuity over a period of time. What I'm describing is a properly constituted hospital ethics committee.

The courts have themselves sometimes recommended the ethics committee route. It was promoted by the courts in the original Quinlan case. That decision was the first to recognize the value of hospital-based ethics committees functioning as a body of review for difficult treatment cases. The more recent Conroy decision by the New Jersey Supreme Court, seems, unfortunately, to diminish the earlier position.

An ethics-trained body of citizens representing a variety of interests, including the clinical, is a valuable asset to the decision making process. Health care providers benefit from working together with others in establishing general guidelines and in providing the flexibility required by special problem cases.

Legal authority must back up such bodies on occasion; however, in general most of the ethical questions that cannot be handled by patients themselves, or by appropriate proxies, are taken care of in this way. Given legal status, such bodies very well serve also to dampen the present intolerable malpractice situation. In any case, this defect in the system is well on the way to rectification.

The other defect to which I referred at the outset may be more difficult to deal with for reasons that will shortly become apparent. This is that we need another official definition of death.

But let us back up a bit. Joseph Fletcher, who must be considered one of the pioneers in Protestant bioethics, once published an article titled "Indicators of Humanhood: A Tentative Profile of Man."[3] Never timorous about rushing past cowering angels, Fletcher proposed his own tentative account of what it means to

[3]Fletcher, Joseph. "Indicators of Humanhood: A Tentative Profile of Man." *Hastings Center Report* 2, no. 5 (1972): 1-4.

be a human being. It contained fifteen positive criteria and five negative ones. They ranged all the way from minimal intelligence to the high neocortical functioning, which we usually associate with distinctively human life, with the subhuman animals in between. The specificity with which Fletcher categorized humanness on the IQ scale was astonishing: below 20 not a person, between 20 and 40 questionably a person.

Reactions to Fletcher's article were both immediate and forceful. After considerable give-and-take, he settled on possessing neocortical function as the fundamental human trait.

Although at a distance this discussion might seem quaint, I think that it is not completely misplaced. "Humanness" is a complicated notion and difficult to define; however, given the present state of our medical technology, being able to decide when "it is all over," when it is hopeless, and when it is appropriate to begin or continue or end a particular therapy, are things which we desperately need to know. Any formula that promises to make these decisions easier can only be helpful.

I suggest such a formula, one based on an ethical definition of death. With our increased ability to intervene in physiological processes we have come, more and more, to think of death as a process rather than as a precise event.

Let us begin at the end of the death process and move backward from there. The final stage of death may be spoken of as *cellular death*. Although not all organs or tissues undergo cellular death at the same time or rate, this is the most obvious and ancient of the definitions of death. When all of the tissues are involved, it can be detected at a distance. At the tomb of Lazarus, the family protested Jesus' request that they open the tomb: "'But, Lord,' said Martha, the sister of the dead man, 'by this time there is a bad odor, for he has been there four days.'"[4]

The next to the last stage of dying gives us our time-honored, and until recently, our legal, definition of death based on the disappearance of the "vital signs" such as breathing, heart sounds, pulse, blood pressure, and ocular reflexes. I choose to call this level

[4]John 11:39, NIV.

of death, *organic or organ system death.*

This is what we meant by death in the past. Our resuscitation skills have now minimized the usefulness of this definition, at least in some settings. This has stimulated most of these United States to enact laws which form the basis for our next level of death—*cerebral or brain death.* Brain death statutes have also, incidentally, legally facilitated the harvesting of donor organs from "pulsatile cadavers" by transplant surgeons. The criteria for brain death are well-established now, and need not be repeated here.

It should be noted, though, that there are special cases where the criteria are difficult to ascertain. Short supply is one of the compounding factors which those who provide transplantable organs for human newborns encounter. Brain-death is exceedingly difficult to be sure about in newborns. No surgeon wants to be guilty of taking a heart from a still living baby to be transplanted into another.

As helpful as it may be legally, the brain-death definition still does not satisfy our ethical needs. Another definition is required and this is where the second defect in our decision-making process is encountered.

Karen Quinlan did not legally qualify as brain dead during the nine years she was in a persistent vegetative state. This is because there was still some electroencephalographic activity present even though she was not conscious. Such patients lie month after month, year after year, drooling, soiling themselves, unaware of their surroundings and the persons in them, or even of themselves, taking up space—and costing a lot of money.

We are aware of this kind of situation, and frequently we have acted appropriately in relation to it. It is just that we have never formalized it or provided it with legal sanctions. For want of a better term, I shall call it *personal-death. Mind-death* as contrasted to *brain-death,* might do as well.

Possibly the reason we have never formalized personal or mind-death is that it is exceedingly difficult to characterize. The indicators are subtle and elusive, calling for subjective judgment rather than for laboratory precision. By contrast, brain-death in adults is usually easy to define, and certainly, when the mind's organ, the brain, is dead, the mind is dead also. But it is possible to be person or mind-dead while the mind's organ, the brain, is still very much alive, even if diminished in function.

Here is where those "indicators of humanhood" for which Dr. Fletcher was searching come into play. I prefer to think in terms of the capacity, actual or potential, for autonomy, self-determination, and self-awareness. These are the qualities which were so important in the initial steps of the decision-making process we outlined earlier.

When autonomy and self-determination are irretrievably lost, or were never a possibility because of serious brain or other defects, we have an individual with person or mind-death and can act accordingly (or ought to be able so to act).

What these appropriate actions should be may be determined by a number of things, such as availability, cost, wishes of the proxy persons, and whether care for the mind-dead individual will deprive others of what they require. It will also be determined by what it takes to keep healthy the social environment of such an individual human.

Man as *Homo Symbolicus* is deeply, if sometimes subtly, affected in his attitudes and sensitivities by how he relates to what may be said to have primarily symbolic value.[5] A non-human, by "non-mind" definition, may still have human claims upon us, symbolically. We cannot simply throw the seriously defective child out with the garbage, or the senile elderly individual for that matter. What "means" human must be treated with human compassion and dignity—for the sake of all of us.

Such care may legitimately exclude extraordinary, heroic, and merely life prolonging procedures. If the mind of such an individual cannot be created or restored, all that is required is what it takes to keep us humane—all of us.

It is on this basis that perhaps it was best that the new ruling by the New Jersey Supreme Court did not make a difference in how Karen Quinlan's caretaker took care of her.

---

[5]Paul Tillich, *Dynamics of Faith* (San Francisco: HarperOne, 2009), 47-62.

It can be argued that some of her measures should never have been instituted in the first place or discontinued much earlier; however, with all the human investments that were made in Karen, at the time of the Conroy decision it was probably best for her care providers—and parents—to continue as they were until the issue was taken out of their hands. The attitude of the parents confirm this, I think.

If Karen suffered cardiac arrest, or came down with a serious infectious disease, or experienced a kidney shutdown or something of similar gravity, the situation would have changed and so would have how she should have been cared for.

This is what happened. Despite the Court's ruling in the Conroy case, her care-givers continued their longstanding routine; however, when she came down with pneumonia, her parents declined antibiotics and she died; however, this might have happened even if they had approved their use.

One of the difficulties with the "person-death" or "mind-death" definition is that it is so difficult to apply. It is for this reason that it should remain an ethical rather than a legal definition. The individualized, case-specific, subjective judgments required in such cases can never have the precision that good law demands.

Legally precise criteria, as in brain-death, will rarely be available. I shudder at the very thought of an aware, responsible patient who is unable to communicate. The patient in a "locked-in" syndrome who has lost all ability to communicate from his eyes down, may still be able to be self-determinate, even if limited to communicating his wishes with his eyes. But what if he also lost the use of his eyes and all other special sense organs? How would we know? The point is, those closest to the patient over a period of time would be in a better position to render judgment than a stranger in a distant judicial chamber.

The difficulty encountered in making such a decision is also the reason that it ought to be a shared decision. Again, there is a role for the hospital-based ethics committee. Constituted as we reviewed earlier, with a representative cross-section of concerned persons, such legally sanctioned committees relieve the health-care providers of much of the onerous burden, or at least they distribute it.

This is a matter in which we all have an important stake if we are to begin even in this small way to turn back the dehumanizing forces at work today. But we also have the right to expect that the other arbiter of moral values in our society, the law, give its full and unstinting support. The courts themselves should insist that others better qualified than they are should usually make these decisions. The courts should also protect the decision makers.

The alternative to taking this definition of death seriously is more of the same. This is a continuation of the practice of playing it very safe, sticking by legal brain-death and continuing to condemn the Karen Quinlans among us to a meaningless existence year after year as the costs mount, while those better able to benefit from our limited health-care dollars remain deprived.

My argument is that such decisions belong in the hands of those best able to make them. My plea is for our legal institutions to guarantee that those decisions remain there.

7
Further Thoughts about Baby Fae

One of the goals of medical research is to discover tolerable and practical alternatives to untimely deaths. Tolerable, because there are worse conditions than death. Practical, because some theoretical alternatives may not, in fact, be available. The investigation that preceded it, and the actual transplantation of a seven-month old baboon heart into Baby Fae's chest, was carried out with this larger purpose in mind. It is important to remember this when reviewing this controversial case.

Organ replacement, either by the transplantation of organs from donor sources or by mechanical devices, is an example of attempts to achieve this therapeutic goal. Unfortunately, there are not, and probably will never be, enough human donors to supply the need. This is especially true for the neonate because of the special difficulties peculiar to that period of life.

For one thing, neonates are rarely involved in deaths by accidents or violence that usually result in the primary sources of donor organs for older members of the population. Finding a newborn who has suffered brain-death but possesses a healthy heart, undamaged by the circumstances often associated with neonatal brain-death, which is of the right size and tissue type, and in the right geographic location so that transport time does not compromise the organ, and for whom proxy donor consent has properly been given, presents a complex of difficulties that render availability of human organs unlikely.

Add to this the difficulty of diagnosing brain-death in the newborn, and we come to see the practical limits of the allograft alternative for newborns. If an allograft were found, it would seem to be an extraordinary coincidence, almost guaranteeing that tissue type selection would be limited. Cardiac allografts do not at present appear to provide a practical alternative. Practical mechanical hearts still remain a distant vision, and no one that I know of is preparing one for neonates.

Two other alternatives must therefore be considered. One of these is the Norwood procedure. It is a surgical effort in several stages to rearrange the structures of the hypoplastic left heart so as to permit the right ventricle to carry the load of the missing left one. The second alternative is the xenograft route taken by Dr. Leonard Bailey at Loma Linda, California. The practicality of this approach derives from the fact that baboon organs are readily available. There are other advantages. For instance, we do not have to wait for brain-death before harvesting baboon hearts. This virtually guarantees healthy, functional organs. The proper size can easily be selected and we have some control over time factors, both for donor transport and for adequate tissue testing.

The main practical drawback of a xenograft is rejection and here the precedents are not encouraging. A fair number of xenograft transplants have been attempted in the past with dismal results in every instance.

There were some interesting innovations in the case of Baby Fae that improved the possibility of a different outcome. First, the immunological investigation of potential animal donors had proceeded far beyond anything done previously. Dr. Bailey and his associates had been studying xenograft techniques on animal models, chiefly sheep and goats, with varying degrees of success, and with the accumulation of a large body of experimental data. The team's work included extensive studies of tissue typing in baboons. It also involved the profusion of a baboon heart with human blood without apparent evidence of rejection.

What remained was the xenograft to a human host. In looking for a human model, the hypoplastic left heart syndrome was chosen because it was within Dr. Bailey's competence as a pediatric thoracic surgeon and because the condition is uniformly lethal. Success would, of course, have had much broader implications. Satisfaction of the criteria noted above seemed assured at the beginning. The animal studies indicated that the procedure was well-tolerated. As confirmation, Baby Fae's condition post-op was not an intolerable one.

One of the startling results of this research was the finding of a much greater histocompatibility between humans and at least some baboons than had previously been expected. Moreover, never had an attempt been made on so young a patient with the possible benefit of an immature immunological system and its diminished tendency to reject transplanted organs.

Another difference was Cyclosporine-A, a newer immunosuppressive drug that had made a great deal of difference in transplant technology. These factors constituted a basis for hope that this alternative might offer a reasonable possibility of success. This possibility was greater than any of the other options, including the human allograft in the rare instances when one was really available. The other alternative was certain death and Baby Fae came close to it more than once prior to surgery.

We had a slightly premature child facing certain death unless something drastic were done to correct her congenital heart defect. There were four options, all but the first highly experimental and none of them good. (1) Death, (2) the Norwood procedure, (3) a human allograft, and (4) a baboon xenograft. The ethical requirement that the incompetent patient's wellbeing take priority over purely experimental purposes demanded that the best available option be selected, even if this interfered temporarily with experimental goals.

Death was unacceptable by all of the tenets of medicine, providing that a reasonable quality of life was a possibility. The Norwood procedure had serious problems, including an unacceptably high mortality rate and a reduced quality of life. A human allograft was an impractical solution to the larger organ transplant problem and presented insurmountable difficulties for the newborn. That left baboon xenograft.

While large questions remained, the newer information and better immuno-suppressant drugs provided a real measure of hope. If the surgery were successful, it would provide a practical solution to the Baby Faes among us, plus a host of other benefits down the line. As questionable as it was, a xenograft offered at least as great, and possibly a greater therapeutic hope than the Norwood procedure and an allograft. We would not know if the xenograft were not attempted.

Much experimental preparation using animal models had been done. Proper consent was apparently provided, including protection for the incompetent infant. The goals were therapeutic rather than purely experimental ones. The baby to be more important than the experiment.

Baby Fae lived almost 3 weeks after the surgery, with apparently at least two good weeks. This was much longer than any other xenograft patient had ever survived. An enormous amount of information has been accumulated that may augur well for the future.

Was it worth it? Only the future will tell us for sure. For now, it at least seems that those who were involved acted with ethical responsibility.

8
Some Ethical Considerations Regarding Artificial Insemination

In a situation of rapid technical and social change, it is difficult to keep all aspects of existence in harmony with each other. Some elements may change more rapidly than others. Technology, for example, as at present may outrun our capacity to accommodate it to values and meanings. As a consequence, we may lose the guidance and control that is essential to keeping the "thing" from turning Frankenstein-like on its creator. When our skills at creating and manipulating the "whats" of our life become greater than those providing the "whys" and the "oughts," that is, if we allow technology to outpace our spiritual or moral value structures, we risk our very humanity.

Unfortunately, there is an almost inevitable lag built in to these guiding values based on the fact that, for the most part, values are inherited from the past, and the past may not always have precisely anticipated the present or future.

In a situation of rapid change it becomes increasingly important, then, that we discover the enduring qualities which we share with the past, and how we may give them the specific application the present moment demands. No moral or value structure can be created de novo for each generation. Such structures belong by nature to continuity not to novelty; however, they must be in contact with what is new. Otherwise novelty becomes merely another name for chaos. Chaos is ultimately incompatible with human existence.

We may draw examples of the kind of troubled sea on which morals and values now find themselves from our newly created capacity to manipulate life itself. In this discussion, just one of these will be singled out—perhaps not even the most important one—that forms a useful illustration of our problem because it is a matter on which the past is largely silent. I refer to procreation by artificial insemination and, more precisely, to artificial insemination involving a donor who is not the husband of the recipient. Giving technical assistance to a husband as he attempts to impregnate his wife appears to be a somewhat different matter, as this discussion will hopefully demonstrate.

A.I.D., or Artificial Insemination involving a donor, is now a matter of general information so that the details of the procedure need not be reviewed here. It usually involves a married woman who wants to bear a child whose husband is sterile. Both agree to obtain semen from a third person. This donor is often a medical student who is given a small fee for his services. Care is taken to assure that the donor is a genetically healthy male.

The semen is usually obtained by masturbation and may be used while fresh or may be preserved for an indeterminate period by freezing. The complete anonymity of both donor and recipient is studiously preserved. When A.I.D. began, the physician who acted as the intermediary was usually the only person privy to information regarding the identities of the persons involved. Increasingly, no one knows both the donor and the recipient because the sperm is frozen in straws or vials and "housed" in a "bank." This requires three "participants" who do not know each other: donor, banker and recipient.

The transfer of the semen is a completely mechanical, instrumental procedure. Occasionally the semen may be mixed with that of the woman's husband if his problem seems to be one of too low a sperm count rather than one of total sterility. In this case, presumably, the husband has at least a chance of being the child's actual father.

There are several pros and cons regarding the procedure. In its favor is the obvious possibility that a fertile woman who wants to bear a child may be able to do so in this manner. There is also the possibility of a measure of eugenic selectivity. Medical students may not all be geniuses but are generally reasonably gifted people. The futuristic implications of being able to select from a variety of gifted males at a frozen sperm bank provides rather exciting eugenic prospects. Imagine being able to draw genetically from some present or future Einstein or Mozart for perhaps generations to come.

The objections are a little more numerous although some are not overly impressive. The legal status of a child born from artificial insemination is sometimes unclear. Suppose, for example, a divorce occurs before or even after the delivery of the child. Who is responsible for child support? Is this the husband, wife, or speculatively, the donor? Does such a child inherit property in the same way that a natural child does? Laws can, of course, be written so as to clear up such ambiguities, and in many places they have been.

There is also the question of the "paternal" attitude toward such an offspring. There have been cases where the husband emotionally rejected the child so conceived. But, of course, natural parents also sometimes reject their offspring.

On the other hand, experience has generally shown that, when artificial insemination is carried out selectively, it does not threaten families. Of course, bringing a child into the world by any method in the vain hope of shoring up a shaky marriage is a risky kind of business and would ordinarily be contraindicated. It is reported that families with children from artificially inseminated donor sperm are usually as happy as families with children who are born naturally.

A perhaps more serious concern might derive from the possibility of consanguinity. A medical student, or any other man, who is repeatedly involved as a donor in a particular geographic area might become the genetic father of fairly numerous progeny because anonymity is the rule. What is to prevent some of these from growing up and falling in love and producing offspring of their own? Recent studies have confirmed statistically what has long been believed, that sexual intercourse between closely related persons produces a disproportionate number of abnormal progeny. Indeed, the statistics indicate a highly disproportionate number. Can anyone who is involved in the process prevent this from happening without violating somebody's trust?

To get at the major moral arguments against A.I.D., however, calls for a more subtle kind of logic. This is probably the reason such objections have not been commonly raised even by conscientious people. Pope Pius the XII, after some deliberation, branded A.I.D. as adulterous in terms of Thomistic natural law theory. But most non-Catholics, plus not a few Catholics, have been unimpressed by his pronouncement.

It will be our purpose here to approach the matter through a backward glance at the general "continuities" that may be involved, and then try to discover, if possible, what may be their application to this situation. These continuities are the principles, especially the Christian ones, which govern sexual and procreative activity.

The truly Christian moralist takes his guidance from what he can discern regarding the divine intention. What God wills is right and, because God's will or intention is by definition orderly and consistent, even if obscure, His intention should be found "written into" the very nature of created things. God's expressed moral law is in fact a description of His creative intention. When He commands "Thou shalt" or "Thou shalt not" in whatever way He commands it, He is not being capricious or arbitrary. He is, as it were, providing an "operator's manual" that outlines the way things He created should function. Moreover, since the intention of God is expressed in the creation itself, as well as in the divine revelation regarding the creation, an investigation of both is appropriate.

A violation of God's law is not merely an offense to God; it is also a violation of the integrity of the "thing itself." In point of fact, I sin against myself, my very being, when I violate God's law for me. This is because my transgression interferes with, or prevents, my achieving the ends for which I was brought into existence. The rules for human existence, expressed or implied, are descriptions of what it takes to make human life truly human.

As we investigate man's created nature, we discover that it contains certain unique features. We discover, for example, that man was made for community. Man is not merely gregarious, though he shares that feature with many animals. He enters into kinds of relationships with other humans unknown to animals. The Bible says "It is not good that the man should be alone."[1] This points to an important feature of man's nature. This quality is related to his intelligence, his freedom, his capacity for symbolic activity, for communication, his self-understanding, his sense of time—his ability to relate past, present, and future—and above all his capacity for certain depths of trust and love. These are all part of what is meant by the statement in Genesis "Let us make man in our image."[2] Man's creation was structured so as to ensure the possibility of achieving these qualities.

His procreative capacity was a part of the structure. When God wanted a world populated with men He created two human beings and let them share in the creation. And this sharing involved more than their mere biologic replication.

To be sure, man also shared reproduction with lower animals, but in man there was this difference. Man was made responsible for his reproductive actions in a way that animals were not. Given little voluntary control over the process, reproduction was largely imposed on lower animals. Reproduction was a part of man's freedom and with this freedom came a creator's responsibility analogous to that of the divine Creator.

Such a responsibility was partly conditioned by the prolonged period of a human infant's dependency. The vast majority of lower

---

[1]Genesis 2:18.

[2]Genesis 1:26.

animals have virtually no influence over or contact with their progeny after they are born. Even those that do have such contact only for a very brief period when compared with man. In the divine economy, this longer time was to produce a double benefit. For the parents, it was to provide an experiential basis for a comprehension of the fatherhood of God. For the child, his parents being God to him in his infancy, it was to establish the matrix for his later trustful, creative dependence on the God beyond his parents. Trust and creative dependence are largely learned qualities, and the home and family were designed by God as their primary learning situation. This could also mean that, if the home failed in its purpose, such qualities might be learned badly or never at all.

To achieve the durability and social closeness that such a learning situation required, God added another dimension to human reproduction not experienced—at least to this depth—in lower animals. God associated reproduction and sexuality with "loving." Animals copulate. Man can also copulate, but only of man do we speak of "making love."

It is well known that one of the major differences between the Protestant and Catholic attitudes towards sexuality in marriage is over which of these two qualities takes priority—the procreative or the social (love). Catholics traditionally opt for the former, Protestants for the latter; however, whichever one emphasizes, the fact remains that in the divine intention the two belong together.

That love is possible independently from frankly sexual, at least gonadal, activity suggests, on the one hand, that love has a kind of priority over procreation. Sexual activity apart from love may seem, on the other hand, base and sensual. Christian moralists generally find this to be the most objectionable feature of the current sexual scene. One of the rules of promiscuous practices is the avoidance of emotional attachment to the temporary sexual partner. Even terms of endearment are taboo. Sex in such a setting obviously has little to do with love-making.

But the durability of the parental relationship, and thus of the family and the home that are so necessary to the achievement of the highest human potentials for the children as well as their parents, requires that the two elements be associated together. Coitus, even reproduction, can occur as a temporary chance encounter, but a family cannot.

One other fact of human experience must also be taken into account. Earlier it was noted that one of the qualities that distinguished the human was his capacity for symbolic activity. Only man possesses this to any significant degree. It is the basis for his intellection, verbal communication, and complex social organization. Certain actions gain their chief significance from the fact that they "mean" something, that they "point to" or communicate ideas and values, and in the process also establish and reinforce them. Many of the actions to which we attribute moral value or disvalue—i.e., right or wrong, depend on such "meaning" for their evaluation.

Suppose we place the recipient of the insemination in a dark room, blindfold her so that she cannot see the donor and insure anonymity as well as impersonality, and drape her body so that only the immediate genitalia were exposed. Suppose that in the same darkened room we place a donor who is unknown to the recipient, and ask him to obtain his semen by masturbating. At the last instant before he ejaculates, we turn on a light which illuminates only the exposed genitalia of the recipient. We then ask him to place the semen in her vagina with his penis and then quickly and anonymously leave the room. Would this be right or wrong? Would it be less wrong to have him deposit the semen in a receptacle first—say a spoon or syringe—and thence into the vagina?

What would make these two situations different? Impersonality and anonymity would be assured in both cases. The point is, the actual contact of the sexual organs would convey a meaning that contact with an instrument would not, and it is this meaning that conditions our moral attitudes toward the act. It is on this basis that the above description is not the way artificial insemination is carried out—even though it might be practical and even efficient.

This point becomes relevant to our discussion when we state, as above, that it was the Creator's intention to associate procreation with what is meant by "making love." Of course many other meanings can also be associated with sexuality—fun, games, guilt, fear, money, filth, nastiness, exploitation, hate—as anybody involved in premarital and marital counseling well knows. But "loving" is what it was supposed to mean and all of these other possible connotations are distortions of sexuality. These distortions may occur because sexual beings do not (or sometimes cannot—sometimes "meanings" are thrust upon us through no fault of our own) safeguard the symbolic significance of their acts.

It is on this basis that artificial insemination must come under closest scrutiny. The practice involves an intended dissociation of sexual activity and love. The effects of such dissociation both on the part of the recipient and donor—but especially the latter—may be subtle and largely unnoticed at first but it cannot but be debasing of the divine intervention in the long run, and especially if a commercial motive is also associated with the act.

Nor is it a justification of the practice to note that such dissociation is already almost universal. It is the task of sensitive Christians to be aware of and to be prepared to deal compassionately and with understanding with that which is less than ideal. Certainly we should never order our activities in such a way as to legitimize or "normalize" the less than ideal even as we attempt to come to terms with it. Always such coping attempts should be redemptive to rather than reinforcing of human shortcomings.

But what shall we do for the wife of a sterile husband who desperately wants a child? Such yearnings can at times be fairly overwhelming. Is there any recourse? Adoptions are becoming increasingly hard to come by. And if artificial assistance is available, is it not perhaps the lesser of evils?

This is a difficult question for a sympathetic human being to turn away. But one could also ask, "What of the single girl who yearns for a child? Shouldn't she have access to this technique?" The objection that she cannot fulfill the family structure requirement by herself is less than convincing in view of the success some widows and divorcees have shown at being both mother and father. Surely under only very unusual circumstance would one suggest that such mothers be deprived of their children—even for their children's sakes.

The objection is, I think, a rather more subtle one, having to do as above with the meaning of the sexual act—a meaning that transcends mechanics or biology. Sensitive Christians will almost intuitively recoil from the mechanization of an event so loaded with possible significance for human good or ill—in the long run.

One cannot "thingify" sexuality without debasing it, that is, without robbing it of its symbolic potential for preserving an important quality of human experience. And this may mean that some persons who want children of their own will have to find other ways of satisfying their God-given cravings. One of the greatest needs in the world at the moment is for affectionate mother and father surrogates in many capacities. The one thing that we must not do is satisfy this need in such a way as to jeopardize the very values which give to such needs their real importance.

Is there not the danger of instilling in the minds of donors for artificial insemination a subtle self-image that involves rejection of responsibility for one's procreative activities? How can the donor possibly be responsible for what is genetically his child in such a setting? Does not this very fact tend to create an irresponsible attitude towards the procreative function?

What a different social world this might be if every person viewed this procreative ability as a gift from God and with the value, respect, and even reverence that should be associated with that awareness. The gift could become one of the most highly prized of the capacities God has given to men. To trivialize it, to commercialize it, or to minimize in any way our sense of value or responsibility for it is to debase it. And the coin of this realm is already devalued enough. It will surely take all of the conjoined efforts of concerned people together to make even a small difference to what has happened to the divine gift—but surely we must try. At least we can avoid helping to push the devaluation along.

Part III

Personal Ethics

9
War and the Christian Conscience

In simpler times, the question of the Christian's participation in war was largely a matter of whether the war was morally justified. War itself as an instrument of national policy could not, on biblical grounds, be summarily rejected. Although the Old Testament examples were related to the theocratic social structure of ancient Israel, it has never been difficult in any age to see God as being on "our side" and thus "our cause" to be just. As a consequence, history abounds with holy wars. Nevertheless, given the social and philosophical complexity of the present, the term "just war" is increasingly difficult to utter in any total sense.

A conflict of competing claims is at issue. On the one hand, there is the Christian's loyalty to his country and his biblical duty to submit to the higher powers. On the other hand, there is his loyalty to God as expressed in sensitivity to the value of human life. How do we accommodate these opposing claims without compromising our personal integrity in the process?

The Adventist accommodation recommends that SDAs not enlist; however, if they are drafted, the church recommends that they make every effort to serve in some medical capacity. This accommodation has failed on logical grounds to be wholly satisfying to all Adventists. A growing number of young Adventists are protesting that it does not go nearly far enough in its rejection of warfare. They increasingly reject participation in war at any level.

"How can those who are accessories to evil acts avoid sharing in the guilt?" they ask. After all, "conscientious cooperators," as Adventists who follow this path call themselves, play a role, even if an indirect and remote one, in the war effort. They contend that, if the war does not qualify as "just" or "holy," the conscientious cooperator is also to blame. Perhaps he does not pull the trigger but, in fact, he holds up the hands of those who do. Any court of law takes account of the guilt of the accomplice even if his is in a noncombatant role.

The question of logic has often been raised by interrogators of young Adventist men. "What would you do if a marauder broke into your home and threatened your family?" The logical argument is won or lost at this point. If the Adventist says, "I would be duty bound to protect my family by whatever means I could," he has started down a road from which there is no turning. This family situation is easily extended to the neighborhood, the community, and the nation. This is not a difficult road to take. What red-blooded man would not come to the rescue of his family in such a situation with all the resources at his command? Wouldn't he argue that God required it?

It is not difficult to contrast a clear cut aggression to our homes with the ambiguous situation of war where the individual enemy may have no aggressive intentions. Unwilling soldiers are drafted on the other side also. Yet there is clear cut aggression in modern war too. Does this not suggest selectivity in combat rather than the rejection of combat itself? Also, if we must engage in combat, selective or defensive, should we not become efficient in it through training?

Here is another hypothetical situation that examiners use. "What would you do if you were a medical corpsman on the front lines and several defenseless wounded men were lying about who were dependent upon you for care and protection? Suddenly the enemy attacks, threatening to overrun your position. You are the only man physically able to act and there are defensive weapons at hand. Would you allow the lives of those defenseless young soldiers to be snuffed out while you stood idly by? Could you do this guiltlessly? If you felt obliged to defend them, should you not also feel responsibility to always have at hand the means needed for their defense, as well as some skill in using protective weapons?"

Short of praying that such a situation would never develop or that God would work a miracle on his behalf, the soldier being questioned faces an obvious logical dilemma. The faulty logic of the Adventist position is attested to at this point by the early retreat of its advocates into responses like, "I don't know what I would do," or "I would just trust the Lord to guide me," or "If I had enough faith and prayed God would work a miracle." Even in such a prayer there is always the possibility that God may use the corpsman himself as the means of providing the answer.

To say that the Adventist position is logically on shaky grounds is not to imply that it is incorrect or unsupportable. It simply means that we must look elsewhere than to simple logic for its support. My view is that the Adventist position is a sound one, albeit perhaps not the only sound one, and I suggest a basis for maintaining and strengthening it.

I propose that the reasons for holding the Adventist position are not logical but "prophetic." The primary function of the prophet in the Biblical sense was communication. As a communicator, the prophet was called to direct attention to truths or values which were either not yet understood or in danger of being lost or disvalued.

Most of the time, the Biblical prophets communicated through the verbal symbols of speaking and writing. As the situation demanded, they sometimes communicated by their actions, even illogical and peculiar actions. Recall Jeremiah walking about with an ox yoke about his neck, Hosea's marriage to a harlot, and the unmourned death of Ezekiel's wife. These were all forms of nonverbal symbolic communication.

As in John the Baptist's attire made of camel hair, even the prophets' manner and dress entered into the messages which they were called to communicate. The messages themselves were often given emphasis beyond proportion. It seemed to be a part of the prophet's role to speak loudly, even violently, in order to be heard above the din of his times.

The biblical prophet was usually an individual; however, God has also called "prophetic" movements into existence for the purpose of restoring lost insights and values and giving new vision. Israel was intended to be a movement when through divine providence it was selected as a "peculiar treasure unto me above all people: for all the earth is mine: And ye shall be unto me a kingdom of priests and a holy nation."[1] All the world was to hear the voice of God more closely through God's chosen prophetic people.

I submit that the Adventist movement was ordained by God for just such a "prophetic" ministry. It was to be a prophetic people, a "collective prophet" through whom God wished to reveal important truths to his larger people or invisible church scattered throughout the world.

There are many things God is trying to say through this prophetic movement and the matter under consideration is among them. In a turbulent world of strife, violence, bloodshed and untold human tragedy, God is trying to remind all people of the sanctity of human life; that He, as a concerned Life-giver, does not sit withdrawn on the sidelines refusing to stain His clothes with the grim and blood of human misery. At great personal risk, He plunges into the gore and mud to bring life and healing and a vision of tender goodness into a world where the lights of human kindness and compassion are fast flickering out. This is the meaning of the incarnation. It is also the message of a prophetic movement as it focuses on the horror fields where war is fought.

It seems entirely in keeping with the divine prophetic action which Jesus Christ expressed that His followers should honor the social order that provides much of the context for meaningful human existence, in other words to give Caesar his due. They should also strive within that order to call attention to the virtues and

[1]Exodus 19:5-6.

values which give significance to life. These are always in jeopardy, especially more so in wartime.

What superficially appears to be illogical may have its own deeper, if covert, kind of logic and this may be true of the non-combatant position. Seen as a "prophetic witness," this position need not be supported by elemental logic in all aspects. Its primary concern is communication. If that communication can also seem logical, so much the better, but it doesn't have to be. All that is absolutely essential is that it be "prophetic."

Although this seems to be what the past and present position of the Seventh-day Adventist church has been, it might not always be so in every possible situation. A flexibility is required which enables the church to speak appropriately to differing circumstances.

There have been conditions requiring vigorous combatancy. The Old Testament is replete with examples. It is conceivable that, at least on a limited scale, this could occur again as, for example, in an aggressive threat to a family or neighborhood. It is not inconceivable that an overwhelming emergency such as that described in the case of the corpsman above, might demand a temporary shedding of the prophet's customary camel's hair coat. Flexibility on the part of the church in the other direction is also required. A situation could develop where any kind of participation in war might, on prophetic grounds, be radically denied.

It turns out, then, that there are three kinds of situations which could in turn call for combatancy, non-combatancy, and partial combatancy, the third being one way to label the Adventist recommendation. Although this is the Adventist position, and it does have an "inner logic," the church must have enough flexibility to do what is morally required in each of the three circumstances.

We still need to add something. This is that the members of the prophetic movement could say different things about the same situation. It would be a mistake for its leadership to speak as it now does about the Christian's relationship to war but to ignore that some of its members are called to embody a more thorough protest against the whole messy business of war. A church which is clear as to its mission must allow and support the conviction, earnestly held by some of its members, that war is always a hopeless instrument of evil.

A church which senses its prophetic vocation must allow for subtle, or even obvious, variations within its general communication. This is especially the case concerning matters as complex as war in our time. This means that it will be prepared to support other viewpoints as legitimate expressions of the Christian message of compassionate concern. In matters of conscience the church must be prepared to speak with as many voices as the varied circumstances of need demand.

10
Shall A Christian Protect His Own?

Now that the United States has shifted to an all-volunteer army, the issue confronting Adventist young men for so long has, at least momentarily, dissipated. There remains the larger question which has always confronted the followers of Christ and now grows in intensity as our cities become ever more barbarous places. It is the question of how much thought and preparation a Christian should give to protecting himself and his loved ones in their little wars with the lawless elements in their own neighborhoods and cities.

The potential draftee seeking conscientious objector status was sometimes faced with the question, "What would you do if someone broke into your home to rob or molest your family?" It was a trap, of course. If he responded according to his normal protective instincts, the next question would be, "What if several homes in your neighborhood were threatened? Wouldn't it make good sense for you and your neighbors to join in mutual defense?" If the young man admitted the logic of this, he would then be led on to the larger community. Finally, he would be asked, "Isn't fighting 'over there' the most logical and effective way of protecting a nation's collective homes?"

That initial question is no longer as hypothetical as it once was. Safety in America's homes, on its streets, in its parks and playgrounds, and even in its lovely wilderness areas can no longer be simply assumed.

How should the Christian relate to a situation of societal disorder bordering on anarchy? The Scriptures tell us that "if any provide not for his own, and especially for those of his own house, he hath denied the faith, and is worse than an infidel."[1] What does such provision include? Food? Clothing? A roof over their head? Probably. Does it also include their safety, protection from marauders, molesters and the like? If so, to what extent? How far should a husband and father go to protect his wife and children?

Our home is situated in a somewhat isolated setting. We have large dogs who are our pets and friends and probably provide us a measure of protection. Although they are not trained as guard dogs and I do not know if they would actually attack anyone, they are vocal in the presence of strangers, and they do appear menacing. To date our home has never been threatened that we know of. Is it wrong for a Christian to own a watch dog, perhaps even one trained for guard duty? If this may be done, what of other defensive weapons such as mace, knives, hatpins, nightsticks, guns? Where should one draw the line?

Is the Christian expected to rely only on prayer and piety for his family's safety? To be sure, prayer is always a Christian's major defense. But we all know examples of good, praying people who were murdered, raped, or robbed even as we've heard of others who escaped. Are we to say that God willed both?

There is always the possibility that God may use man's efforts as the means of accomplishing His ends. Does it make any moral difference whether God sends defending angels or employs human defenders? If He can use the latter, may that not include us husbands, fathers, and brothers?

It seems clear, both from experience and from an understanding of the issues in the Great Controversy about the character of

[1] 1 Timothy 5:8.

God, that He cannot miraculously intervene in every threatening case, even though He might wish to, without jeopardizing the future. The security of that future results to a great extent upon a full portrayal of the consequences of sin, even those remote and indirect results which sometimes hurt or kill his pious and praying children.

Consider these comments by Ellen White regarding miracles and our efforts.

> God does not work miracles where He has provided means by which the work may be accomplished. Use your time and talents in His service and He will not fail to work with your efforts. If the farmer fails to plow and sow, God does not work a miracle to undo the results of his neglect.[2]

> There are great laws that govern the world of nature and spiritual things are controlled by principles equally certain. The means for an end must be employed if the desired results are to be obtained. Those who make no decided efforts themselves are not working in harmony with the laws of God."[3]

Does this principle apply to the protection of our families?

The statement in 1 Timothy about providing for our loved ones should be accompanied by another one in Romans; "Put ye on the Lord Jesus Christ and make not provision for the flesh to fulfill the lusts thereof." What "provision for the flesh" constitutes may be judged by the previous verse, "Let us walk honestly, as in the day; not in rioting and drunkenness, not in chambering and wantonness, not in strife and envying."[4] In line with the last phrase, lusts of the flesh may apparently include such passions as hatred, hostility, vindictiveness and vengeance.

---

[2]Ellen G. White, *Fundamentals of Christian Education* (Mountain View, CA: Pacific Press, 1923), 123.
[3]Ibid., 174.
[4]Romans 13:13-14.

The follower of Christ will avoid danger wherever possible. It is presumptuous to take unnecessary risks and then expect God to work miracles for us. We must deport ourselves defensively. Extravagance and display of wealth may be asking for trouble. We should also avoid risky places. Avoidance is not the whole answer, of course. Things being what they are at present, there is almost no way to lead a normal life and remain entirely free from peril.

Christian attitudes toward self-defense are in the main conditioned by Jesus' own words and example. It was Jesus who said, "Whosoever shall smite thee on thy cheek, turn to him the other also."[5] What does this injunction mean? Is "turning the other cheek" clearly a non-defensive action? Or is it, as in Mahatma Gandhi and Martin Luther King, Jr., a most potent kind of defensive action which involves profound moral force?

The Christian who thinks of Jesus' way as passive may have missed the point. "Turning the other cheek" is not an act of passive cowardice but a deed which is designed to exert the maximum possible moral pressure on the enemy. Its effectiveness depends entirely on the moral sensitivity of the enemy. "Turning the other cheek" may be an effort wasted on a madman because he cannot respond to its moral thrust!

"Turning the cheek" as a moral reaction to abuse comes out differently when it involves turning someone else's cheek, perhaps that of one's defenseless child. What does it mean to my wife or daughter who is about to be raped by a sex maniac? Or to me who may be in a position to intervene?

Although making a voluntary display of vulnerability may be an important way of dealing with an enemy, it loses some of its force when we ask others to take this risk. This is especially so when the enemy is a madman. We must remember that there is such a thing as "moral madness." Even God deals differently with persons whose "cup of iniquity" is full.[6]

Jesus once said as He faced an enemy, "My kingdom is not of this world: if my kingdom were of this world, then would my ser-

---

[5]Matthew 5:39.

[6]Genesis 15:16; Revalation 16:19; Revalation 18:1-8.

vants fight?"[7] What are we to make of this?

Surely Jesus' words indicate that the sword is not an appropriate instrument for the promulgation of the Gospel. Moreover, its use is not to interfere with the life and mission of Jesus. But does my intervention to prevent injury to my wife or child fall into the same category? The senseless jeopardy in which I may place them if I do not fight seems like a different matter.

What about what Jesus said to Peter who was trying to defend him? "Put up again thy sword into his place: for all they that take the sword perish with the sword."[8] This is surely a valid appraisal of a general way of life which has been confirmed again and again throughout history. But what of our encounters with mad men?

We also have in the Scriptures Paul's respect for the one who "beareth not the sword in vain: for he is the minister of God, a revenger to execute wrath upon him that doeth evil."[9] If it is proper for me to support such "ministers," in this the soldiers of the Roman Empire, with my encouragement, cooperation and taxes, is it not also proper for me to share in their responsibilities as I am able?

A "called people" may be asked to emphasize certain truths by their behavior, perhaps even to overemphasize them, so that they will not be lost in the general turmoil. Such overemphasis may sometimes lose in logic what it gains in results.

Recall the somewhat extreme behavior of certain of the prophets such as Jeremiah with the ox-yoke about his neck, the peculiar garb of Elijah and John the Baptist. Few would have listened to them otherwise. On the other hand, the exceptional behavior demanded by the "prophetic role" must not be allowed to obscure the general principle.

Finally, we have these thoughts from Ellen White:

> In the parable of the unjust judge, Christ has shown what we should do. "Shall not God avenge His own elect, which

---

[7]John 18:36..
[8]Matthew 26:52.
[9]Romans 13:4.

> cry day and night unto Him?" Christ, our example, did nothing to vindicate or deliver Himself. He committed His case to God. So His followers are not to accuse or condemn, or to resort to force in order to deliver themselves.[10]
>
> However unjustly one may be treated, Let not passion arise. By indulging a spirit of retaliation we injure ourselves. We destroy our own confidence in God, and grieve the Holy Spirit."[11]

The setting of this statement is a chapter which begins, "Christ had been speaking of the period just before His second coming, and of the perils through which His followers must pass."[12] Christ's counsel is in complete harmony with the manner in which Jesus endured His own "time of trouble," and the avoidance of making provision for the "lusts of the flesh" about which we spoke earlier seems clear.

Yet it also seems likely that none of this precludes the use of restraint to control the ordinary criminal. The perils Christ's followers pass through at the end of time are not precisely the same, nor are the issues the same, as those involving everyday acts of violence such as now stalk our streets and haunt our neighborhoods.

Ellen White offers the assurance in this chapter that "If we surrender our lives to His service, we can never be placed in a position for which God has not made provision." But what provision? Paul's earlier statement suggests that "God's ministers," the police or soldiers, might be such a provision. Are there ways in which we can cooperate with the divine providence in preventing us from being mugged or beaten senseless in a city park or having one's wife raped in a shopping center parking lot by madmen?

The Christian is involved in a dual set of obligations that sometimes appear to conflict with one another. On the one hand, he is

---

[10]Ellen G. White, *Christ's Object Lessons* (Mountain View, CA: Pacific Press, 1900), 171-172.
[11]Ibid.,164.
[12]Ibid.,173.

given the sacred trust of providing for those dependent upon him and surely this must include their safety. On the other hand, he is required to love the enemy.

This love is derived from the Greek word *agape* which does not necessarily include such sentiments as "liking." The Lord did not ask that we be fond of the enemy, only that we deal kindly with him. All of our actions toward the enemy are to be with his redemption, restoration and preservation in view. Never must we make provision for hatred, hostility, vindictiveness and vengeance toward him.

Both of these obligations will be served best by a demonstration of kindliness and non-offensiveness toward even the invader of our homes if we have the opportunity. Unfortunately, many crimes of violence do not give us this option. Being suddenly accosted on a dark street may make the possibility of exercising the power of moral influence fairly academic. If the enemy reveals an inability to respond by still behaving like a moral madman, is this perhaps the time to employ whatever minimal force is required to prevent his crime for his sake as well as the innocents involved?

This does not seem to be inconsistent with Jesus' admonition to "resist not evil"[13] particularly if we interpret this as Paul does when he says: "Recompense no man evil for evil."[14] The use of restraining force against an enemy may be for his own good, to keep him from the evil from which he seems unable to restrain himself.

Such a course of action is fraught with hazards, including immediate physical hazards if one is not prepared by ability, training, experience, and equipment to exercise such restraint. If restraint is insufficient or ineffectively applied, the results could be worse than those that would have come from not resisting at all. It will usually require the assistance of equipped and trained people.

Resistance must also be conditioned by what is endangered. If I am awakened in the middle of the night by the sounds of a burglar rifling my desk, it probably would be wise to feign sleep. On the other hand, if he gives evidence of planning to inflict bodily harm

---

[13]Matthew 5:39.

[14]Romans 12:17.

on us, or if he moves towards my daughter's bedroom, it might be the time for me to become very much awake.

There are perils which are even greater than physical risks which include rationalizing what the Apostle Paul called "the lusts of the flesh." Abraham Lincoln once asked how many legs a sheep would have if we called his tail a leg. His answer was that it would still have only four because calling a tail a leg doesn't make it so. Likewise, calling hatred, hostility and vindictiveness "righteous indignation" doesn't change the moral pathologies that they are.

It is not enough to suggest to persons in threatening circumstances that they simply pray and everything will be all right. Pray? Yes! Yet prayer is rarely something one does "simply." In the words of Ellen White, "Let there be most earnest prayer; and then let us work in harmony with our prayers."[15]

Prayer is not a magical solution to difficult problems. Prayer is the means by which we draw on the resources of heaven for goodness that casts out the "lusts of the flesh," for wisdom that clears our minds, for sharp discernment, for endurance for what must be borne in patience, and for strength that steadies our hands to do what has to be done. Prayer is the means by which we store up such resources in advance of the crisis so that what may seem to be the impulse of the moment is a reflection of a clear design written by God into a consistent life.

Genuinely following Jesus makes a man responsible, not irresponsible, strong not weak, active not passive and courageous not cowardly. Above all, being a true disciple helps a man to know what has to be done and it gives him the moral presence to do it in the right way and for the right reasons.

---

[15]Ellen G. White, *Testimonies for the Church,* vol. 5 (Mountain View, CA: Pacific Press, 1948), 714.

11
What's Wrong with Gambling?

Until I was told why, I was surprised that I was invited to address this topic. It does not seem to be a high priority among the ethical issues that we should be addressing. I can think of several more pressing concerns—racial justice, equality for women, church-state relations, bioethical issues such as abortion, overseas wage-scale inequities, even some things going on in our national government which ought to disturb us.

My mind got busy when I was told that some Adventists had become interested in the ethics of gambling because one of their own had won a lot of money in a lottery. I wondered if they would have viewed the matter differently if the winner had given all the money to the church. Would his winning at the lottery have been excused if it had been committed in advance to the Sabbath School investment program? In that case, might we assume that God aided in turning up the winning number? Would they have allowed the winner to build a new school gymnasium with the money? Would it have been less wrong if he hadn't won so much, say ten dollars instead of thousands? Can we overlook small-time gambling and condemn only those in the big money? With all the sales promotion gimmicks of today's competitive business enterprises, there could be a large number of unnoticed small-time gamblers functioning in our midst. Or are they really gambling?

The more I thought about it, the more I realized how ambiguous this issue could be. Christians have traditionally opposed gambling, but without really clarifying the reasons. They simply say that it is wrong, we shouldn't do it, and we should try to keep others from doing it.

The City Council of Loma Linda, California, a predominantly Seventh-day Adventist town in southern California, once found itself torn between its intentions to keep the municipality free from "vice," on the one hand, and extending religious freedom, on the other. The precipitating event was a request by a local church of a different denomination to operate Bingo games in order to raise money for its parochial school. The members of the Council had very little to help them decide either way.

In all of my books on ethics I have been unable to discover a single one that deals candidly with this question. We do not even have a clear definition of what constitutes gambling.

Where is the line between investing and gambling on the stock market? Is it not easy to differentiate between "playing the stock market" on Wall Street and "playing the ponies" at Santa Anita or Churchill Downs? This question might keep some executives who manage the church's investments awake at night. It might be bothering a rank and file church member or two as well. We could be plowing new ethical soil—or, at least, soil that has lain fallow for quite a long time.

It seems obious that sound business investment, even in stocks and bonds, is not what we typically condemn when we oppose gambling; however, we know that it is possible to gamble in this and other business practices. There must be a line that qualitatively distinguishes investing and gambling. This quality might be what makes gambling wrong.

The largely unexamined apprehension most Adventists feel

toward gambling is partly due to cultural conditioning. It is, of course, also influenced by a number of statements in Ellen White's writings where she simply assumes that it is a tool of the devil, without clearly telling us why.

The larger culture out of which the Adventist movement grew had similar negative feelings, as expressed in the numerous anti-gambling ordinances in effect across America. While these restrictions have gradually been relaxed in most parts of the country, due to shifting demographic factors, many citizens still continue to think of gambling as, in some way, immoral.

A poll I once read revealed that 80% of Roman Catholics and 77% of Jews identified themselves as bettors as compared with only 54% of Protestants. This suggests that antipathy toward wagering may be associated with the Protestant ethic. This should not be surprising to anyone who is familiar with the sociological literature on the subject. The many references in the writings of Ellen White to economy, avoiding the waste of time, and maintaining of faithful stewardship are all very much reflections of the Protestant work ethic.

The Protestant ethic was a compound of several different things. One of these, the idea of "vocation," was a part of the sixteenth century protest against Roman Catholicism. Whereas it had long distinguished between "religious" and "seculars" lines of work, the first more sacred than the second, people like Martin Luther and John Calvin taught that each person has a "calling" which is as holy as any other.

A second factor was the way Isaac Newton and others from the seventeenth century forward increasingly pictured the universe as governed by a comprehensive and unexceptional law of cause and effect. According to this deterministic model, nothing happens by luck, fortune, accident, spontaneous generation or transnatural caprice. Things happen the way they do because they are supposed to occur that way and no other.

In Newton's terms, the vast clockwork of causal events did not eliminate the supernatural. Rather, the supernatural operated within and through the causal sequence complex. Many of the intellectual progeny of Newton did not retain the idea of God. They came to believe that the causal sequence operates by itself.

In a contradictory way, this sense of an all-pervasive orderliness conditioned the work ethic. Many believed that how one made money was totally determined but that one should choose to do it well. This incoherent integration of determinism and voluntariness was doomed to fall apart and in time it did. Some jettisoned the idea of vocation in favor of strict determinism, others made the opposite move and still others tried to maintain the seemingly unintelligible synthesis.

As a theological descendant of John Wesley, Ellen White was among those who rejected absolute determinism but retained the idea of vocation. According to this view, in God's universe effects typically follow causes. If one wants certain things to happen, it is necessary to put forth the requisite effort. Reaping presupposed the sowing.

This principle comes through nicely in a statement by Ellen White:

> God does not work miracles where he has provided means by which the work may be accomplished. Use your time and talents in His service and He will not fail to work with your efforts. If the farmer fails to plow and sow God does not work a miracle to undo the results of his neglect. Harvest time finds his fields barren—there are not sheaves to be reaped, no grain to be garnered. God provided the seed and the soil, the sun and the rain, and if the agriculturist had employed the means that were at his hand he would have received according to his sowing and his labor.
>
> There are great laws that govern the world of nature and spiritual things are controlled by principles equally certain. The means for an end must be employed if the desired results are to be obtained. Those who make no decided efforts themselves are not working in harmony with the laws of God.[1]

[1]Ellen G. White, *Fundamentals of Christian Education* (Mountain View, CA:

If a culturally conditioned apprehension were all that were involved, the issue would not warrant much attention. But we know that beliefs and practices which persist over long periods of time are often based on underlying realities that give them their survival value even if they are not always obvious on the surface. Sometimes it is the "hidden agenda" that constitutes the real basis for continuity. It is this "hidden agenda" that I think should concern us here.

It turns out that we are dealing with two views of reality. In the first, man's activities are a part of the same divine ordering of cause and effect which we see in the natural world and to obey God is to work in harmony with it. Our ways of making money should be in sync with how the world actually is.

Games of chance, on the other hand, suggest another view of reality which involves myth, magic, caprice, luck, miracle and fortune. It is based on the notion that man is not "bound by the rule of causal orderliness." The implication is that man may under certain circumstances transcend the laws of cause and effect. It may be that this feeling of "law-transcendence" constitutes the psychological power of risk-taking and the attempts to "beat the odds" that is the essence of wagering.

Some commentators speak of the illusions of power with which an addicted gambler faces the next day's roll of the dice. This is a sense of power flying in the face of rational calculation as though it were the magic, omens, rituals, superstitious incantations and so forth as in days of old. The ecstatic appearance of the face of one who has taken a chance and won seems not unlike the description of the unnatural excitement Ellen White described Eve experiencing following the eating of the forbidden fruit.

If the primal sin is autonomy, self-sufficiency apart from God, a sense of not being subject to the law of cause and effect, it may be that there is a deeper reason for concern about gambling than appears on the surface. Could it be that games of chance become a symbolic reinforcement of this false feeling of escaping the usual rule of cause and effect? Is it possible that rebellion against God, the source of order, is the Ultimate Gamble and that ordinary gam-

Pacific Press, 1923), 123-24.

bling is a potential contributor to the larger, more deadly, game?

If so, all who persist in making the Final Wager may ultimately do so under some of the same illusions that operate in ordinary games of chance. They may be cut from the same cloth, ordinary gambling being the microcosm and the Final Wager against God the macrocosm.

Investing *defers* to the law of cause and effect while gambling *defies* it, or at least it tries to, and this is their most basic qualitative difference. In real life, this difference is not absolute but relative. At one end of a continuum there is financial activity that involves a high level of careful calculation and orderly planning. At the other end there are financial endeavors that amount to high levels of speculative risk-taking.

This difference can be seen in the contrast between those who operate the games of chance in places like Las Vegas and those who play them. Those who run gambling institutions do not take big risks in their management of them. They may be in a dirty business of exploiting human weakness; however, they do not wager with the institution's resources. Calculating to the extreme, theirs is the sin of exploitation. The difference is diligence in business as over against resting on luck, fortune, magic, or even miracles.

Some might object that we have an example of a kind of "chance" mechanism in the biblical custom of "casting of lots." We do well to remember, as a principle, that God does sometimes identify with the less than ideal in order to bring us up to the ideal. If He hadn't, we should all be in trouble. At a later time, He might work through His preferred method, that is, through thoughtful, consecrated, prayerful, dedicated people.

Would we really want to go back to replacing people at top levels of leadership, as the early church did in the case of Mathias, by casting lots? I prefer a thoughtful nominating committee, and I think God does, as well!

To summarize, then, gambling reflects an essentially unbiblical, un-Christian attitude toward the nature of things. It is based upon fortune, luck, accident, and caprice. By contrast, God's universe is an orderly place in which causes produce their effects. One who conforms to the law of God carries out his activities in a way that acknowledges that fact.

Any practice that symbolizes transcendence of that orderly universe, that one is in some small sense not subject to its laws, must be, on these grounds, suspect. Sin is the Ultimate Wager. To the extent that lesser wagering contributes to the Final Gamble, it participates in its ultimate error.

12
The Problem of Pornography

When the Roman general Pompey conquered Jerusalem in 63 B.C., it took three additional months of desperate siege to breach the walls of the Jewish temple. In the carnage that followed it is said that no fewer than twelve thousand Jews perished. Through it all, many of the priests solemnly carried on their daily services in spite of the horror about them. Others, dressed in sackcloth, sat immovable in their seats in the Temple courtyard as had the Roman senators two centuries earlier during an invasion by rude barbarians from Gaul.

Pompey had long been curious about the Temple and the fanatical zeal it inspired in the Jewish people. There were many rumors about the Jewish god it contained. Some said the head of an ass was enthroned in the Holy of Holies. Others said the Temple housed the venerable lawgiver of the race. Still others reported it contained a god or goddess in human form after the fashion of Greeks and Romans.

To the profound dismay of the survivors, Pompey forced his

way into the innermost enclosure, past the sacred candlesticks, the golden table of showbread and the altar of incense until he came to the sacred veil. Beyond lay the mystery of the Jewish religion. None but the high priest ever entered this place, and he but once a year on the holiest day of the Jewish calendar. Rudely, Pompey thrust the veil aside, to find that the room was—empty! All that remained at this time in the ancient Holy of Holies was a low stone on which the high priest placed his censer.

Whether Pompey was impressed by the notion of an unseen, spiritual deity we do not know, but it is recorded that he left the Temple treasures untouched and ordered that the place be cleansed and purified and that the Temple services be carried on as usual.

What made the Holy of Holies holy? There was, of course, a great deal of history and ceremony behind the feeling of awe the mysterious place inspired in the heart of the faithful Jew, including the fact that none but the most consecrated of the priests could enter it, and then only once a year after special preparation.

The question may partly be answered by asking it in reverse. What would have rendered the Holy of Holies common or profane? Probably one of the quickest ways to transform the Most Holy Place into a marketplace would have been to run main street though it. The Holy of Holies, to the believing Jew, was consecrated by the presence of the invisible God. Only the unbelieving Pompey found it empty. Pompey simply did not have a belief that was stimulated and reinforced by the awe and mystery that were keys for the Jews to the Temple ceremonies. Allow the thoughtless crowd to drift through it with daily indifference whenever they wished, and its holiness would dissipate. Soon it would become as empty to everyone as it was to the Roman general who desecrated it. There is a lesson here for what may seem on the face of it a quite different matter, the problem of pornography.

Charles Wittschiebe, formerly of Andrews University, wrote a book with a provocative title: *God Invented Sex*.[1] A fitting subtitle to the book might have been: "And God Saw That It Was Very

[1]Charles E. Wittschiebe, *God Invented Sex* (Nashville: Southern Publishing Association, 1974).

Good." The fact that such a book could be published reflects some interesting changes in the attitudes of a people traditionally restrained in such matters.

Not all of these changes have been for the worse. At least some things can now be openly talked about that need to be talked about. But this also reflects, at least in part, the more relaxed climate of the larger society of which the Adventist Church is a part. Which brings us to the question raised by the Pompey story. Is it an unmixed good that there seem to be no limits to what may be freely looked at, displayed, and talked about by everybody in almost every conceivable situation?

Let us back up for a moment. This God who created sex, what did he have in mind? And what was so very good about this aspect of His creation?

The human creature differed relatively from the rest of creation in a number of important ways, but chiefly in his potential for relating to his Creator. To ensure that possibility, the Creator designed, among other things, that human babies would experience a proportionally longer period of infant dependency.

Many of nature's babies do rather well without parents, except for the mere act of bringing them into existence. Most are not even aware that they have parents. Even among those mammals more nearly resembling man, infancy is relatively brief. But for humans the period of at least some dependency persists for well over a decade and a half. This provides for human offspring a unique sense of the need for someone greater than themselves. It also allows parents the privilege of participation in the divine responsibility of the Creator. Both form the basis for a consciousness of God. It is thus no accident that of all of God's creatures, only man has the capacity for worship.

Whether this possibility is fully realized depends largely upon the quality of the dependency experience. What can be a foundation for achieving the Creator's intention in creating humans can also constitute a situation of vulnerability to a host of destructive, dehumanizing tensions countering the Creator's purpose. The difference is largely a question of whether it is a prolonged, stable, situation of love.

While all sexual animals copulate in one way or another, humans were created to "make love." For them alone sexuality was placed in the context of "loving." Human sexuality was thus given the possibility of meanings no other creature could ever know, meanings with power to blend the lives of two people into a unity and possibly a family that would last and last. God surrounded the relation with safeguards to assure that His intention would be achieved. When he created human sexuality, He created something sacred and precious. He intended that man should celebrate it as such.

There is more than one way to profane the gift of sexuality. It can be done by prudery and narrowness as easily as by reckless abandon. Sexuality is profaned whenever humans come to think of their sexual powers in negative terms. The devil triumphs as readily when misplaced prudery devalues the sacred gift into an evil to be rejected as he does when the gift is abused. But inappropriate sexual repression and the common reaction to it, moral laxity, are in one sense but two sides of the same coin. Both attitudes depreciate the divinely-given treasure.

We use the word pornography to refer to various misuses or distortions having to do with human sexuality. This term is apparently of uncertain definition, judging from the contention that has reached even the highest decision-making centers in the land. What is pornography? Where is the dividing line between pornography and art?

The legal ambiguities point up the necessity of developing a definition of pornography based on a norm provided by an understanding of the Creator's purpose in creating human sexuality. What God had in mind was two people, a man and a woman, committed to each other in trust and openness, their moments of sexual ecstasy blending them into a oneness that would bind their every day together year after year after year. God intended marriage to be forever. Their sexuality was designed to be a basic cement of their enduring love relation, a love nest into which it might even be safe to bring children into the world.

In light of this purpose, anything or any experience—visual, tactile, or otherwise—which devalues the treasure, that trivializes God's precious sexual creation, anything that weakens that cement, is pornographic.

By this definition a recent motion picture, reported to have displayed eighteen acts of sexual intercourse openly on the public screen, is profoundly pornographic. What can be the net result of so wanton a display? Not love, surely. Eventually, not even titillation. Under such circumstances sexuality becomes only debased, common, and unimportant, like Pompey's desecrated Temple.

In a topless bar in San Francisco the bartenders became so accustomed to the half-dressed waitresses that they eventually didn't even bother to look. One of them reported how one day a tastefully dressed young lady entered the establishment with a friend. All the bartenders' heads turned to look at her with approval.

Every great lover—and God created great lovers, even if it is difficult for some of us to think in those terms after all of those centuries—has always known that this kind of love achieves its peak when there is long-term commitment, trust, and tenderness, but also where there is an element of romance, mystery and magic. Great lovers set the mood with candlelight and flowers and whispered caresses. But the result of our current inundation with the sexually provocative in the public media—press, television, literature—and in dress styles can only be an increased lack of inhibition in sexual activity, accompanied by a corresponding diminished capacity for great love-making, and ultimately a net weakening of the ties that make for community: the family, the home, and thus of the whole social fabric. If the family disintegrates, lost also is at least a major part of man's capacity to enter into meaningful relationship with God.

Ours is not an age of sexual prowess, but of sexual triviality. That is what is really wrong with those "dirty" pictures. They are an insult to refined sensitivity. Every connoisseur of good food, fine art, and music appreciates the significance of the subtle. By outraging the senses, ours is an age that has debased the talent for experiencing the really fine and the good. It has certainly done this in matters of sex.

> How is the gold become dim! How is the most fine gold changed! The stones of the sanctuary are poured out in the top of every street.[2]

The new mood has tried to justify itself with an emphasis on individual freedom. But real freedom is to be responsible, not merely to be uninhibited or, as one has put it, to be "unbuttoned."

Anti-pornography laws have been opposed as undue restraint on individual liberty to do our own thing as long as it doesn't hurt anybody. Laws against "victimless crimes," usually referring to deviant sexual behavior between consenting adults, have been opposed as a contradiction of terms. "How can there be crimes without victims?" the new libertarians ask.

Now let's think about that for a moment. Given the depth of inter-human involvement, is there such thing as a victimless crime? If no man is an island, our beliefs and value systems may not always be a private matter, least of all in this area.

Each generation is the guardian of the values of the future and has a responsibility toward those that follow. Hugh Hefner and his friends are helping to shape the world in which my children and my grandchildren must live. How they shape it is, then, very much my business and yours.

God created men and women for great love. Do you want to experience great love? Then preserve yourself for the right person, the right place, the right setting, and the right time. Meanwhile, guard well your senses; don't allow the Hefners in this world to jade them for you.

God created sex to be very good. Sexual sins are an affront to the Creator. They are also destructive of the truly human. They are so bad because sex was meant to be so very good.

---

[2]Lamentations 4:1.

13
The Christian, Homosexuals, and the Law

Changing attitudes toward homosexuality, expressed both by the freedom with which the gay community is able to campaign for recognition and acceptance, and the way these are being granted by previous religious and legislative adversaries, are placing many informed Christians in a dilemma.[1] True to their Christian intuitions, they are likely to be inclined to react to examples of prejudice, deprivation, and oppression with tolerance, compassion and even passion. It is characteristic of Christians who are fully informed by their moral sources to be on the side of the underdog, almost instinctively. The oppressed and downtrodden have from the beginning usually been able to rally Christians to their support.

Yet the heightened moral sensitivity which often accompanies

[1]This chapter is an integration of two papers: "Ethics and Law" and "The Christian, Homosexuals, and the Law."

vigorous Christian commitment is likely to experience a certain outrage at the present open flaunting of centuries-honored standards of conduct. These give him explicit as well as implicit injunctions that are difficult to explain away. Consider these passages from the New Revised Standard Version of the Bible:

> You shall not lie with a male as with a woman. It is an abomination. If a man lies with a male as with a woman, both of them have committed an abomination; they shall be put to death; their blood is upon them.[2]

> For the wrath of God is revealed from heaven against all ungodliness and wickedness of those who by their wickedness suppress the truth. For what can be known about God is plain to them, because God has shown it to them. Ever since the creation of the world his eternal power and divine nature, invisible though they are, have been understood and seen through the things he has made. So they are without excuse; for though they knew God, they did not honor him as God or give thanks to him, but they became futile in their thinking, and their senseless minds were darkened.

> Claiming to be wise, they became fools; and they exchanged the glory of the immortal God for images resembling a mortal human being or birds or four-footed animals or reptiles. Therefore God gave them up in the lusts of their hearts to impurity, to the degrading of their bodies among themselves, because they exchanged the truth about God for a lie and worshiped and served the creature rather than the Creator, who is blessed forever! Amen. For this reason God gave them up to degrading passions. Their women exchanged natural intercourse for unnatural, and in the same way also the men, giving up natural intercourse with women, were consumed with passion for one another. Men committed shameless acts with men and received in their

[2]Leviticus 18–22.

> own persons the due penalty for their error. And since they did not see fit to acknowledge God, God gave them up to a debased mind and to things that should not be done. They were filled with every kind of wickedness, evil, covetousness, malice. Full of envy, murder, strife, deceit, craftiness, they are gossips, slanderers, God-haters, insolent, haughty, boastful, inventors of evil, rebellious toward parents, foolish, faithless, heartless, ruthless. They know God's decree, that those who practice such things deserve to die—yet they not only do them but even applaud others who practice them.[3]

> Do you not know that wrongdoers will not inherit the kingdom of God? Do not be deceived! Fornicators, idolaters, adulterers, male prostitutes, sodomites, thieves, the greedy, drunkards, revilers, robbers—none of these will inherit the kingdom of God. And this is what some of you used to be. But you were washed, you were sanctified, you were justified in the name of the Lord Jesus Christ and in the Spirit of our God.[4]

> Now we know that the law is good, if one uses it legitimately. This means understanding that the law is laid down not for the innocent but for the lawless and disobedient, for the godless and sinful, for the unholy and profane, for those who kill their father or mother, for murderers, fornicators, sodomites, slave traders, liars, perjurers, and whatever else is contrary to the sound teaching that conforms to the glorious gospel of the blessed God, which he entrusted to me.[5]

The Christian moralist who is informed by his contacts with living people as well as by the Bible has an additional dilemma.

---

[3]Romans 1:18–31.

[4]I Corinthians 6:9–11.

[5]1 Timothy 1:8–11

He is committed to the conviction that no one should be held accountable, blamed, condemned or even looked down upon for something over which he has no control. Such people deserve only tolerance, helpful understanding, and genuine acceptance. He is also aware, if he is informed, that a homosexual may not have chosen to be one.

The etiology of homosexuality is obscure, as we all know. There are a number of theories as to its cause and it is not necessary to review them in detail here. It is probable that the identity of a person as a homosexual is at least in part situationally conditioned; however, it is also possible that there is something more than this which prenatally predisposes at least some individuals to it. What this is, or what these things are, is presently unclear.

The "Kinsey Heterosexual–Homosexual Rating" makes at least one thing clear, and this is that we are not either heterosexual or homosexual but each one of us is somewhere on a continuum which stretches between them. See the figure on the following page.

While homosexual behavior may frequently involve volition, the homosexual state or identity itself may not be necessarily so. This is especially the case at the bottom of the continuum which represents "Exclusive Homosexual." Persons nearer the bisexual center of this spectrum might be able, within limits, to select which way they wish to go, or at least they might be more influenced by environmental factors.

Perhaps this is the way to deal with the Pauline statements. If Romans and I Corinthians are read carefully, they suggest an element of volition. Possibly the passages refer only to individuals who could do otherwise. On any other grounds, a serious conflict appears, arguing condemnation, rather than acceptance. This expresses bigotry and intolerance, both essentially non-Christian attitudes.

It is a commonplace that we can often gauge the strength of a temptation by the vigor with which the object of temptation is rejected. The heat of many expressed anti-homosexual aversions may indicate latent homosexual tendencies being denied, repressed

0	Exclusively Heterosexual
1	Predominantly Heterosexual (Only Incidental Homosexual Contact)
2	Predominantely Heterosexual (More than Incidental Homosexual Contact)
3	Equally Heterosexual and Homosexual
4	Predominantely Homosexual (More than Incidental Heterosexual Contact)
5	Predominantely Homosexual (Only Incidental Heterosexual Contact)
6	Exclusively Homosexual
X	No Socio-Sexual Contact or Reactions

or projected. Crusading reformers often have problems, as we all know.

The Christian moralist is also aware of the horrors which have been perpetrated by religious people who have taken recourse to civil power to support their beliefs and convictions. He knows that the proper sphere of social legislation is to protect possible victims against criminal or other malicious actions. Social legislation only applies when the exercise of one person's rights infringes on the rights of another. Whatever may be the additional functions and duties of education and exhortation, "victimless crimes" are generally not the law's business.

Although there is considerable overlapping of effort between ethics and law, it is important to distinguish them. Ethics must often be far more sensitive to circumstances than law can permit itself to be. Ethics must also be prepared to intrude into highly personal, private matters which may not be the proper domain of the social legislator.

When law oversteps its boundaries into private morality, injustice and bad law almost always result.

"Victimless crimes" are usually outside of law's purview; however, they are not outside the jurisdiction of teaching, preaching and the "doing" of ethics. It is the proper function of law to regulate the exercise of individual rights so that they do not infringe on the rights of others, especially when these rights have become a matter of consensus. It is the function of ethics to probe the fundamental basis of these rights so as to lay out the ways in which they may come into conflict.

Law usually does its work after ethics has prepared the way. Reversing that order also usually results in bad law. We must ask "is it right?" before we ask "is it legal?" It is for this reason that law is sometimes spoken of as "frozen ethics." Although "congealed" or "jelled" might be preferable terms, when social norms have become a consensus law gives them substance, form, and continuity so that they faithfully serve their proper ends. Ethics and law are complimentary.

It is on this basis that laws governing the private sexual behavior of consenting adults have generally been falling by the wayside, as well they might if such activities are in fact "victimless." This is one of the questions I wish to pursue. Let us do this by turning to a different issue which shares a number of important points with the one before us. It is incest.

Incest is one of the most universally proscribed of all the possible human sexual liaisons. Almost all cultures have treated it with horror, disgust and abhorrence. The reason for the forcefulness of its rejection probably derives from its universal threat to the family. This is caused by the propinquity of the sexes in the isolated family as well as other factors such as the apparently normal Electra and Oedipal attachments of mother and son and father and daughter. We know that in isolated families incest may never be very far away.

In spite of the new moral picture in other areas, we still do not hear advocacy of incestuous alignments. We might say, and correctly so, that incest differs from homosexuality in the possibility of offspring. This is a hazard because, according to every study, such offspring face a vastly increased incidence of fetal abnormality which is directly proportional to the degree of consanguinity.

So, to make the point, let us consider only those incestuous relationships which cannot result in pregnancy. Would our gay liberation friends really wish our legislative bodies to eliminate all laws governing incestuous sexual behavior involving consenting adults, provided they are sterile or agree to abort their issue? What about sexual behavior between a post-menopausal mother and her grown son or between a vasectomized father and his grown daughter? Would they perhaps favor solemnized marriages for such couples? Why not?

To most of the world the notion is inherently repugnant. Yet if "victimless crimes" are not to be the subject of social regulation, why shouldn't this also apply to incest between consenting adults which does not entail childbearing? Most of us find incest, even on these terms, disturbing. This is partly due to our centuries of conditioning. It is also because the victim or victims which rightly concern us are not always the obvious ones. Society itself may be the victim.

Such liaisons threaten the family structure which is the basic fabric of society. In spite of the radical experiments going on which question the viability of the traditional family—complex marriages, open ended marriages, sexual communes and so forth—the majority opinion remains that no structure has yet been discovered that adequately substitutes for a Mom and Dad who care about each other enough to remain faithfully committed to each other year after year. They provide the enduring configuration of persons in interaction which gives children the secure sense of acceptance and identity which is the optimal context for the development of healthy personalities. Culture is probably secure enough to survive a measure of experimentation; however, if too many people get involved in alternative family arrangements, we may be in for real trouble down the road.

We are speaking of homosexuality, of course, and not of incest; however, the two issues parallel each other in certain particulars. This is mainly in revealing that "victimless crimes" may not in fact be victimless. They may only have a different victim. A society's norms, and thus the society itself, may be the victim.

Some are advocating the total acceptance of homosexual unions as a legitimate alternative to the heterosexual family. This may be illustrated by two statements made by leading figures in the homophile movement. The first is from Franklin Edward "Frank" Kameny. An astronomer and physicist with a PhD from Harvard, he was one of the earliest and most influential gay rights activists:

> Homosexuality is not an inferior state, that it is neither an affliction to be cured nor a weakness to be resisted, that it is not less desirable for the homosexual than hetero-sexuality is for the heterosexual; that the homosexual is a first-class human being and first-class citizen, entitled, by right, to all of the God-given dignity of his humanity—as the homosexual that he is and has a moral right to continue to be, that homosexuality is nothing to be ashamed of, nothing to be apologetic about, nothing to bemoan, but something around which the homosexual can and should build part of a rewarding and productive life and something which he can and should enjoy to its fullest, just as heterosexuality is for the heterosexual. Homosexuality per se cannot properly be considered a sickness, illness, disturbance, disorder, or pathology of any kind, nor a symptom of any of these, but must be considered as a preference, orientation, or propensity, not different in kind from heterosexuality, and fully on par with it. In their entirety, the problems of the homosexual as such are—or stem directly from—problems of prejudice and discrimination directed against this minority by the hostile majority around them....Homosexuality can only be considered to be as fully and affirmatively moral as heterosexuality. It thus follows that homosexuality, both by inclination and by overt act, is not only not immoral, but is moral in a real and positive sense, and is good and right and desirable, both personally and societally.

The second is a statement by Barbara B. Gittings, a former editor of *The Ladder: A Lesbian Review*:

> Homosexuality is not a sickness, not an impairment, not a failure, not an arrested development, not a flaw, not an incompleteness, not a distortion, not a sin or a sinful condition. It is not something to be regretted in any way; it is not something to be resigned or endured. The majority of homosexuals would not change even if they could. More important, they should not change even if they could. What the homosexual wants—and here he is neither willing to compromise nor morally required to compromise—is acceptance of homosexuality as a way of life fully on par with heterosexuality, acceptance of the homosexual as a person on par with the heterosexual, and acceptance of homosexuals as children of God on an equal basis with heterosexuals. Therefore we are not interested in compassion, or in sympathy as unfortunates. We do not wish to be looked down upon. Our homosexuality is a way of life as good in every respect as heterosexuality.

This advocacy might not affect exclusive homosexuals at the extreme end of the heterosexual and homosexual spectrum in one way or another. Yet wholly accepting homosexual unions might greatly condition the attitudes and behavior of other persons more nearly at the center of the spectrum. I'm thinking of bisexuals, or those nearly so, for whom sexuality more clearly involves volition.

A Christian moralist bases his perception of right and wrong on a certain understanding of man. This includes man's ability to deal with "meanings" and "values" as well as with objects. An act is right or wrong often in terms of the meaning of the act rather than the mere fact that it takes place. Man may thus be defined not only as *Homo sapiens* (thinker) and *Homo faber* (maker), but more importantly for ethics, as *Homo symbolicus* (symbolizer). Man is able to read meanings into actions or objects. The symbolic action or object in this sense becomes the means to an end other than the end itself. The symbol "refers to" or "stands for" this other thing and in doing so the symbol modifies or creates attitudes toward it.

Symbolic meanings are the basis for man's civilization, for his intellection, communication, and economic and social interaction. In our present context, a sexual relation may be a symbol which points beyond itself and conditions attitudes toward certain social values which serve the common social good.

With this in mind, traditional Christian teaching usually limited legitimate sexual expression to the context of the permanent commitment of two persons. These are the husband and wife, who may in the course of their sexuality become father and mother and thereby establish an enduring constellation of persons, the family, in which healthy growth and maturation of offspring might occur. Sexuality in such a context symbolizes trust, openness and permanence. These are the cement that binds two lives and those of the progeny into an enduring unity. The durability of the larger society depends on the degree to which the integrity of these units is maintained by a majority of its members.

Sexuality can come to have other meanings. It can serve purely hedonistic ends or it can even become an end in itself. It can be dissociated from love and commitment, as we hear in the claim that it is not necessary to be in love to make love. It can, of course, also be dissociated from procreation, as the pill has shown us, so as to selectively control the creation of a family, or as is frequently the case, to separate sexuality from the family altogether. But both in the dissociation from loving, and in the total dissociation from family, sexuality may come to mean something else and lose its capacity to serve these traditional ends.

It may be no accident that freer sexuality, the dissolution of the family and such movements as the "gay liberation" movement are occurring simultaneously. They may belong to the same general phenomenon. This development should give us all pause.

It seems very important to some of us that there be resistance in every legitimate way to the dissolution of the family because it is a social structure which is very important to the future of our civilization. Such resistance should, of course, be directed to its proper ends. It is a miscarriage of justice to deny homosexuals their rights in unrelated areas, such as the right to meaningful employment and to the same level of personal fulfillment which we demand for others.

Society has the right to demand the same degree of responsible behavior of the homosexual minority that it demands of the heterosexual majority. Being a heterosexual does not give one freedom to behave sexually however, whenever, wherever, and with whomever one chooses. Neither does being a homosexual. Private behavior not involving individual victims is usually not the law's business; however, their public expression and advocacy may be, particularly if these involve persons of immature judgment.

It is wrong through prejudice and bigotry to deprive individuals of the opportunity to fulfill themselves in every way consistent with membership in a healthy society. No one should be denied the chance to contribute to that society with all his native gifts simply because he is a homosexual, or a heterosexual, for that matter.

It is also necessary that both homosexuals and heterosexuals be prevented from weakening the social structures upon which the society depends for its long-run viability. Heterosexual sins in this sense can be as destructive as homosexual sins and both must be placed under appropriate strictures if the health of a society is to be preserved. Society itself may become the victim of these so called "victimless crimes."

If we deny to our children the chance to experience and in turn to pass along to their children a fairly clear picture of what an enduring family is about, or if we allow persons whose attitudes and behavior are inimical to the family, to weaken the family by modifying its necessary norms, we hazard our children and thus our society's future.

A Christian should always be willing to grant acceptance and support to persons who are different, especially when that difference is through no choice of their own. But this does not include a willingness to allow them to undermine the things most people value for their children and their children's children. Among other things, this means that society has the right to ask heterosexuals and homosexuals alike to mind their manners. If they cannot or will not do this, if they insist on being overt in their behavior, or publicly advocate for a life style that undermines society's valued institutions such as the family, society has not only the right but also the duty to restrain them.

14
Answers to Anxiety

Some emotional experiences persist as moods for hours, days, weeks, months or even longer. One of these moods is so universal a problem that it deserves a somewhat extended consideration. This is the problem of anxiety.

The easiest way for us to define what we mean by anxiety is to contrast it with fear. By fear we indicate the normal emotional reaction of a person in the presence of a real danger. It is what puts the threatened person on his guard and prepares him for fight or flight as the situation may indicate. It is a useful emotion if it is not so overwhelming so as to paralyze appropriate action. Fear is a tool for survival, a saving asset in the business of living, disappearing when the actual threat is over.

Anxiety, on the other hand, is generally not an asset but a liability. Its object is usually more imagined than real, moving the individual to self-defense when no self-defense is called for and causing him to react in ways inconsistent with actual preservation and relationship with other persons.

We want ourselves and our children to retain the kinds of survival fears that keep us from being run over, drowned, or burned to death. We dread with reason the nameless anxieties that prevent us from appropriately reacting to reality. They hold us back from progress or make us plunge ahead in advance of the actual threatening situation, all the while desperately holding on to them in spite of what the real situation is like.

Anxiety's origins in a person's past make it difficult to deal with it effectively. In fear, a real and present threat can often be managed by appropriate action. In anxiety, the cause may lie deeply hidden in a past failure to deal meaningfully with a disturbing situation by repressing it into the unconscious. Here, beyond easy recall, the defeat still stirs like some unseen, underground monster, conjuring up all sorts of fancied and nameless visions of disaster but itself remaining beyond conscious control. This is why expert help from a trained pastor, counselor, clinical psychologist, or psychiatrist, depending on the depth and character of the disturbance, is often needed. It will be helpful for us to consider at some length some of the causes of anxiety, the results, and then suggest some answers to the questions it raises.

The major cause of anxiety may be summed up in the one word, "insecurity," and it often stems from early childhood. Every grown-up person is in some ways the child he used to be. If the little child he used to be came into a world where his emotional environment did not provide him with a sense of belonging and a measure of self-trust, if it was a world of shifting landmarks and values, he may well discover the burden of adulthood too heavy to carry.

Each child is a helpless bundle of unfulfilled potentials, sensitive to his environment to a degree almost undreamed of in later years. Unbelievably dependent, he reacts to the interplay of tensions and actions of the older persons who make up his personal world in subtle ways which are often unnoticed but nonetheless may be fateful.

Most of the time the almost inevitable moment of tensions

between parent and child are brief and inconsequential; however, they can result in more or less permanent fear-guilt-hostility relationships which damage his personality.

It is possible to identify several damaging types of parental behavior. His parents may have plunged him into feelings of rage or failure by forcing him to learn bodily or emotional controls before he was ready for them. They may have been so stern and rigid that he never experienced them as rewarders of his efforts or comforters of his needs. He may find his parents so vacillating or changeable —sometimes timid, sometimes demanding and stern—that he can never be quite sure what to expect. Insufficiently aware of the uneven nature of the growth, they may expect him always to perform at the peak of his ability and they may demonstrate anger and disappointment at his backslidings. Children, as well as their parents, under the influence of fatigue and emotional stress, may temporarily regress to more infantile forms of behavior. Drawing attention to these lapses may well fix in the growing personality feelings of guilt and lack of self-confidence that bode ill for the future.

The child learns to deal successfully with other people in his home. It may also be the place which inhibits his natural outreach and his absorbing interests. It may be where his explorations are met with an unnecessary, impatient and finicky "no," which gives him the distinct impression that what he does is not worth doing or that he is not worthy of doing it well. Such children often react to life at the adult level in terms of their childhood defeats and they often express those defeats in the language of nameless anxiety.

All of us from time to time face situations which make us feel self-distrustful and isolated. We feel self-distrustful because we have not developed habitual patterns of responding that enable us to meet new demands, or because we do not know how to revise our responses or what to substitute for them. We feel isolated because we experience people as strangers, not only in themselves but in what they expect from us. Under these circumstances we often interpret situations in ways that throw us into crises.

Childhood and adolescence are replete with such conflicts and if during these years parental support is lacking or operated with too stern a hand, the result may be insecurity, negativity and rebellion. The years of adolescence are particularly crucial. During this period changes are so rapid, the demanded adjustments are so great, and the organism is so emotionally vulnerable that a variety of anxiety reactions are virtually inevitable.

People often reach adulthood before they are emotionally mature and this leaves them unprepared to face the responsibilities and make the decisions it requires. Here the often forgotten defeats of childhood may raise their ugly specter in ways that are destructive to purposeful and successful living.

Too often childhood attitudes toward freedom in work and marriage prevent people from making mature adjustments when they are adults. Whenever boredom threatens on the job, or with the marriage partner, they want to shift their interests or change their minds. They enter into marriage as if it were only a prolonged adolescent love affair. If they have children, they feel tied down by them instead of feeling the normal parental interests of adults. This sets the stage for the anxieties of insecurity in another generation.

Adults often retreat from situations which they do not feel competent to handle and which they can tolerate only if they look temporary. But adulthood is not simply a "passing phase." It is "for keeps." Inability to cope with its challenges brings into sharp relief all the accumulated earlier failures. If past conditions have made the young adult reluctant, anxious and resentful in the face of responsibility, adulthood will "find him out."

Most of the adult's problems center on his work. This is where his emotional maturity is often most put to the test and where his weaknesses become cruelly manifest. Here is where his old false solutions, his old fears, guilt feelings, hostilities, and insecurities are likely to break out in overt or disguised panic responses of various kinds. Here the opinion he holds of himself, especially his place in relation to other persons, is constantly tested. If his self-esteem has never been more than precarious, competition on the job may well threaten him beyond his capacity to bear.

The neurotic reactions of such individuals are almost too common to mention. The sacrifice of life's pleasant qualities, health, love, hobbies, recreation and contentment for the sake of material status symbols, or their vulgar display, often mark the unsure and inadequate person in ways he little realizes. So do the psychosomatic complaints which are part of the price he pays for his lack of inner resources.

Accumulated feelings of guilt often work themselves out in various forms of self-punishment, including persistent failures of one sort or another. Children whose parents abnormally fenced them in with overly strict patterns of "dos" and "don'ts," which were usually symptoms of their own insecurities, may well have instilled in them a sense of guilt and unworthiness which is the basis of their "need" to scourge themselves.

Marriage is another arena where the defeats of the growing years are often refought. Its stern tests may brutally bring into the open a failure to mature, as this is expressed by an inability to turn outward from the self, to face reality, to affirm other persons as real people who have rights, and to recognize that they are valuable in themselves as unique individuals. Marriage provides more opportunities for releasing hatreds and fears than do many other human relationships.

It is true: the child is father to the man. The adult is not a new person unrelated to his past, and his present anxieties may represent a failure to come to grips meaningfully with the emotional problems this past has bequeathed to him, but this is only a part of the story of anxiety.

Adulthood has its own quantum of insecurity produced by problems of employment, illness, and natural disasters of various kinds to name a few. Although these are unsettling to everyone, they are unduly so to persons who are poorly equipped emotionally to deal with them.

A sometimes unrecognized cause for anxiety is derived from the failure of many persons to achieve the fulfillment of their potential abilities. The child or adult who finds himself caught up in a situation where his talents are not challenged or utilized reacts in terms of uneasiness, loss of interest, and boredom.

Another primary source of anxiety in contemporary society

with its increased concentration in vast metropolitan centers, and the personal isolation that is so characteristic of city living, is the lack of a "feeling of belonging." Gone from many lives is the close-knit structure of family, relatives, church, and the social intimacy of life-long friendships that was so characteristic of a less-hurried yesterday. Largely gone are also are the systems of value, the codes of conduct that provided strong in-group feelings. No one denies that the "good-old days" were not always so good, but the increasing anxiety of our times may be a nostalgic cry for values that are fast disappearing. Most of us need at least a measure of the permanent and familiar in our emotional environment from which to take our bearings, to know as it were who we are, where we are and where we are going.

Aging is another source of anxiety. It is usually accompanied by a gradual contraction of life. The horizons of activity and interest gradually close in and point inexorably to the day when life will slip away altogether. Physical resources once taken for granted are no longer abundant. A late night out means a tired day tomorrow, injury or illness mean a longer convalescence. There is the shortness of breath on the stairs, the weariness at the end of the day, the aloneness that follows the passing of loved ones, and old friends, the relative isolation of retirement, the limitations that increasing physical disability places on freedom, the feeling of decreasing worth, the curtailment of material resources can all become overwhelming to many individuals who formerly seemed to handle the crises of life with relative ease.

Yet, despite all this, if there is one present cause of anxiety and inner restlessness that now stands out above the others, it is the increasing conviction on the part of many that nothing "makes any difference," and "nothing really matters." All human beings require, for health, something to dedicate themselves too. This dedication rallies the otherwise often conflicting and scattered elements of the personality around a common integrating center which provides a sense of inner unity. A strong sense of purpose provides the security of an ordered and patterned existence without which most persons become distraught and anxious.

Insecurity and the anxiety it produces usually disguise themselves as something better. There is anxiety that masks its weakness behind a show of strength. This often marks the life where emotional insecurity has deep roots. It is a part of the alienation of man from man that characterizes today's world. Such persons tend to interpret strength as power over others and seek a substitute for security in the domination of others. Genuine strength resides in a feeling of self-confidence that does not need to prove its prowess. It can afford to let others be themselves. Insecure people must be in endless competition with others and are often condemned to run till they drop. No amount of achievement will reassure them. They also tend to belittle the achievements of others as a means of building up their own self-esteem. They cannot enter into relaxed give-and-take relationships with others. They use their knowledge to manipulate, control, and dominate. They are ever ready to persecute and oppress. They cannot be compassionate; even their giving must be a sign to them of strength. Philanthropic rather than spontaneously generous. They are incapable of real gentleness and courtesy. Only the really strong can afford to be gentle.

Anxiety that wears the guise of moral correctness has often cast a shadow on real goodness. It frequently hides guilt, fear, and hostility behind a façade of meekness, selflessness, and seemingly virtuous behavior. The clue to its true face is its negative rather than positive orientation, its emphasis on "not doing" rather than "doing." It tends to be hypercritical of others, making some robust and life-affirming individuals feel uneasy in its presence. It pries into others' affairs—particularly their "morals." It tends to be rigid and tense. And as in the case of the false strength, it needs to dominate others. The whole morally rigid, legalistic structure of such a personality seeks to serve its needs by making others feel guilty and obligated.

Another mask for anxiety is an apparent love. A person who has not received or is unable to accept love for some of the reasons discussed earlier is likely to think of love only in terms of his own needs. He cannot give of himself. Love to him is not to affirm the other for himself, but to possess the object of his "love." Such a husband cannot permit his wife to be a person; such a mother ties their children to her with cords that often are mistaken for utter selflessness but are in reality the very opposite, derived from a fear of being left alone.

These false faces are particularly dangerous because of the false messages they convey. Anxiety which masks itself as righteousness does profound damage to the concept of it besides the damage it does to the anxious individual and the ones he exploits.

If these are conscious disguises, they are bad enough; but if, as it is in most cases, they are unconsciously assumed, their falseness is particularly dangerous because the one who in self-deception wears them actually prevents himself from receiving the help he so desperately seeks. They are all exploitive and tend to confuse us about the kind of human qualities we ought to value.

It is apparent to many who deal understandingly with anxious persons that a major source of the anxiety which characterizes so great a portion of contemporary life is the loss of connection with the realities that have sustained countless men throughout the centuries. The renowned psychologist Carl Jung, said,

> It seems to me, that, side by side with the decline of religious life, the neuroses grow noticeably more frequent.

He also reported that:

> Among all of my patients in the second half of life—that is to say, over thirty-five—there has not been one whose problem in the last resort was that of not finding a religious outlook on life. It is safe to say that every one of them fell ill because he had lost that which the living religions of every age have given their followers, and none of them has been really healed who did not regain his religious outlook.[6]

The reason for this is not difficult to discover. Religious faith is all

[6]Carl Jung, *Modern Man in Search of a Soul* (New York: Houghton Mifflin, 1933), 230–231.

about the very things that are relevant to the problems of anxiety.

What does religious faith have to say to the situations that produce anxiety? It says some rather practical things about the kinds of interpersonal relationships in the home and elsewhere that provide the warmth, love, and acceptance which are so vital to emotional health of adults as well as their children. If every child were born into a "love nest" in the religious sense of that expression, most of the inadequate responses of adults to life's threatening experiences would be avoided.

Religious faith at its best also says some larger things about a universe in which God is the proper center of everything, including each person's life. To feelings of isolation and loneliness, it speaks of a watchful Father who cares about the details in each individual's life.

> Are not two sparrows sold for a farthing? and one of them shall not fall on the ground without your Father. But the very hairs of your head are all numbered. Fear ye not therefore, ye are of more value than many sparrows.[7]

To the feelings of guilt and unworthiness, religious faith speaks of forgiveness, the rediscovery of value, and it identifies ways that these may be realized in experience.

> Come now, and let us reason together, saith the Lord: though your sins be as scarlet, they shall be as white as snow: though they be red like crimson, they shall be as wool.[8]

To the feelings of meaninglessness, boredom, unfulfilled abilities, lack of direction and purpose, religious faith has more than an ample answer. This vacuum in contemporary society, which is all too easily filled with false solutions, exists only because man has not remembered God. It exists because people have forgotten about His purpose, His tasks, and His call.

---

[7]Matthew 10:29-31.

[8]Isaiah 1:18.

> He hath shewed thee, O man, what is good: and what doth the Lord require of thee, but to do justly, and to love mercy, and to walk humbly with thy God?[9]

To the life threatened by contracting horizons and the final threat of death itself, religious faith points to the One from whom nothing can separate us:

> For I am persuaded, that neither death, nor life, nor angels, nor principalities, nor powers, nor things present, nor things to come, nor height, nor depth, nor any other creature, shall be able to separate us from the love of God, which is in Christ Jesus our Lord.[10]

It also points to the surety of a reality beyond the grave:

> And God shall wipe away all tears from their eyes; and there shall be no more death, neither sorrow, nor crying, neither shall there be any more pain: for the former things are passed away.[11]

Man has not only a past which has contributed mightily to what he now is, he also has a present and a future which contribute something of their own. While he is inclined to react to these contributions according to the patterns he developed from his earlier period, this is not inexorably so. To be human is to possess a certain capacity for meeting life creatively and it is this fortunate fact that alleviates some of the hopelessness of our common human predicament.

There is an old Dutch legend about a spider. It was a respectable, well-behaved spider, and it lived high up under the rafters of a barn. It said to itself one day, "I wonder what things are like down there," and being quite adventurous, it dropped on the end

---

[9]Micah 6:8.

[10]Romans 8:38, 39.

[11]Revelation 21:4.

of its long, slender thread until it came to rest on a beam many feet below. It liked the look of its new surroundings so it spread its web and set up home. There it lived as the long days went by. It caught flies, and grew fat and prosperous. Then, one day it noticed a long, slender thread running up into the darkness high above. It was puzzled, and said, "I wonder what that's for?" It serves no purpose that I can see. I can do without it." So it broke the thread and its little home and its little world collapsed.

Has your world been collapsing about you? Have fear and anxiety filled your days and nights with a nameless dread and uneasiness, robbing you of health and making your life empty and miserable? The answer is the forgotten slender thread from above. The answer is God.

15
Forgiveness and Guilt

If you were born into a healthy family where you were surrounded by an abundance of love and emotional security, where you were free of destructive conflict, and you never committed a known sin, would you need salvation? Would you need God's forgiveness? Could you experience guilt?

In *What Ever Became of Sin,*[1] psychiatrist Karl Menninger captures our changing climate by describing the disappearance of "sin" from much contemporary life. We have behavior disorders, character defects, dependencies, obsessions compulsions, narcissisms, sociopathologies and many more, but we don't have "sin." What does he mean by "sense of sin?" Does he mean a sense of evil? Or is he referring to a sense of guilt?

This question is important because the concept of "sin" virtually presupposes a religious belief structure. It has nearly always meant some act which was against God. Even sins against our fellow men

[1]Karl Menninger, *Whatever Became of Sin?* 2nd edition (New York: Hawthorn Books, 1973).

were primarily sins against God. Recall King David's lament after the Bathsheba incident had been exposed. "Against thee, thee only, have I sinned, and done this evil in thy sight."[2]

Against God? I should have thought his sin was primarily against Bathsheba or at least against Bathsheba's husband. Perhaps they both sinned against Uriah. Was not David's sin also against a whole people? He let them down by his folly. They looked to him as their leader and example and he failed them. But against God?

As a matter of fact, "against God" is the forgotten connotation of the word "sin" and it might be useful to recapture it in our time. Sin strikes at God, who is the very center of reality. The loss of the sense of God is the fundamental reason why this sense of sin has disappeared.

It is interesting that "guilt," when we define it broadly enough, has not disappeared. This illustrates the important fact that "sin" and "guilt," though often associated, bear no necessary relation to each other. We can be guilty without a sense of or belief in sin. Legally, of course, this has always been true, even in atheistic settings. A trial in a court is for the purpose of establishing guilt, not sin.

I was once called to be a juryman; however, fortunately, I was able to talk my way out of it by pleading hardship because my class for freshman medical students had just begun and an absence of four to six weeks would have been a minor disaster. Before I left, the presiding judge gave us a long, articulate and intelligent speech in which he distinguished between civil and criminal law. The case in question was one involving criminal offenses including murder, rape and numerous robberies. At one point in his presentation he made an interesting observation. We were not, he told us, to make a moral judgment about the accused. Only a legal one. Had he broken the law? That was the question; whether he was a sinner was not.

Although the judge's point could have been debated, he was a sophisticated child of his time when he stated the difference between "moral" and "legal." My guess is that he might not have been able to give a precise response to the question of whether the man,

---

[2]Psalm 51:4.

if legally guilty, was also a sinner. It would have depended on the judge's religious beliefs and orientation, if indeed he had any positive feelings in that direction.

There can be "guilt" without "sin." Is the reverse possible? It surely is the case that some people seem to feel no remorse for what is to many of us sinful behavior. The "sexual liberation" of recent years is in the general direction of "sex without guilt." I recognize that the destructive, repressive qualities that have sometimes distorted even legitimate sexuality in the past were not always healthy. Fortunately, the pendulum seems to be swinging back the other direction now.

It is important that we achieve a measure of consensus as to what we mean by "guilt." First, we must make a distinction between technical, objective or even legal guilt, which is a part of society's attempt to regulate its social interactions, on the one hand, and the feelings of remorse or a smitten conscience on the part of the guilty party, on the other. If a person does not accept the regulations, he may feel put upon or persecuted by what he perceives as an injustice. Objective, technical guilt may have little to do with forgiveness, although a "legal pardon" may be somewhat analogous.

The guilt which is associated with forgiveness, what we might call "sin-guilt," involves the subjective experience of uneasiness, discomfort and remorse which all of you know when you have violated your conscience. It is universally present as a normal function of our being human. It is not that animals totally lack something that appears to be equivalent. But in man the conscience is so highly developed that we give his actions moral meanings which we do not apply to the lesser creatures. Terms like "right and wrong" are distinctly human terms.

What is understood to be right or wrong may vary widely from culture to culture. Some say almost anything which is thought to be right in one culture may be thought to be wrong in another. The picture is not quite that scrambled. There is far greater cross-cultural agreement on moral matters than there is disagreement. This is because most of the "rules" derive from our being human, not from our being Tibetan, Ethiopian, Hottentot or whatever.

Nevertheless, when it is properly qualified, the observation is valid. In ethics, there is much cultural diversity.

Having a highly developed moral sense, call it superego or whatever, is a universal fact of our common humanity. The sensitivity of this moral sense varies widely from individual to individual. Those with highly sensitive consciences may suffer profound pangs of guilt from what might appear to most of us to be very minor infractions. Others may seem little disturbed by even fairly major deviations from the norms; however, all of us by virtue of being human, experience something.

It is not easy to describe "guilt sensations." It is a little like defining "time." Augustine said that when he didn't think about "time" he knew what it was but when he thought about it he didn't. Guilt can range from mild feelings of psychic stress or discomfort, which you can experience when you neglected to brush your teeth as is your custom, to anguish and remorse which can be almost life-threatening.

The young Luther was so ravaged by a sensitive conscience that his constant compulsion to confession began to weary the vicar of his Augustinian monastery. He finally exclaimed, "God is not angry with you. You are angry with God." The leftovers with which Luther kept trotting in appeared to Staupitz to be only the samples of a sick soul. 'Look here', said he, 'if you expect Christ to forgive you, come in with something to forgive—parricide, blasphemy, adultery—instead of all these peccadilloes.'"

The capacity for experiencing subjective guilt was there from the beginning. As soon as the first couple sinned in that Garden, they experienced nakedness. What a profound metaphor for the alienation, self-disesteem, self-loathing, weakness, and vulnerability that came as a reaction to their sin! The essence of guilt is a feeling of a loss of self-respect, of unworthiness, of not being worthwhile, of being disvalued, inferior, bad, alone, separated. We could multiply the adjectives endlessly.

The capacity to feel this was created by God because of man's high destiny which is to be a member of God's universal family. Like pain, it was a protective mechanism. The potential experience of pain protects us from damaging our physical organism. Without it we could not survive. Just so the potential feeling of guilt is there to protect our social well-being. The capacity for guilt is a good gift from God.

But also, as in pain, unremitting, unresolved guilt can itself become destructive disease. This experience of guilt is a warning flag that something is wrong and must be righted and, if the signal is functioning normally, you ignore it at your peril.

As David Belgum, who taught for many years in the University of Iowa's School of Religion, tells us, there are different kinds of guilt.[3] There is *real guilt*. It is the normal or healthy psychological discomfort which is caused by real sin, when this is defined as deviation from the Creator's intentions. This guilt is properly associated with forgiveness.

There is also *false guilt*. This is the kind of guilt that no one should have to carry. It is based on misinformation, miseducation and faulty conditioning. It may result from the attempts of others, especially parents, to cope with their own problem of guilt. Sometimes it results from the general moral ignorance of our families, teachers, role-modelers, and culture.

How do we know what is really right and what is really wrong? Christians believe that we can know this by divine revelation—the teachings of the Bible, Sinai, the prophets and so forth and Jesus most of all—plus intelligent application of their principles to particular times and places. This isn't always so easy and that's why there are ethicists and ethics centers.

Without such norms we become vulnerable to false guilt, or to confusing real with false guilt. There has obviously been a lot of false guilt about sexual matters. But there is real guilt too and it is important that we don't play conceptual tricks on ourselves in our efforts at unloading guilt. We must not turn real guilt into false guilt in order to be rid of it.

In addition to *real guilt* and *false guilt* there is *neurotic guilt*. This guilt is true in its experience and false in its appearance to

---

[3]David Belgum, *Guilt: Where Psychology and Religion Meet* (Englewood Cliffs, NJ: Prentice-Hall, 1963).

others and to ourselves. Because it is unresolved, we often give it a false face in our attempts to cope with it. It can appear as legalistic, self-righteous moral pride, or even as false humility. Or it can be covered with a variety of escape mechanisms. It can even appear as somatic illness. But whatever its face, it is one of the consequences of not dealing forthrightly and correctly with guilt.

Because *false guilt* is based on mistaken information, it should succumb to correct information and reconditioning even though the reconditioning may take some time. A good example is what compulsive people feel when they are supposed to be on vacation. This "guilt" can feel very real. Even if our minds tell us that we are being stupid, it may take considerable, prolonged, and conscious reconditioning before we are able to bring about the rest and relaxation that vacations are supposed to provide.

When, as in *neurotic guilt,* our inappropriate sense of being in the wrong is built into us by the inadequate coping behavior of others—often those with whom we first lived as infants, children and adolescents—the causative factors are so deep that they often require the skills of a clinical psychologist or psychiatrist. Pastors, teachers, and other professionals can help by consistently being the kinds of persons by whom we should have been surrounded much earlier in our lives.

Religious resources can be especially helpful in addressing *real guilt.* This means uncovering the true problem and eliciting a sense of God's forgiveness. It also means taking advantage of all the aids to faith and acceptance which God has provided. This includes aids such as the truth about God in the Bible and elsewhere. It includes symbolic aids to faith such as baptism and the Lord's Supper. It includes actively participating in the life of a healthy community of faith. It includes the practical aids to self-acceptance and feelings of value that naturally come from "making things right," insofar as this is possible, and serving others. The Gospel replaces guilt with worth. When it is accepted by our assisted faith, divine forgiveness is the vehicle of that transformation.

Part IV

Faith and Reason

16
Toward an Ethic of Responsibility

Many serious-minded Christians share in the alarm expressed by conservative believers over the present moral climate of America, including the American church. Overly rapid change in almost every aspect of life has left large segments of our country in a situation of virtual anomie, or at least considerable confusion about what constitutes a good life.

Above all there is a need for clarifying language. Take, for example, the terms "Situationism" and "situationism." Although they are spelled the same, they refer to quite different entities. The former is a technical term with a fairly precise definition. It is an ethical posture also referred to as "Contextualism" or "Contextual Ethics," terms we shall use interchangeably. The latter has come by usage in conservative circles to mean irresponsibility, immorality, impulsive, capricious behavior, antinomianism, and the like. Those who decry it see it as characterizing a "generation adrift," often particularly with regards to sexual behavior. The term "New Morality" enjoys a similar distinction between it and the "new morality;" however, it is mainly employed in a pejorative sense.[1]

Little need be said here about "situationism" because its meaning appears obvious. Apparently, much more needs to be said about "Situationism" as a method for dealing with moral dilemmas. We shall direct our attention primarily to the use of this word.

Situationism is a method which assumes that answers to moral questions may be found within the context in which they arise. The Situationist or Contextualist looks at moral dilemmas and when asked, "What am I to do?" responds, "it all depends on the situation." "What are the facts in the case?" It thus involves the inductive method applied to morals.

Contextualism is an antagonist of a kind of rule ethic which simply turns to prescriptions for all of its answers, an ethic which asks in turn, "What do the rules, the fathers, the authorities say about the matter?" To illustrate: some years ago when a well-known Jewish religious thinker was asked regarding Judaism's position on a medical moral issue, he responded by saying that he did not know because the Rabbis had not spoken on that subject.

A rule ethic underlies the almost total dependence of some church members on authoritative pronouncements handed down from institutionalized leadership as the way to dispel ambiguity in moral matters. The Contextualist, on the other hand, places great store on individual reason and responsibility. He rejects the rule-ethicist's tendency to emphasize conformity for conformity's sake. He prefers to utilize in matters moral his ability to read, listen, and be taught.

This is not to imply that the Contextualist rejects rules as of no value simply because he objects to rule conformity. He knows that most of life can be, and indeed must be, lived "by the numbers" to

---

[1]Joseph Fletcher, *Situation Ethics: The New Morality*. Library of Theological Ethics (Louisville: Westminster/John Knox Press, 1997); Paul Lehmann, *Ethics in a Christian Context*. Library of Theological Ethics (Louisville: Westminster/John Knox Press, 2006); Paul Tillich, *Morality and Beyond* (New York: Harper Torchbooks, 1963).

use an old army phrase. He hopes that the people who share the freeways and airports with him and scrub for his surgical operations will be committed to fairly dependable prearranged patterns of behavior. He also knows that life would simply be chaotic if every momentary possibility were turned into a major moral struggle. Habitually good behavior on the part of the majority of people is the very basis of social existence.

The Contextualist has a point to make. It is that life is complex and that no two situations can be exactly alike. If we are insensitive to this fact, we may discover ourselves in circumstances where our "habitual behavior" may be inappropriate, even morally destructive. Account must be taken of all the circumstances in which an action takes place if we are really to do the right thing.

The Contextualist is also aware that he may encounter novel situations for which previous experience, or even "divine revelation," has not precisely prepared him. What does he do when he finds no rule ready to guide him? Or worse, what if the rules express competing claims so that they seem to contradict one another? Are we then reduced to moral impotence? Unfortunately, our rapidly changing world has thrust many such situations upon us.

The Contextualist is likely to be intrigued by moral issues raised by the newer technology such as medicine. One Contextualist recently expressed the wish that all rule-ethicists could spend a few months wrestling with the moral problems with the world of medicine to test whether their astounding ability to separate the moral "black sheep" actions from "white ones" could stand up under the pressure of the physician's shadowland of confusing shades of gray. It is one thing to know that killing is wrong and that saving life is right. But what of the situation where to kill or not to kill are not the alternatives, but one in which the question is who lives when not everybody can.

Often the physician would prefer to shift the responsibility to someone else and how often he cannot! What he clearly needs is an ethic that tells him how to act responsibly as an individual, on his own.

It should be obvious that an ethic which concentrates on the moment of decision and the situation in which it occurs will be greatly conditioned by its reading of the situation. Situationism seems to be no single entity for this reason, at least in terms of the specific answers it gives to moral questions. There is a uniformity of method that is in the form of its question, "What am I as a morally responsible agent to do in light of this particular situation?" There may be great diversity, however, in how "this particular situation" is perceived. Thus there may be a very broad spectrum of possible situational answers given by persons using the identical method.

Some situational answers may represent a very narrow reading of the "situation" indeed. This is a reason for the pejorative use of the word "situationism." Such persons might, for example, see the extent of the situation as the impulses of a boy and girl on a lonely road in the back seat of his car who are oblivious to the larger personal and social consequences of their actions. It might also be so broadly perceived as to include the revelation of God and the wisdom of the community as well as the future, even eternal consequences of human behavior. In other words, the validity of the conclusions of this method is only as valid, as in all matters involving logic, as their premises.

If this is so, the alarms of the conservatives, while understandable, are misdirected. It is not Situationism as a method which is at fault but the individuals who use the method. If we oppose some of Joseph Fletcher's answers to ethical questions, it must be for his misreading of the situation and not because he is a Situationist.

What is new about the "New Morality" is not the ethical method involved but the fact that many of the moral premises have changed. The "situation" is being perceived in a new way. We should criticize the premises upon which many in our time are basing their moral decisions, not the fact that they are involved in personal decision making.

How we perceive God and His revelation to man, for example, is likely to prove most crucial to moral decision. A belief in a highly personal God who is deeply concerned about man and elects to guide him into the way of love is one kind of premise. An abstract notion of God who is impersonal, with an accompanying view of the commandments of Scripture as an accumulation of human folkways, is quite another. Each radically modifies the perceived situation in its own way.

Anyone who is sufficiently open to be able to see it cannot but be struck with the fact that from one end of the Scriptures to the other moral imperatives were constantly adapted to the circumstances in which they were to be carried out. This was so even with the Ten Commandments. The "Thou shalt not kill" was given immediate exception—sometimes of a chilling nature. The same can be said of Jesus' dealings with the Sabbath, David with the showbread, Paul and the matter of circumcision. We could go on endlessly.

Never should a rule, even a Ten Commandment rule, be so applied as to oppose love. This is the situational method and it is thus as old as morality. This is what men have always done when they were morally sensitive and accepted responsibility for their actions. It is what most of the detractors of "situationism" themselves do when they wrestle with morally ambiguous issues, whether or not they realize it. Indeed, it is what they had better do if they do not wish to be involved in unloving actions!

A second semantic misunderstanding in this conflict derives from the use of the term "absolute." The Christian Contextualist insists that there is only one absolute which is love. When the opposition objects that this minimizes the significance of the Decalogue he is not aware that each is using the term "absolute" in a different way.

When the anti-"situationist" speaks of the Ten Commandments as God's "absolutes," he means by this that they are to be taken with the utmost seriousness and that they possess an exceedingly broad range of applicability and durability. He may also mean they are the highest expressions of moral principle that God has revealed to man, carrying with them the very authority of God Himself.

The Contextualist, who may also take the Ten Commandments seriously, employs the term "absolute" in its philosophic logical sense, meaning the ultimate, beyond which there can be nothing.

In such usage there can never be more than one absolute under any circumstance, just as there can only be one "first." If we speak of Ten Absolutes, we commit a semantic error because these Ten, even if prior to all lesser values, would necessarily have to be relative to each other.

Note this relativity in the Ten Commandments. Imagine, if you will, a situation where the Fifth Commandment, if strictly followed, would put us in conflict with one of the first four. Few persons who take the Decalogue seriously would hesitate to place their obligation to God above that to man even if that man were his earthly father. The Fifth Commandment is, therefore, secondary and thus relative to the one taken from the first four. In a sense it is relatively less binding.

Recall that Jesus seems to have made a distinction something like this when he said that "the first and great commandment" is, "Thou shalt love the Lord thy God with all thy heart, and with all thy soul, and with all thy mind. This is the first and great commandment." He went on to say, "And the second is like unto it, Thou shalt love thy neighbor as thyself."[2] Conceivably, we might in desperation be forced to give one of the last six commandments priority over another one of them, as in that intriguing case of Rahab and the spies.[3]

It is clearly consistent both with the words of Jesus and the writings of Ellen White to say that the Ten Commandments are *expressions* of God's law. But, please note, that which is an expression of something is relative to it even if it is its highest expression.

The love "absolute" which is commanded is no mere sentimentality or feeling, even less the biological urgency suggested in the assurance that "it must be right because we love each other so." The love commanded is *agape*. It is a principle involving reason, choice, will, commitment, loyalty and the acceptance of responsibility. It can even be directed against one for whom one has no positive feelings, even the enemy. Such love is alone without exception eternally valid. It is indeed the very character of God.

---

[2]Matthew 22:37-39.

[3]Joshua 6:1-24.

All expressions of this love are conditioned, however, by time and space. Stated as "*Thou shalt nots,*" they are sublime descriptions of how love operates under the conditions of our being human. But these descriptions might have to be restated so as to be appropriate to other conditions as, for example, the Fifth Commandment and Seventh Commandment when applied to angels.

They may even be amplified so as to apply in spirit to new situations. Paul's observations regarding the "Governing Powers" is an illustration of such an amplification of the Fifth Commandment. The same can be said for Christ's descriptions of *agape* in action in His well-known Sermon on the Mount.[4]

That this can be done attests to the truth that it is not their wording that is sacrosanct but their principle, the absolute value, which undergirds them. If we say this, we have become Christian Contextualists in essence. The conservative critic tends only to give these descriptions of love greater practical authority because of his presuppositions about God and what happened at Sinai.

A final point of contention uncovers a semantic error on the other side. This concerns the word "legalist." Both sides vigorously reject "legalism;" however, the antagonists mean different things even though they use the same word. When a situationist rejects legalism, he is likely, as an antinomian, to be rejecting rules per se. On the other hand, Christian Contextualists, whether self-consciously or not, are more apt to be simply objecting to a misuse of the rules.

Because legalism constitutes the stimulus and point of departure for the whole Contextual enterprise, it is important that we understand it. The Christian moralist who views God's commandments as the supreme expressions or descriptions of love, must always insist that the rules serve love. If any rule is stated or applied in such a way as to conflict with love, it is no rule, or a bad rule and must be suspended or abrogated. One of God's commandments can never contradict love and be God's commandment without introducing an unthinkable contradiction into God's nature and character.

---

[4]Matthew 5:1–7:29

Legalism consists not in having rules or even in their precise application. Being careful may indicate the depth of one's concern or even a quality of personality or character. The careful surgeon who takes great pains with his operative procedure may be revealing something very important and valuable about himself. The same might be said about a housepainter, bricklayer, or anyone else who takes pride in his workmanship. He is not thereby necessarily a legalist—though, of course, he also may be.

The legalist is one who is morally "careful" for the wrong reasons. For the legalist, law, rather than serving love, serves law, or perhaps even more accurately, unworthy motives, or unresolved psychological conflicts.

It is one thing for a surgeon to practice his art with all of the skill and precision he can muster, including scrubbing before the operation in a fairly well-defined manner for the sake of reducing his mortality rates to the barest minimum, but quite another if it is done for his own status in the medical and larger community, or even deeper, as a way of compensating for or resolving hidden conflicts within himself.

The legalist is one who keeps the rules not so as to be more loving but most often as a way of solving personal problems, such as deep feelings of guilt, which prevent him from really accepting himself and thus other people.

Guilt need not be clearly identified as such by the individual. Psychologists and psychiatrists also speak of "free-floating guilt" which is tied to no clearly recognized act or situation. Such guilt may, for example, be related to forgotten parental perfectionism internalized by the child as an enduring sense of frustration, failure and unworthiness, only to appear later as attempts to earn feelings of "righteousness" by a life of high-level moral rectitude. Theologians call this "salvation by works." Unable to feel worthwhile and accepted, even if he does not understand the basis for his anxiety, such a person attempts to earn the acceptance of himself and others. Unfortunately, he most often only succeeds in compounding the difficulty.

The theological solution to his problem is "salvation by grace" rather than works, by accepting God's loving acceptance, through trusting in God's freely given forgiveness. This grace is often mediated through accepting, non-condemning, loving persons in one's life. The one who can accept himself because he has truly learned to trust God is thereby released from his frenzied struggle for superficial moral purity to an unstrained and natural outflow of loving behavior where the rules serve as useful guides.

The legalist often identifies himself by the way the rules function in his life. Most often they are either the means by which he receives the punishment he so deeply feels he deserves (masochism) or they become the vehicles by which he critically projects his own guilt on others (sadism). They are not easy persons to live with. Such legalism is rejected by all Christian Contextualists.

To summarize: Christian Situationationism or Contextualism, as opposed to "situationism" or "contextualism," is a clearly defined ethical method for dealing with moral dilemmas. Such dilemmas occur in the presence of conflicting and competing moral claims or where there is a lack of adequate, clear, and applicable moral guidance. It recognizes the complexity of human life as it is lived morally and the difficulty of anticipating all of the factors which make up any particular moment of decision. It admits to only one absolute norm for human behavior. This is love as *agape*, as a concerned commitment to others in ways that are guided by the needs of particular circumstances.

As a method it is inductive and it depends on a marshaling of all of the relevant facts which make up the situation. It accepts full responsibility for determining the most "loving" action in the light of these facts.

Individual Contextualists may differ widely in how they interpret the "facts" of the context or situation depending on their antecedent beliefs and experiences. As in any enterprise involving logic, the ethical conclusions reached will reflect such premise differences. These differences may demonstrate the world view or *Weltanschauung*, of the individual observer, including his conceptions of God, the meaning of existence, man's eternal destiny, and the relative value and authority he gives to such revealed guidance as the Bible.

Persons with little respect for the "authority" of the Bible are likely to appear antinomian, capricious, and impulsive as they draw ethical conclusions, and this is part of the reason why conservative Christians find them disturbing. A Christian Contextualist who takes the Bible authoritatively may, on the other hand, include in his perceived situation the whole of human history and destiny. This is the largest and most important situation.

17
Can Christian Bioethics Be Based on Reason Alone?

This question is a child of the modern world, if one identifies the modern period with the so-called "Age of Enlightenment" or roughly the last three centuries. Not that the role of reason in moral matters was unappreciated before that time. Although in the 13th century St. Thomas Aquinas believed that man needed divine revelation to be aware of some moral truths, he also held that the most basic ethical axioms or propositions are self-evident.

It is difficult to overestimate the impact of this heroic figure on ethics, even today. Practically all of Roman Catholic thinking on such matters has been conditioned by St. Thomas. Conservative Catholic attitudes regarding contraception are largely Thomistic.

St. Thomas said that everything in Nature has its proper purpose or end. The proper goal of sexual intercourse is reproduction of the species; therefore, anything that interferes with this end is against nature and is thus a violation of nature's law. He thought that all rational persons would agree.

The Apostle Paul seems to have something similar in mind when he wrote this in his *Epistle to the Romans* more than a millennium before:

> For when the Gentiles, which have not the law, do by nature the things contained in the law, these, having not the law, are a law unto themselves: Which show the work of the law written in their hearts, their conscience also bearing witness, and their thoughts the meanwhile accusing or else excusing one another; in the day when God shall judge the secrets of men by Jesus Christ according to my gospel.[1]

The major Protestant reformers, partly as a reaction against the excesses of Scholasticism, were unimpressed with nature and with human reason as reliable sources of moral truth, or almost any other truth for that matter. They believed that human reason is too damaged to depend on.

With the advent of "The Enlightenment" an attempt was made to breathe the new spirit into philosophical and ethical areas. A morality fitting the mood of the times—inductive, scientific and rational, rather than merely authoritarian—became the watchword of the best ethical minds of the period.

Utilitarianism was conceived in this spirit. It was a scientific attempt to establish moral principles on rational observations, to discover the "ought" by observing what "is." According to the Hedonistic Utilitarians, when we observe what men in fact do, we discover that they invariably pursue happiness or pleasure and avoid unhappiness or pain. John Stuart Mill wrote that happiness is the only desirable end because all people desire it more than anything else.[2] He could think of no better way to determine whether something is desirable than establishing that most people desire it.

We speak of this kind of ethical thought as "naturalistic."

---

[1]Romans 2:14, 15

[2]John Stuart Mill, *Utilitarianism* (Indianapolis: Bobbs-Merrill, 1979), 34-43.

Although there are other examples of the attempt to derive the "ought" from the "is," the Utilitarians largely held the stage during the eighteenth and early nineteenth centuries. As the new science filled in the gaps in our understanding, which formerly had been filled by God, He became largely unnecessary or so remote so as to not concern us overmuch. What remained was for someone to describe how nature could be self-operating, and "naturalism" in ethics as elsewhere would come fully into its own.

Charles Darwin's *Origin of the Species*[3] provided that description. Darwin's contribution to social theory is more apropos to our present discussion than its scientific implications. His *Origin* gave us the basis for a rationalistic, humanistic materialism. Marx and Engels were delighted. They tried to induce Darwin to allow them to use his name in the forward of *Das Kapital* but, to his credit, he politely declined.

The most inclusive of all the moral "naturalisms," certainly the most consequential, came into being. "Right" was now defined as what furthered survival and served the interests of those who were "fit" to survive. We can know what we ought to do by observing the natural world around us!

A philosopher was born in the latter half of the nineteenth century who, in terms of the devastating impact of his life and thought, was one of the most influential thinkers who ever lived, although I am not aware that this fact is commonly appreciated. His name was Friedrich Nietzsche and he was raised in a somewhat straight-laced religious home, mainly by aunts and sisters. When he was eighteen years of age he gave up his Christian faith. Later he was to say that it was the easiest thing he ever did and then he proceeded to spend the rest of his life proving that it was the easiest thing he ever did.

Friedrich Nietzsche's main claim to fame derives from the fact that he took Darwin very seriously in matters moral. The book which said this most clearly was his *The Antichrist*. He chose the title with care because he believed that Judaism and Christianity

---

[3]Charles Darwin, *On the Origin of Species by Means of Natural Selection* (London: John Murray, 1859.

were responsible for most of the world's ills, especially the world's social ills. Jews and Christians had "transvalued" the values. They had veritably turned morality on its head in service of their own decadence. Here are his words:

> What is good? Everything that heightens the feeling of power in man, the will to power, power itself. What is bad? Everything that is born of weakness. What is happiness? The feeling that power is growing, that resistance is overcome. Not contentedness but more power; not peace but war; not virtue but fitness. What is more harmful than any vice? Active pity for all the failures and all the weak: Christianity.[4]

Where did Friedrich Nietzsche get this? The key words tell us. They are "will to power," "self-preservation," "law of selection." These all come straight out of *Origin of the Species*.

That the fit survive in the competitive struggle for existence by possessing more wits, greater agility, stronger muscles, longer claws, and more powerful teeth is in fact the nature of evolution. "Power" is the name of the survival game. We are talking about power over the weak and the will to use it. This is the way it is in nature, and when he is true to himself, according to Nietzsche, man participates in the general configuration of the rest of nature. Thus the truly great men of the past were men like the Roman legions who marched through the world conquering and displacing its weak and decadent.

Ideas have consequences. It would be naïve to attribute to ideas, even those as forceful as these are, more credit than they deserve. Surely the causes of our two great World Wars were vastly more complex than anything Friedrich Nietzsche had to say; however, there is strong evidence that Nietzsche furnished much of the philosophic undergirding of these two major human catastrophes.

It is said that Hitler slept with Nietzsche under his pillow.

---

[4]Walter Kaufman, ed. *The Portable Nietzsche* (New York: Penguin Books, 1977), 569.

The similarity between the superior type of human that Nietzsche championed and Hitler's Aryan superior race is no accident, nor is the Holocaust, and all that it represents. Similar attitudes were also at the center of the Kaiser's war. Two horrible World Wars, more terrible than all the wars of history combined, can be said to have been at least conceptually conditioned by a view of nature that gained currency in the mid–nineteenth century.

According to naturalistic ethics, observations regarding nature at work are the stuff with which reason works out its solutions to ethical dilemmas. St. Thomas had said much earlier that at least some solutions were "self-evident to unaided reason;" however, if we cannot depend upon the observed laws of nature to give us moral guidance, as is suggested by our reading of Nietzsche, reason as a tool for making ethical judgments is in trouble. What was the source of Nietzsche's error? Our conclusions are only as good as the facts on which they are based, even if the rational process is without flaw. His "facts" were in error.

If human reason cannot handle human problems, the only alternative would seem to be to appeal to some kind of supernatural guidance for answers, which is, of course, what some folk think we should have been doing all along. Unfortunately, even through the writings of inspired prophets, God has not chosen to involve himself directly in very many of the perplexing issues the new technology has thrust upon us. Where, for example, does prophetic precedent come to grips with the issues raised by the new fertility and reproductive techniques: artificial insemination, in vitro fertilization, embryo transfer, cryo preservation of human embryos, surrogate parenting? What chapter and verse shall we consult to give us guidance in relation to the marvels of genetic engineering? The Bible admonishes us to refrain from killing, at least murdering people. But where in the Bible is there anything that tells us when to or when not to institute life-prolonging procedures, or when to stop them and under what circumstances?

The naturalists were correct in attempting to derive the "ought" from the "is." Their usual mistake was in their incorrectly identifying the "is." A Christian ethic, biblically based, must conclude that ethics is based primarily on creation, although as we shall shortly be pointing out, it may take divine revelation to acquaint us with the reality of creation. What now "is" may not be the same "is" of creation.

The original creation is no longer available to us, no matter how assiduously we search for it in the field or laboratory. The Bible is clear about a Fall affecting the whole of creation. Fallen nature formed the basis for Nietzsche's rational moral system. Because he had already rejected any possibility of knowing about any other kind of nature, his conclusions were inevitable and wrong, and appropriately named "Anti-Christ," I might add.

Ethics is based on Creation before the Fall. That ancient "is" forms the true basis for what "ought" to be. Unfortunately for human pride, that fact denies us human self-sufficiency in matters ethical.

The original Creation is available to us only by revelation. Only the inspired pictures of Eden and of Eden restored, and Jesus' disclosure of the Creator and His character, can provide a sufficient basis for knowing what "ought" to be.

A rational Christian bioethics will be one that stresses the restoration and fulfillment of the Creator's original intentions, insofar as these may be ascertained from the inspired sources. The rules, such as the Decalogue, are descriptive of those intentions rather than being merely prescriptive. God made us to behave in such a manner. To be true to our moral charter is to be self-fulfilled rather than self-denied.

This principle also applies to the new questions. Any biological engineering discovery that has the potential for restoration of creation is to be supported. Those that lead in Nietzsche's direction are to be deplored. Those fertility and reproductive innovations that contribute to what God had in mind in creating the procreative family are to be welcomed. Those that place the family in jeopardy are to be opposed. Any action whose total effect is to diminish the Creation in any significant way is immoral. That, finally, is what morality and ethics are all about.

The Creation as an expression of the Creator is made known

to man by revelation. The Creator has also given general moral descriptions of it. In addition, the Creator has provided man with a mind capable of perceiving the true nature of that Creation, if he would apply himself with persistence and dedication and if he did not reject out of hand the Bible a major source of truth. Together, inspiration and dedicated reason persistently applied can arrive at moral truth.

Before the Fall, reason alone would probably have sufficed. The "is" was good, perfect, undistorted. Ethics could be a scientific enterprise. We could discover the truth about behavior as we discovered the truth about atoms, and planets, and the stars. Nature's laws were God's laws and thus there would be special compartment for ethics apart from science, or the rest of natural truth.

In such an ideal world the answer to the question, "Can Christian bioethics be done on the basis of reason alone?" would be "Yes, of course!" But in the world in which we live, man needs help with the premises even as he reasons his way to proper conclusions. Here, the answer is both "yes" and "no." It all depends upon where reason begins its work and to what end.

18
Is the Scientific Method Appropriate for Religious Knowledge?

A major source of conflict in the minds of many contemporary youth is the apparent contrast between the stuffy platitudes of their fathers in an increasingly distant past and a supercharged age of technological magic and wonder. These new developments appear to deny former beliefs; worse yet, they also render the older convictions as unnecessary and irrelevant. On many college and university campuses, the impression is that all the fascinating things are happening in places like the science research laboratory instead of where religion is being taught. To many young people, traditional religion appears out of date and isolated from the real world, with all of its precision, certainty, and shiny new technology and vocabulary.

The enormous fruitfulness of the scientific method is partly why religion suffers by contrast. When applied to the natural world with courageous abandon, it has issued in the positively staggering technical developments of our times. When applied to the issues with which religious faith has been concerned, the results have been, in the eyes of many, little short of disastrous. Not only has the Bible been called into question as the revealed word of God to men, but the very belief in a divine providence controlling the forces of nature and shaping the destiny of man is rendered more or less incredible.

The modern story of religious belief in the face of the onslaughts of the scientific method is a dismal one of almost constant retreat by the proponents of religion. A large segment of the church has remained viable either by denying science's development or by an interesting and tempting intellectual maneuver. This maneuver consists in so defining "the things of the Spirit" that the scientific method is inappropriate. Such a solution to the conflict was in fact, ready made in the theology of the churches in the early centuries.

During the early centuries of our era when Christianity migrated from the soil of its ancient Hebrew heritage and established itself in a largely Hellenic cultural world, a fusion of viewpoints occurred which was to prove fateful to Christian theology in a number of ways, not the least of which was its misunderstanding of ultimate reality. The wholism of Israel's biblical monotheism, where one God was the creative source of all that is, was modified by contact with Greek Platonism, Gnosticism, and even Manichaeism. The result was that reality was conceived by many of the church fathers in the dualistic terms of a radical disjunction of spirit and matter which was quite foreign to the Hebrews.

According to Plato, spirit and matter, expressed particularly as soul and body in man, were categorically different entities. Matter occupied time and space, was temporary and changing, while spirit or soul was beyond all time and space and belonged to the eternal and changeless. All of reality was divided between these two categories.

According to the Platonists and Neoplatonists, to speak of the soul or the spirit in spatial terms was to misunderstand reality. For example, to say that Jesus after His ascension sat down at the right hand of the Father is to speak only in metaphor. God as Spirit could have no right or left hand, nor can He sit. These are spatial metaphors and thus belong to matter. Freedom and God's foreknowledge presented logical difficulty since ideas such as past, present and future, or before and after, are temporal terms and God as Spirit is not involved with time.

Probably the most influential Christian after the apostle Paul was Augustine who became Bishop of Hippo in North Africa. He accepted his mother's Christian faith only when he was able to conceive of God in non-material, non-temporal terms. His was a better mind than mine, apparently, for I confess that I cannot understand how anything unrelated to time and space can exist as any more than an abstraction.

Such thinking bequeathed to Christian theology the classical doctrine of the immortal soul inhabiting a body from which it escapes at death to return to its eternal spiritual abode. This included the concept of a radical gulf between supernatural and nature.

This formed the matrix of the solution of the science-religion conflict to which we referred, a solution in which science can be no threat to religion since its categories and methods do not apply to the realm of the spirit, a solution which could also allow science to go its merry way untrammeled by the strictness of religious sensitivity. The results, as we all know, have been well nigh disastrous.

In contrast to this implicit, if not always explicit dualism, what is the message of the Bible? It is that God is one in number, nature and character: "Hear, O Israel: The Lord our God is one Lord."[1] It is that God is the Creator and Sustainer: "All things were made by him; and without him was not any thing made that was made."[2] It is that He is "Upholding all things by the word of His power."[3] It is that God is good: "O taste and see that the Lord is good."[4] It is that "God saw everything that He

---

[1]Deuteronomy 6:4.
[2]John 1:3.
[3]Hebrews 1:3.
[4]Psalms 34:8.

had made, and, behold, it was very good."[5]

In short, the Bible teaches that everything can ultimately be traced back to one eternal reality, which is God. Because God is a unity, there are no contradictory or disharmonious principles within Him. All that comes from Him belongs together as a single and internally integrated whole. The Bible also teaches that this whole as derivative from a good God is itself also good. The Manicheans were wrong. Evil is not an entity on its own; it is always a distortion or privation of good.

There is a truth in pantheism. As in all error, pantheism has been a viable doctrine precisely because it contained a partial truth. Error can never stand solely on its own two feet. Pantheism's truth, which is a Bible teaching, is that there is no place in God's entire universe where we can go to escape from God's presence, where God is not.

Pantheism's error is the assumption that this "everywhere, in everything" is all there is to God. In biblical faith, beyond the creative and sustaining activity of God is the *Person* of God who is the proper object of our adoration and worship. The believer's right response to the skeptics taunt "show me where God is and I'll believe" is "First show me where God is not." In other words, reality is one.

What, then, can we say of the applicability of the scientific method to religion? Logic would lead us to respond that, if reality is one, the method which is applicable to a part of that whole cannot be sharply excluded from the remainder. So it is. This is worth exploring in terms of (1) the similar spirit, or dedication, of religion and science and (2) their common appeal to experience for validity. It is also worth investigating how they differ about (1) repeatability and (2) the scope of appropriate scientific research.

Let us begin with the spirit or dedication of religion and science. Although the scientific method has been defined variously, first of all it is an attitude. Let us deeply breathe the atmosphere of this attitude in the following words by Ralph Waldo Gerard who had a distinguished career in the United States as a neurophysiologist and behavioral scientist:

---

[5]Genesis 1:31.

> Let me tell you now what was told me as a beginning investigator by a great teacher and what I have religiously told my beginning students over the years. I don't think there is a better epitomizing of the moods of science, one not to be violated by loose talk, by banding half-understood words and concepts, by unsupported mystifying conclusions. The advice is simply this: "Young man, take care lest you find what you are looking for.[6]

By contrast how often religious people and scientists alike have been guilty of fitting facts to their prejudices and wishes.

Gerard tells of a patient who constantly snapped his fingers while visiting a psychiatrist. The psychiatrist did what almost everyone would: He asked the patient why he kept doing it. The answer was that he kept snapping his fingers in order to keep the wild elephants away. The psychiatrist explained that there was no danger because the closest wild elephant was miles away. The patient's response: "Certainly effective isn't it?"'[7]

Gerard goes on to say, "Perhaps my most precious value, probably of scientists in general, is a dedication to honest and, if possible, clear thinking. I would echo that famous statement of Huxley: "God give me courage to face a fact, though it slays me." After criticizing what often happens in the realm of religion, this great scientist then described the similarity of both religion and science at their best:

> The question was asked whether religion is the quest or its results. To me, both religion and science are the quests, not the results. The results may change from year to year or from generation to generation. I still thrill to hear one of the finest of man's sentences, "carry fire from the altar of the past, not the ashes."[8]

---

[6]R.W. Gerard, "Comments on Religion in an Age of Science" in Harlow Shapley, *Science Ponders Religion* (New York: Appleton-Century-Crofts, 1960), 99.
[7]Ibid, 96.
[8]Ibid. 98.

Granting the validity of his criticism of what often passes for religion, is the spirit Gerard expresses as the attitude of true science really so different from that which breathes in the following?

> The fact that there is no controversy or agitation among God's people should not be regarded as conclusive evidence that they are holding fast to sound doctrine. There is reason to fear that they may not be clearly discriminating between truth and error.[9]

> There is no excuse for anyone in taking the position that there is no more truth to be revealed, and that all our expositions are without error. The fact that certain doctrines have been held as truth for many years is not proof that our ideas are infallible. Age will not make error into truth, and truth can afford to be fair. No true doctrine will lose anything by close investigation.... There are those who oppose everything that is not in accordance with their own ideas and by so doing they endanger their eternal interest.[10]

Many of us would say "Amen" to this from Ellen White provided such investigation didn't conflict with our private prejudices. I'm utterly amazed at the number of persons who cry out for freedom of investigation of everything except their own pet theories. Then they are not nearly as daring as they thought.

Surely in the light of these statements the spirit of religion and science is one. Note how the following statement by scientist Hudson Hoagland captures what is best also in religion. He was a renowned specialist in neuroendocrinology who also helped develop the birth control pill.

> Often the most important ingredient in really major scientific creativity is not imagination—one must have that to

[9]Ellen G. White, *Counsels to Writers and Editors* (Nashville, Tennessee: Southern Publishing Association, 1946), 38-39.
[10]Ibid., 35, 36.

> do anything, of course—but courage. And courage carries the conviction: 'What I am doing is right—which is faith.' The great physicist, Clark Maxwell, truly said that the credit for a new idea does not belong to the first man who has it, but to the first man who takes it seriously.[11]

Sometimes we have witnessed science even outdistancing religion in religion's own domain. Many Christians might hang their heads in shame over the church's past shortcomings but they cannot deny the religious quality in Hoagland's further observation:

> The scientist has developed a high regard for truth and spends much time in trying to ascertain it, and the fraternity of scientists transcends national boundaries and class and color distinctions. As Bronowski has pointed out, a scientist can be wrong without being wicked, in contrast to thinking in spheres that are dominated by authoritarianism in religion and politics. Scientists can function effectively only when they have mutual respect for each other's integrity. The scientist has learned to say "I don't know" to questions where others are sure they do know the answers on the basis of meager evidence or no evidence acceptable to him. He knows that some of the most unethical conduct of history has been the result of religious belief.[12]

In these last words Hoagland refers to religious wars, inquisitions and so forth, which we recognize as having little to do with true religion. When science and religion are both true to themselves, they breathe the same spirit of eager dedicated quest and an open mind and heart.

In addition to an open mind and courageous dedication to the truth, the scientific method is concerned with confirming and verifying the facts. Science ultimately appeals to experience. Claims

---

[11]Gerard, p. 94.

[12]Hudson Hoagland, "Some Reflections on Science and Religion" in *Science Ponders Religion*, 25.

are true or false according to the degree that they are confirmed or disconfirmed by experience.

Experiments are ways of controlling experience in order to test reality. Faith at its best also speaks of "experimental religion" as over against merely theoretical formulas of belief. Does not the Bible from one end to the other appeal to experience as the basis for trust and commitment? "Taste and see that the Lord is good"[13] and "Come now, let us reason together."[14] The old conflict between faith and reason is a false one. Faith is action in the presence of favorable evidence without final proof.

Again and again the New Testament witnesses to the zeal, courage and conviction of those who had seen and handled the resurrected Lord. Paul appealed to experience regarding the resurrection of Jesus. "After that he was seen of above five hundred brethren at once," he wrote, "of whom the greater remain to this moment."[15]

The major difference between science's experimental method and the Bible's experimental method is that science, by insisting on repeatability and prediction, has narrowed the range of experiences which it allows itself to consider. What the Germans call *einmaligkeiten,* or things that happen only once, are in principle virtually excluded from scientific investigation. Science as often practiced has often cut itself off from understanding creative personality as well. By "creative personality" I mean an individual who *can* act as well as *react* and be *acted upon*.

It is interesting that those behavioral sciences which insist on a rigid application of a narrow scientific method—namely the behaviorists—are forced to deny human freedom. This narrow application of the scientific method is an arbitrary limitation which science imposes upon itself. Broadly defined as methodologically reliable appeal to all experience, the scientific method is most appropriate for religious truth.

In order to enlarge the scientific method so as to apply it to

[13]Psalms 34:8.
[14]Isaiah 1:18.
[15]I Corinthians 15:6.

religion or religious knowledge, it must change in an additional way. This is that it must include the kind of knowledge that takes place between persons.

To know another is more than being aware of certain propositions or facts about him; it also includes a kind of relation *with* him that is more than knowledge *about* him. To know God is more than knowing about God. And it is this kind of knowing—again experiential—to which the ordinary application of the narrow scientific method proves not false but inadequate. Such knowing involves love, trust, intuition, commitment, faith, and all of the other elements of interpersonal experience as well as the use of sense and reason.

Is the scientific method appropriate to religion? The answer is "yes" if the method is not arbitrarily limited so as to exclude the most significant quality of reality, namely the personal. Religious faith is all about the total experience of my person with the person of God.

There is only one valid way of knowing. Scientific and theological investigation, while emphasizing differing aspects of reality, when true to themselves belong to each other in method as well as in ultimate object. This is the meaning of the statement that nature and revelation speak with but one voice.

19
Knowing with the Heart: An Adventist Theory of Perception

The purpose of what follows is to explore the implications of a number of statements in Ellen White's writings bearing on the knowing process and to suggest a conceptual model that may hopefully tie them together into a consistent theory of perception. The consequences of such an analysis may be felt in a number of different directions, but at the very least it may underscore the conviction held by many of us as to the essential soundness of the writings of Ellen G. White on deeply philosophical matters.

I also hope that this enterprise may shed light on an issue that is gaining importance with the church's increasing intellectual sophistication. This is the relation of the prophet and his temporal and cultural context to the truth revealed through him. No single issue in Adventist theology may have greater momentary urgency. How it is resolved may condition rather fundamental attitudes toward the inspired sources and thus to the entire body of received truth.

I shall begin by quoting a selection of statements that bear directly on perception and then develop the model in the pages that follow.

> "My teaching is not mine," said Jesus, 'but Him that sent me. If any man willeth to do His will, he shall know of the teaching, whether it be of God, or whether I speak from myself" (John 7:16,17). The question of these cavaliers Jesus met, not by answering the cavil, but by opening up truth vital to the salvation of the soul. The perception and appreciation of truth, He said, depends less upon the mind than upon the heart. Truth must be received into the soul; it claims the homage of the will. If truth could be submitted to the reason alone, pride would be no hindrance in the way of its reception. But it is to be received through the work of grace in the heart; and its reception depends upon the renunciation of every sin that the Spirit of God reveals. Man's advantages for obtaining knowledge of the truth, however great these may be, will prove of no benefit to him unless the heart is open to receive the truth.[1]

> The value of man is estimated in heaven in accordance to the capacity of the heart to God. This knowledge is the spring from which flows all power. God created man, that every faculty might be the faculty of the divine mind; and He is ever seeking to bring the human mind into association with the divine. He offers us the privilege of co-operation with Christ in revealing His grace to the world, that we may receive increased knowledge of heavenly things.[2]

---

[1]Ellen G. White, *The Desire of Ages* (Mountain View, CA: Pacific Press, 1953), 455-56.
[2]Ellen G. White, *Christ's Object Lessons* (Mt. View, CA: Pacific Press, 1900),

> Looking unto Jesus we obtain brighter and more distinct views of God, and by beholding we become changed. Goodness, love for our fellow men, becomes our natural instinct. We develop a character which is the counterpart of the divine character. Growing into his likeness, we enlarge our capacity for knowing God.[3]

It is obvious that such knowing involves a number of parameters, including the character of the knower, as in the following quotations:

> Men estimate character by that which they themselves are capable of appreciating. The narrow and worldly-minded judged Christ by His humble birth, His lowly garb, and daily toil. They could not appreciate the purity of that spirit upon which was no stain of sin.[4]

> Let none suppose that they can live a life of selfishness, and then, having served their own interests, enter into the joy of their Lord. In the joy of unselfish love they could not participate. They would not be fitted for the heavenly courts. They could not appreciate the pure atmosphere of love that pervades heaven.[5]

> Selfishness prevents us from beholding God. The self-seeking spirit judges of God as altogether such a one as itself. Until we have renounced this we cannot understand Him who is love.[6]

> Every impure thought defiles the soul, impairs the moral sense, and tends to obliterate the impressions of the Holy

---

354-55.

[3]Ibid.

[4]White, *The Desire of Ages*, 136.

[5]White, *Christ's Object Lessons*, 364-65.

[6]White, *The Desire of Ages*, 302.

> Spirit. It dims the spiritual vision so men cannot behold God.[7]
>
> That the Son of God should come to this earth as a man filled him with amazement and apprehension. He could not fathom the mystery of this great sacrifice. His selfish soul could not understand such love for the deceived race.[8]
>
> The brain nerves which communicate with the entire system are the only medium through which heaven can communicate to man, and affect his inmost life.[9]
>
> Whatever injures the health not only lessens physical vigor, but tends to weaken the mental and moral powers. Indulgence in any unhealthful practice makes it more difficult for one to discriminate between right and wrong, and hence more difficult to resist evil. It increases the danger of failure and defeat.[10]
>
> Anything that lessens physical strength enfeebles the mind, and makes it less capable of discriminating between right and wrong. We become less capable of choosing the good, and have less strength of will to do that which we know to be right.[11]

Knowing "with the heart" apparently incorporates elements not ordinarily prominent in knowing "with the mind." In the above statements phrases like "homage of the will," "work of grace," "renunciation of every sin," "heart is open," "spring from which flows all power," "goodness, love for our fellow men," "joy of unselfish

---

[7]Ibid.

[8]Ibid., 115.

[9]Ellen G. White, *Testimonies for the Church*, vol. 2 (Mountain View, CA: Pacific Press, 1948), 347.

[10]Ellen G. White, *The Ministry of Healing* (Mountain View, CA: Pacific Press, 1909), 128.

[11]White, *Christ's Object Lessons*, 350.

love," "spiritual vision," and "love" appear. Undoubtedly the list includes Pascal's "heart's reasons that the mind knows not of." However, it entails than these: the "will," "commitment to God," "renunciation of sin," are terms that plainly suggest the preservation of freedom of the will in the process. The knower retains the capacity to choose or to reject such knowing.

Two qualities in man, then, condition the perception of divine truth. One is something bound deeply to the kind of person he is, and the second is based on his willingness to know. The first of these is, of course, subject to numerous hereditary and socio-environmental factors which may not, at least directly, be subject to man's volition; things "happen to" him, accidents of time and place, resulting from his having been "born there."[12] Such factors may include the "propensities" that trip us all up sooner or later that come from wading in the larger genetic pool, as well as the inerasable scars that are early imprinted upon us by the propensities of others. They also include the linguistic and other cultural prisons that confine us to certain ways of looking at things long before growth and maturation make volition a possibility.

This second quality is the one with which "heart knowing" is chiefly concerned. Insofar as a man is a man in God's image, he also possesses a real, if limited, possibility of choosing to do something about what these other factors have done to him.

> Let no one say, I cannot remedy my defects of character. If you come to this decision, you will certainly fail of obtaining everlasting life. The impossibility lies in your own will. If you will not, then you cannot overcome. The real difficulty arises from the corruption of an unsanctified heart, and unwillingness to submit to the control of God.[13]
>
> The tempted one needs to understand the true force of the will. This is the governing power in the nature of man—the power of decision, of choice. Everything depends on the

---

[12]Psalm 87:6

[13]White, *Christs Object Lessons*, 331.

> right action of the will. Desires for goodness and purity are right, so far as they go; but if we stop here, they avail nothing. Many will go down to ruin while hoping and desiring to overcome their evil propensities. They do not yield the will to God. They do not choose to serve Him.[14]

> God has given us the power of choice; it is ours to exercise. We cannot change our hearts; we cannot control our thoughts, our impulses, our affections. We cannot make ourselves pure, fit for God's service. But we can choose to serve God, we can give Him our will; then He will work in us to will and to do according to His good pleasure. Thus our whole nature will be brought under the control of Christ.[15]

> Through the right exercise of the will, an entire change may be made in the life. By yielding the will to Christ, we ally ourselves with divine power. We receive strength from above to hold us steadfast. A pure and noble life, a life of victory over appetite and lust, is possible to everyone who will unite his weak, wavering will to the omnipotent, unwavering will of God.[16]

How this comes about is a question that should interest all of us. We cannot expect, of course, to grasp fully the mysterious ways of God but since God works through the central nervous system, the "brain nerves," an understanding of the mind and its functions may aid us in cooperating with the divine purposes. The following diagram is an attempt to create a conceptual model that may contribute to this understanding:

---

[14]White, *The Ministry of Healing*, 176.
[15]Ibid.
[16]Ibid.

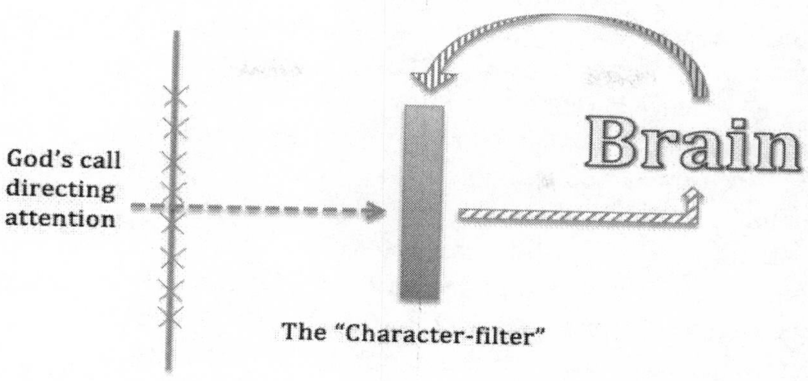

The vertical line at the left of the diagram represents the whole of possible experience. In its entirety it would, of course, be available only to so unlimited a being as God. The single continuous line is somewhat misleading in that it fails to do credit to the multiple dimensions of which reality consists. However, for our present purposes this is not an important over-simplification.

The central portion of the line, drawn here disproportionately large, represents that part of the whole available to human senses and their artificial extensions. These extensions include the various devices by which we extend our senses into areas not ordinarily available to us—the marvels of radio, electron microscopes, and the like. Included in the region available to us are the usual and obvious, as well as those more subtle and mysterious senses that may be involved in phenomena like extrasensory perception—if, indeed, there is such a thing—a somewhat open question at the moment.

The x's drawn on this central portion symbolize the various possibilities that may be available to experience at any given moment. These may in practice seem almost infinite in number and kind, and enormously complex in quality. Again, however, for our purposes, that fact should not be allowed to confound the simplicity of the model.

The broken line leading from possible experience to the right represents "incoming" actual experiences. In the process of being perceived such experience must pass through a complex "character" filter here drawn as a symbolic lens. Imagine the lens as a colored filter, if you will, which modifies the experience in important ways. This experience is then picked up by a sensory end organ—drawn purposely vague so as not to represent any specific receptor system—and thence on through Ellen White's "brain nerves" to the cerebral cortex.

If this analysis of cerebral function is correct, this experience is, in turn, reflected into the quality of the filter itself. This is represented by the upper broken line and arrow. Each experience thus conditions subsequent incoming experience by altering the character of the perceiver. "By beholding we become changed." Thus new experience is perceived largely in terms of what has gone on before. This is how I understand the difference between sensation (feeling) and perception (seeing with understanding). Understanding is largely a function of previous experience and perception. The past inevitably shapes the present. We are to a major extent the prisoners of our own pasts.

This is not true totally, however, since each new experience also adds its own contribution to the "past." That is to say, we see things in terms of the persons we are or have been, in terms of our characters, which are in a state of potential flux and open to subsequent experience. We see things not as they are but as we are, living as we usually do in a state of "becoming." Even memory is creative and an expression of change in the one who remembers—as all of us are aware if we think about it. I use the word "potential" because we can in practice come to experience reality only repetitively.

The perceptual "ruts" we tend to sink into, especially as we become older, are well known to all of us. This tendency may be to some extent ego-defensive, that is, the familiar and established offers a measure of protection to the self, but there may also be other reasons for perceptual stabilization, including organic change in nervous and other tissues, as well as a narrowing of experience possibilities. The feeble and infirm are often bound by the narrowing limits of their physical world and social resources—just because they are infirm.

The possibility of change is relative at best and it is often subject to fortune. This would rule were it not for one fact. This is that God is interested in changing us and is actively involved in trying to bring this about. God is interested in our being changed because He wishes to be known—and to be known as He is without perceptual distortion and misrepresentation. Recall this from the book *Christ's Object Lessons:*

> It is the darkness of misapprehension of God that is enshrouding the world. Men are losing their knowledge of His character. It has been misunderstood and misinterpreted. At this time a message from God is to be proclaimed, a message illuminating in its influence and saving in its power. His character is to be made known. Into the darkness of the world is to be shed the light of His glory, the light of His goodness, mercy, and truth.[17]

Let us now explore the manner in which God attempts to achieve this revelation—the word "attempts" is appropriate since His relation to man is non-coercive even as He reveals Himself.

If God directs His revelation to the "brain-nerve" system, as noted earlier, and values human freedom—which is in part to say the same thing—He is bound by the process that all "knowing" involves. For the "brain nerves" and freedom are involved in other kinds of knowing as well—at least insofar as freedom is retained by the knower. Such freedom can be lost in a variety of ways, including the perceptual stabilization referred to above.

On the diagram, man's range of possible experience is marked by multiple representative x's. We are unable to attend to all, or even very many of these, at any one time. We therefore select, or have selected for us, what we are to experience out of the vast number of possibilities available at any given moment.

Unfortunately, selectivity itself may be severely limited in practice, being also largely at the mercy of the kinds of persons we are. Mostly experience is simply thrust upon us. The behaviorists are

---

[17]White, *Christ's Object Lessons*, 415.

right—up to a point. They would perhaps be totally correct were it not for the activity of God, at least in the world as we now find it.

God enters man's history as one who calls in His word, in nature, in human institutions and social interactions. And thus there is freedom. "The truth shall make you free." But it is possible to lose the ability to hear God's voice, or, to shift the metaphor, it is possible for the lenses through which one sees God, His character, to become opaque to the truth like the blind man's cataracts. Ellen White says of men in the days of Christ:

> In the days of Christ these lessons had been lost sight of. Men had well-nigh ceased to discern God in His works. The sinfulness of humanity had cast a pall over the fair face of creation; and instead of manifesting God, His works became a barrier that concealed him….Not only the things of nature, but the sacrificial service and the Scriptures themselves—all given to reveal God—were so perverted that they became the means of concealing Him.[18]

Presumably if this has become total, man's sin has become unpardonable and God must say, "Ephraim is joined to his idols: let him alone."[19]

Reference was made to the fact that God's communication to man is limited by the central nervous system—the "brain nerves," in a situation of freedom. It is through this system that God has His only contact with the character-filter, which may be obscuring the perception of truth. His call is thus distorted, but even so, as it is listened to, there comes the possibility of modifying that filter, even if ever so little. Even small changes make it possible for subsequent truth to be perceived with greater accuracy. We speak of "progressive truth."[20] Each experience of truth, though partial and

---

[18]Ibid., 18.

[19]Hosea 4:17

[20]Francis D. Nichol, *The Seventh-Day Adventist Bible Commentary; the Holy Bible with Exegetical and Expository Comment*, vol. 2 (Washington: Review and Herald Pub. Association, 1953), 1000.

out of focus, changes the one who perceives it so that the next experience comes through with greater clarity. Unfortunately, however, the reverse is also true and freedom to know God may slip through our fingers.

Since the role of freedom in perception is vital, it is important that we examine this human quality in some detail. Ellen White has written a fair amount on the subject.[21] Here Mrs. White pointedly rejects determinism in favor of "uncaused" actions as being crucial to the divine plan and the controversy with evil.

Freedom can mean a variety of things, as the history of ideas has shown us. It can refer to a state of being as in St. Augustine's usage. It can also refer to a state of release from restraints—free from iron bars and the like *a la* Hobbes. In our present model the term is applied to the ability to select between alternative possibilities.

Such alternatives must be practical alternatives before they become matters of option. William James has written of "live" and "dead" options in his *Essays on Faith and Morals.*[22]Although it is an alternative in theory, one is not free to choose a "dead" option. To be "alive" in James' sense, the alternatives must truly compete with each other in some way for our attention. This means that they should be close to equivalent to each other, if not qualitatively, in the force they exert upon us.

The following diagram—a minute portion taken from the range of possible human experience in the earlier diagram—illustrates live and dead options. The relative size of the above cross-markings suggests the relative strength of the demand for our attention exerted by possibilities available. Given alternatives (a) and (b) as they call out to us for attention, in (1) there is no contest. If, however, (b) is strengthened or reinforced in (2), the one who attends is brought to a moment of decision, to what Heschel calls the "parting of the ways," where the choosing will comes into play.

---

[21]Ellen G. White, *The Great Controversy* (Mountain View, CA: Pacific Press, 1950).

[22]William James, *Essays on Faith and Morals,* edited by Ralph Barton Perry (New York: Meridian Books, 1962), 34.

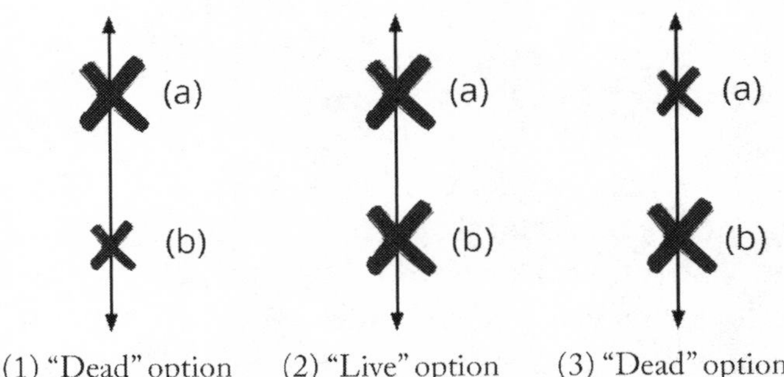

(1) "Dead" option (2) "Live" option (3) "Dead" option

This is at least a partial illustration of the active role God plays in human perception. God calls, and at times He must call loudly, in order to compete with the background noise of man's sinful condition. Sometimes this has involved a very great expenditure on God's part, as at Calvary. But this also explains why God sometimes obscures Himself, Luther's Deus *absconditus*. He gives evidence enough for faith, but He will not remove all doubt for freedom's sake. Over-reinforcement as in (3) also "kills" an option; again, however, because truth must be presented to the heart, the will, and not merely to the mind. The "truth" is given to make us free and not to enslave us—and freedom means at least the freedom to choose.

Nothing that has been said above may seem new, but the application of this model to one of Ellen White's problem statements may be. I now turn to this application, both as a means of understanding the problem passage which has far-reaching implications to a people who take inspired Scripture seriously and to illustrate the utility of the model. The context of this paragraph is also worth reading in this connection.

> It is not the words of the Bible that are inspired, but the men that were inspired. Inspiration acts not on the man's words or his expressions but on the man himself, who, under the influence of the Holy Ghost, is imbued with thoughts. But the words receive the impress of the individual mind. The divine mind is diffused. The divine mind and will is com-

bined with the human mind and will; thus the utterances of the man are the word of God.[23]

It should be obvious from what has been said that God cannot just pick up anyone off the street to receive the prophetic gift. "If there be a prophet among you, I the Lord will make myself known unto him in a vision and will speak unto him in a dream."[24] If God is to reveal the truth with the least possible distortion, He must choose the best possible medium for that revelation. This means choosing one whose character (the lens-filter) is as transparent as possible; that is, the best person available at the time. But having chosen such a person, He brings him (or her) to one experience after another provided the prophet will pay attention, because He cannot bypass the mind and will of the person who is the perceiver and still leave him free.

Guaranteeing the prophet's freedom, just as He does that of any man, He makes himself known to the prophet in essentially the same way as He does to the rest of us—that is, through the "brain nerves." The alternative would involve the direct affecting of character. And if God can manipulate any man's character in violation of his volition, then He must do it to all men, and there can be no untruth and no one can be lost in the end. Neither, however, would being saved make a great deal of difference.

Most of the ways in which the prophet and ordinary men differ, therefore, are relative—mainly a relative capacity to perceive divine truth. Prophets are, of course, also provided a certain status in the community. Not only must the truth be presented clearly. It must be taken seriously—on authority. To achieve such authority, prophets are provided charismatic roles by whatever means local cultural meanings and values dictate—Elijah's and John's camel- hair coats, Jeremiah's ox-yoke, Ellen White's "glory, glory, glory" and her evident lack of respiration during vision, all things that time and place require if men are to be made to sit up and take notice.

---

[23]Ellen G. White, *Selected Messages,* vol. 1 (Washington: Review and Herald Pub. Association, 1958), 21.

[24]Numbers 12:6.

The only absolute difference is the action of God in the revelation. God may elect to say some things through a prophet that He says through no one else. But, we repeat, the method by which the prophet perceives what God has said remains the same as for all men, and this point may be of considerable importance if we are to avoid undercutting faith in the prophetic gift by subjecting it to impossible demands. The word of God is clothed in the words of men. "The word was made flesh."

The incarnation of the Word, in all the ways that this occurs, also involves accommodation on God's part. The making flesh, that is, the placing within the narrow limits of human experience that which cannot really be flesh, is the major problem of revelation. How can God take something from the area in the diagram normally outside man's perceptive range and translate it into human terms? How can God speak the unspeakable to *this* man or woman in *this* particular time and place under *these* conditions and at *this* level of growth without mystifying or even seeming absurd to other sets of conditions? This underlines God's use of symbols, types, parables and metaphor, perhaps to an even greater degree than may seem immediately obvious.

The temptation is always easy to take as a literal description of reality what is in fact a divine accommodation to human frailty—particularly if the metaphor does not advertise itself as such. In any case, the absolute difference setting prophetic inspiration apart from human discovery is the One who acts in a special way, but, and mark well, at a level that does not bypass the freedom of the perceiving individual. Prophets, too, perceive with their hearts and thus add their own accommodations to the process. It is this fact that made necessary the large number of prophets covering so broad a spectrum of time and place. The initiation of the message was not subject to their will, "for prophecy came not in old time by the will of man,"[25] although they could will to refuse it. And each could not avoid accommodating in his own way. However, in the total community of prophets there was the possibility of complementarity and balance. The Word of God comes in a whole Bible.

---

[25]2 Peter 1:21

Fortunately, a norm was also provided in Jesus who, as God, was the only Person who knew God in the fullest sense. He especially was the "Word incarnate." This does not eliminate the difficulty entirely, of course. Even the words of this Word were listened to and passed along by fallible men who had to perceive Him not only with their minds, but xalso with their hearts.

If God did not call, if God did not enter human history—our history and the prophets' history—calling us to pay attention, no freedom to perceive truth would now exist and we would all see things totally in terms of the things that have happened to us, as the behaviorists say.

But God did and does call to men. His call is not a coercive demand and man's freedom is retained in revelation. Thus the perception of truth, *the* truth, is not merely an autonomous act of human calculative reason, a function of the mind. It involves freedom to refuse to pay attention and thus it is also an affair of the heart, whether perceived by ordinary men or those who are specially chosen who are entrusted with special revelations of truth.

20
The Philosophical Roots of a Wholistic Understanding of Man

Brain transplant. What staggering ethical and social implications that possibility raises! Beside the usual transplant questions—who shall receive the organ, from whom, and when—such a possibility raises additional perplexities peculiar to the tissues involved, such questions as who the new individual would be, or the confusing dilemmas resulting from transplanting a female brain into a male body. Would the new combination of John Jones' body and Mary Smith's brain still be John Jones or Mary Smith? Or would it be John Smith or Mary Jones?

What we now know about man's makeup renders such questions presently fairly academic. Even if the almost insurmountable technical difficulties involved in accurately connecting the severed end of a spinal cord from one body to the cord of another were to be successfully overcome, a serious problem remains. Individual neurons and their extension pathways do not precisely correspond in different individuals. The situation that would follow would then be something like severing the major telephone connections of San Francisco and trying to graft them onto the complex system of Los Angeles simply by pushing the severed cable ends together.

I present this illustration not only to draw attention to the enormous complexity of the human organism but also to make the point that man is not a mind and a body, or a mind in a body. He must be considered as an interrelated whole if we are to accurately appraise his makeup and behavior. As my college psychology professor used to say, man is "an integral entity and not an additive aggregate."

The term "wholism" when applied to this idea can be used in the sense of "healthy." Whole and heal are derived from the same etymological base. It will be used here, however, with connotations of "totality" (which is, of course, not entirely unrelated).

To view man in wholistic terms is to take into account the now well-accepted fact that every part and function of a man is interrelated with and interdependent on every other part and function. What happens to the part happens in some way to the whole—as in a cube what happens to one dimension affects the whole cube. A cube has depth, width, and height. Shorten or lengthen any one of these dimensions and the whole cube is affected.

The term dimension is a particularly apt one and it is used by one of the more perceptive thinkers of our time, Paul Tillich. In an address delivered before the New York Society for Clinical Psychiatry in 1960, he said:

> Man should not be considered as a composite of several levels, such as body, soul, spirit, but as a multidimensional unity. I use the metaphor "dimension" in order to indicate that the different qualities of life in man are present within each other and do not lie alongside or above each other. One can expediently, but not necessarily, distinguish the physical, the chemical, the biological, the psychological,

> the mental, and the historical dimensions. Different distinctions as well as more particular ones are quite possible. What is important, however, is to see that they do not lie alongside, but within each other, as in the metaphor "dimension" the dimensional lines cross each other at one point.
>
> This point, in our consideration, is man. He is a multidimensional unity; all dimensions distinguishable in experienced life, cross in him. In every dimension of life, all dimensions are potentially or actually present: he does not consist of levels of being, but he is a unity which unites all dimensions. This doctrine stands against the dualistic theory which sees man as composed of soul and body; of body and mind; or body, soul, and spirit, etc. Man is one, uniting within himself all dimensions of life—an insight which we partly owe to the recent developments of medicine especially psychiatry.
>
> As confirmation of this idea, one may refer to psychosomatic medicine. Although this is not incorrect, one should not forget that a hyphen between "psycho" and "somatic: represents the statement of a problem and not a solution.
>
> The multidimensional unity of life in man calls for a multidimensional concept of health, of disease, and of healing, but in such a way that it becomes obvious that in each dimension all the others are present.[1]

The dualism to which Tillich refers comes to us associated with the name of the pre-Christian Greek philosopher Plato. Plato was, of course, not the originator of such a perspective. It is traceable in other Greek literature back to at least the twelfth century B.C. Plato receives the credit, however, for having honored the idea with his considerable wit and literary skill.

Plato's view is apparently easy to come by judging from the fact that it has been almost universally held by men, at least during

[1]Paul Tillich, "The Meaning of Health," *Perspectives in Biology and Medicine*, Volume 5, Number 1 (Autumn, 1961), 92-100.

primitive stages of their acculturation. A number of factors undoubtedly account for this. Dreams, for example, suggest that there is a conscious entity not tied to the body and its limitations, possessing the ability to travel to strange places and engage in exploits quite apart from the body. Having little understanding of association factors in recall, such an entity also provides an easy explanation for the sense of the continued presence of the departed that many bereaved persons feel for a time.

For Plato, the dualism of spirit and matter, or soul and body, was not only a way of understanding man. It was also a way of looking at the larger reality of the universe as it reflected itself in man. Follow Plato as he discusses the soul and body in dialogue between Cebes and Socrates in "Phaedo."

> "Well then," added Socrates, "let us suppose that there are two sorts of existences—one seen, the other unseen."
>
> "Let us suppose then."
>
> "The seen is the changing, and the unseen is the unchanging?"
>
> "That may be also supposed."
>
> "And, further, is not one part of us body, another part soul?"
>
> "To be sure."
>
> "And to which class is the body more alike and akin?"
>
> "Clearly to the seen – no one can doubt that."
>
> "And is the soul seen or not seen?"
>
> "Not by man, Socrates...."
>
> "And were we not saying long ago that the soul, when using the body as an instrument of perception, that is to say, when using the sense of sight or hearing or some other sense . . . were we not saying that the soul too is then dragged by the body into the region of the changeable, and wanders and is confused; the world spins round her, and she is like a drunkard, when she touches change?"
>
> "Very true."

"But when returning into herself she reflects, then she passes into the other world, the region of purity, and eternity, and immortality, and unchangeableness, which are her kindred, and with them she ever lives, when she is by herself and is not let or hindered; then she ceases from her erring ways, and being in communion with the unchanging is unchanging. And this state of the soul is called wisdom?"

"That is well and truly said, Socrates," he replied....

"And which does the soul resemble?"

"The soul resembles the divine, and the body the mortal—there can be doubt of that Socrates."

"Then reflect, Cebes: Of all which has been said is not this the conclusion?—that the soul is in the very likeness of the divine, and immortal, and intellectual, and uniform, and indissoluble, and unchangeable; and that the body is in the very likeness of the human, and moral, and unintellectual, and multiform, and dissoluble, and changeable. Can this, my dear Cebes, be denied?"

"It cannot."

"But if it be true, then is not the body liable to speedy dissolution? And is not the soul almost or altogether indissoluble....?"

"That soul, I say, herself invisible, departs to the invisible world—to the divine and immortal and rational: thither arriving, she is secure of bliss and is released from the error and folly of men, their fears and wild passions and all other human ills, and forever dwells, as they say of the initiated, in company with the gods. Is not this true, Cebes?"[2]

Christian theologians were to argue later about the exact nature of the soul. Some said it was beyond all time and space and that special and temporal language was inappropriate for it. Be-

[2]Plato, Phaedo, in *Plato: Five Great Dialogues*, translated by Benjamin Jowett and edited by Louis Ropes Loomis (New York: Walter J. Black, 1942), 112 ff.

cause time did not apply, such theology had no problem with divine foreknowledge. Augustine, for example, could speak of past, present and future as being simultaneous to God.

Some sought the "seat of the soul" somewhere in the body—perhaps the blood, the brain, or the pineal gland—from whence it used the "body" to its ends as the ghost within the machine. It is easy to think in such terms, to feel as though somewhere we are inside our head peering out through our eyes, listening through our ears, using our lips, and using our hands, which feel like mechanical tool extensions.

Others saw the soul as exactly paralleling the body but simply existing at another level of reality unavailable to ordinary sense experience. In any case the two levels of reality were thought of as qualitatively different and functionally independent entities. Hence the term dualism. And it was a dualism that extended throughout the whole of what is, including the divine.

A later revival of Platonism in the early centuries of the Christian era called Neoplatonism added an interesting variation to Plato's theme. In the interval between Plato and Plotinus, Gnosticism had made an impact on the western world. According to the Gnostics, pure spirit emanated downward through various levels of reality until it finally became matter which was thus a kind of degraded end product.

A logical consequence of this belief was, of course, a disvaluing of matter. The Manicheans, whose view of matter was strongly conditioned by Gnosticism, frankly branded matter as evil. The Manichean hope was for the liberation of spirit from its material burden by present behavior and ultimate redemption. The Manichean ideal, for example, eschewed sexuality—not for its own sake but because procreation further entrapped spirit in evil matter. Manichean ethics involved certain dietary and other restrictions designed to prevent the strengthening of the material nature. They established water purification laws not because they anticipated the "germ theory" but because clean water was thought to evaporate more freely, and thus return more easily to "spirit," where it belonged.

This bit of obscure history is important because the most significant figure in Christiandom in post New Testament times, St. Augustine, Bishop of Hippo, counted Plotinus as one of his chief philosophical mentors and was an ardent Manichee for a decade before his conversion to Christianity. Even though he eventually turned against the Manicheans, he was never able entirely to shake off his distrust of the body, nor did the Christianity he did so much to shape. Puritanism, Victorianism, even our present, reactionary, sexual libertarianism were all touched in one way or another by him.

The committed Christian learned early, thanks to Augustine, that his body was a drag on his spiritual pilgrimage, to be struggled against as an alien element now, to be controlled, and ultimately, joyfully, to be dispensed with altogether. Not only were there two categorically different kinds of reality in the universe and the microcosm that is man, spirit and matter, but only the former was to be wholeheartedly affirmed.

Such a view could scarcely be favorable soil and climate for the development of scientific medicine, and it wasn't. Justinian I closed down the medical schools at Athens and Alexandria as centers of Pagan learning unfitting a Holy Christian empire. The excesses of Monasticism, the desert fathers and their extreme physical privations, even the relative value hierarchy in which the various professions were held in the Middle Ages—clergy at the top and medicine men at the bottom—all reflected the disesteem with which the body came to be held.

All of which seems more than passing strange in the light of the ministry of Jesus, who spent more time healing men's bodies than almost anything else. The fact is, the healing ministry of Jesus was informed by a quite different worldview.

Scientific medicine has traditionally given a place of honor to a Greek as its father, but the true creator of its spirit, if not its methods, was not Hippocrates of Cos, but Jesus of Nazareth. The fertile soil in which His ministry flourished has in fact also nourished every science worthy of the name. The developments of the modern period in the western world are virtually unthinkable apart from a major presupposition of that soil—biblical, and thus Judeo-Christian, monotheism.

According to a radical monotheism there is above all a unity at the heart of things. Monotheism does not demand that everything everywhere be equivalent nor is it necessarily a matter of number. The Trinitarian expression of God is also monotheistic if the essential unity of the Godhead is maintained. Monotheism is a larger expression of the truth contained in Tillich's "multidimensional unity." In monotheism we are but looking at "wholism" on a cosmic, universal scale.

Such was the way of looking at things that the Judeo-Christian culture bequeathed to the world, not two levels of reality as suggested by the Platonists, but one, a unity of many interdependent, interpenetrating and interacting dimensions.

Note that this monotheistic wholism is implied in this familiar passage of Scripture:

> In the beginning was the Word, and the Word was with God, and the Word was God. The same was in the beginning with God. All things were made by Him; and without Him was not anything made that was made."[3]

Everything that is comes from God, including its continued existence. There are in God's universe no independent levels of reality. All is tied together by the creative power of the divine unity.

See this same wholistic unity implied in the following passage from the pen of E. G. White:

> In dwelling upon the laws of matter and the laws of nature, many lose sight of, if they do not deny, the continual and direct agency of God. They convey the idea that nature acts independently of God, having in and of itself its own limits and its own powers wherewith to work. In their minds there is a marked distinction between the natural and the supernatural. The natural is ascribed to ordinary

[3]John 1:1-3.

causes, unconnected with the power of God. Vital power is attributed to matter, and nature is made a deity. It is supposed that matter is placed in certain relations and left to act from fixed laws with which God Himself cannot interfere; that nature is endowed with certain properties and placed subject to laws, and is then left to itself to obey these laws and perform the work originally commanded.

This is false science; there is nothing in the word of God to sustain it. God does not annul His laws, but He is continually working through them, using them as His instruments. They are not self-working. God is perpetually at work in nature. She is His servant, directed as He pleases. Nature in her work testifies of the intelligent presence and active agency of a being who moves in all His works according to His will. It is not by an original power inherent in nature that year by year the earth yields its bounties and continues its march around the sun. The hand of infinite power is perpetually at work guiding this planet. It is God's power momentarily exercised that keeps it in position in its rotation.

The God of heaven is constantly at work. It is by His power that vegetation is caused to flourish, that every leaf appears and every flower blooms. Every drop of rain or flake of snow, every spire of grass, every leaf and flower and shrub, testifies of God. These little things so common around us teach the lesson that nothing is beneath the notice of the infinite God, nothing is too small for His attention.

The mechanism of the human body cannot be fully understood; it presents mysteries that baffle the most intelligent. It is not as the result of a mechanism, which, once set in motion, continues its work, that the pulse beats and breath follows breath. In God we live and move and have our being. Every breath, every throb of the heart, is a continual evidence of the power of an ever-present God.[4]

---

[4]Ellen G. White, *Testimonies for the Church*, vol. 8 (Mt. View, CA: Pacific Press. 1948), 259, 260.

This suggests that God is directly responsible for the elemental energy present at every level of existence from the electrons spinning in their orbits clear out to the distant galactic systems. Nothing would exist at any level apart from the basic energy that is God's power. The universe is thus tied together by God's own essential unity. That two-story universe of the ancients in which God's dwelling and activity is largely limited to the spiritual realm of the supernatural was a myth. God dwells on both floors! The laws of nature are God's laws and descriptions of His usual activity.

The implications of this are far-reaching. They provide, first of all, for an affirmation of nature quite unlike the posture of Hinduism, where things of sense, time, and space are illusory and ultimately irrelevant. This affirmation differs as well from Gnostic-influenced Neo-Platonism or Christianity where reactions to material substance are profoundly negative. A sophisticated natural science, even a healing science, could develop in neither of these contexts.

Biblical wholism, radical monotheism, is the necessary presupposition of all truly significant scientific achievements, even if this is unrecognized and unacknowledged. That is why it happened first in the western world. The scientist who credits his philosophical undergirding knows that in his laboratory he is but thinking God's thoughts after Him.

Theistic wholism also implies something else. Because God dwells on both floors, there is no gulf between supernature and nature. They belong together. A miracle is not an irrational or unnatural event, but rather an unfamiliar, unusual, hence mysterious divine action. It "belongs" to the whole of God's activity which is usually predictable, repeatable, and thus reducible to observable laws.

Reflecting this larger point of view into the microcosm which is man we discover that similar truths prevail. Again we find an elemental unity of all dimensions, interpenetrating, interdependent. Nothing occurs in one of man's dimensions in total isolation from all the rest of him.

Observe this in Jesus' understanding of man as it is expressed in His healing of the man with the palsy, let down through the roof by his friends, "Whether is easier, to say, thy sins be forgiven thee; or to say, Rise up and walk?"[5]

Jesus may not have been referring to specific sins this man had committed such as lying, stealing, or even sexual immorality, but rather to the underlying state of alienation out of which these acts may occur. But the fact remains that in the eyes of Jesus the man's attitudes and behavior had implications for his physical health.

Out of similar soil spring statements such as the following by Ellen White:

> Whatever injures the health, not only lessens physical vigor, but tends to weaken the mental and moral powers. Indulgence in any unhealthful practice makes it more difficult for one to discriminate between right and wrong, and hence more difficult to resist evil. It increases the danger of failure and defeat.[6]

> The relation that exists between the mind and the body is very intimate. When one is affected, the other sympathizes. The condition of the mind affects the health to a far greater degree than many realize. Many of the diseases from which men suffer are the result of mental depression. Grief, anxiety, discontent, remorse, guilt, distrust, all tend to break down the life forces, and to invite decay and death.[7]

It should not be expected of the Bible or of the above statements, all written before psychosomatic medicine had been conceived and elaborated in scientific terms, that they should be set forth in modern technical language. But certainly the seeds are there, the seeds and the fertile soil. Psychosomatic medicine has its roots in a wholistic view of reality, and especially as that view is reflected in man.

---

[5]Luke 5:21.

[6]Ellen G. White, *The Ministry of Healing* (Mt. View, CA: Pacific Press, 1909), 128.

[7]Ellen G. White, *Counsels on Health* (Mt. View, CA: Pacific Press, 1951), 344.

This perspective contrasts sharply as we have said with the earlier Greek, Platonic dualism. Almost all Biblical scholars now recognize this fact. Hebrew monotheism issued in human wholism. For example, contrasting the two, John A. T. Robinson, Bishop of Woolwick in the Church of England and then Lecturer and Dean at Trinity College in Cambridge, says that:

> The third and perhaps most far reaching of all the Greek antitheses, that between body and soul, is also foreign to the Hebrew. The Hellenic conception of man has been described as that of an angel in a slot machine, a soul (the invisible, spiritual, essential ego) incarcerated in a frame of matter from which it trusts eventually to be liberated. The body is nonessential to the personality: it is something which a man possesses, or, rather, is possessed by. "The Hebrew idea of the personality," on the other hand, wrote the late Dr. Wheeler Robinson in a sentence which has become famous, "is an animated body, and not an incarnated soul."
>
> Man does not *have* a body, he *is* a body. He is flesh-animated-by-soul, the whole conceived as a psycho-physical unity. There is no suggestion that the soul is the essential personality, or that the soul (nephesh) is immortal, while the flesh (basar) is mortal. The soul does not survive a man—it simply goes out, draining away with the blood.[8]

For another example, Victor White, Dominican priest and collaborator with psychiatrist Carl Jung, quotes New Testament scholar G. W. A. Lampe as follows:

> The body in Hebrew thought . . . is neither a tomb nor a prison house for some "spiritual" or "intelligible" man buried or imprisoned within the flesh. Man is essentially a unity. His physical aspect is not to be rigidly separated in thought from his intellectual or spiritual character. It is the

---

[8]John A. T. Robinson, *The Body: A Study in Pauline Theology* (London: SCM Press, 1952), 14.

> whole man who is the object of God's dealings, and salvation is concerned with the relation of the whole man to God, not with any triumph of the human "spirit" over the corrupt and transitory "flesh." It is man as a single whole who was created by God.
>
> It is the whole man who, as a sinner, is alienated from God, at enmity with him and the object of his wrath: and it is the whole man who is the object of God's grace and is redeemed into the fellowship of a son with his heavenly Father.[9]

The Greek, Platonic heritage of the translators of the King James Bible is apparent, of course, in the way they frequently translated the Hebrew *nephesh*, *ruach*, and the Greek *pneuma*, and *psyche* into "soul" and "spirit." But the terms could also have quite different connotations more nearly corresponding to ideas like "life" and "personality" (as in fact they were translated numerous times). Unfortunately these presuppositions were thus passed on to generations of Bible readers.

Only in fairly recent times has it been possible to read ourselves back into the Hebrew thought forms and recapture something of what they intended to convey by those words. The discoveries of psychosomatic medicine made, of course, an important contribution to this development. The Bible on its own terms projected the unity of God into its view of man who was created in the divine image.

Words like "soul" and "spirit" point, however, to an addition that needs to be made to what was said earlier about the "multidimensional unity" conception of man—something toward which those biblical expressions were pointing. Man is a multidimensional unity but the graphic portrayal of that unity as a tridimensional cube is misleading if it conveys the notion of homogeneity or uniformity. Nearer the facts is the expression "*centered* multidimensional unity," suggesting that not all portions of a dimension are of

---

[9]Victor White, *Soul and Psyche: An Inquiry into the Relationship of Psychotherapy and Religion* (New York: Harper and Brothers, 1960), 22, 23.

equal importance to the whole. Some areas are central; others are peripheral.

In the larger, universal concept of wholism, this notion of centrality prevents monotheism from becoming monism or pantheism. In the biblical, Christian view, God is omnipresent. "Whither shall I go from thy spirit," asks the Psalmist, or "whither shall I flee from thy presence?" We spoke earlier of the power of God as the elemental energy that everywhere pervades the universe, the energy of electrons, tying together molecular particles, objects, etc. But one does not say of an object, say a stone or a chair, "*There* is God." Rather one says, "There is an expression of God's power."

This universal presence is "centered" in the person of God at the heart of the universe. One rightly speaks of God sitting on His throne, even if somewhat metaphorically. Yet there is also a truth in the notion of omnipresence, God extending throughout His universe both in power and awareness.

Something like this also prevails at the level of the microcosm that is man. His various dimensions have a center and a periphery. It may not be possible to delineate precisely where one shades into the other. Where, for example, does the peripheral nervous system, at least functionally, shade into the central nervous system?

The mind is not fully reducible to its chief organ the brain, even though it is with the brain, and especially certain portions of the brain, that its most central functions appear to be associated. Something similar to this may probably be said of all of man's dimensions. Some of his physiologic functions are also more crucial than others even though not isolated from them. The same is true for his social dimension.

These and other dimensions, central and peripheral in relation to themselves, enjoy a complicated interrelationship with each other, touching and overlapping in various complex ways, but usually not precisely coinciding with or paralleling each other. Some events or experiences may affect man more or less centrally in one dimension and at the same time peripherally in another.

To illustrate, a relatively minor piece of surgery such as a vasectomy on a male is physiologically and anatomically quite peripheral to the organism but it may in some cases have rather important central implications to other dimensions such as the social and psychological. There, the "meaning" of the surgery may outweigh in significance any of the physiologic and anatomic changes produced. More than one vasectomized male has found it necessary to "prove" his masculinity afterwards in socially unacceptable ways.

Any physician or surgeon who does not take into account the "meaning" of changes produced in his patients by his actions or therapies may be in for some surprises. Such illustrations might be drawn from any of man's dimensions.

It may be, as was stated, that it is to the central function of man's mind that the older dualistic concept was dimly pointing in its reference to the "soul" and if by "soul" we understand this it may still be a useful term. There is, in fact, almost something like that older definition in one aspect of this central mental function—namely his freedom.

When the superstructure of that two-story universe was swept away during the modern period, a highly materialistic worldview was left as a residue. So also was it with man. When his soul was denied, man remained as a highly complex physiochemical organism whose actions were as determined by cause as any of the rest of a mechanical universe.

Such a view, one in which every human action is reducible to causes that determine it—where everything a man does, including all of his supposed choices could not be otherwise, the causes being what they are—where what he does he *has* to do, has very grave consequences. As a denial of human creativity it is the death knell for every meaningful use of words like "responsibility," "blame," "praise," and "sin!" No one doing what in fact he *has* to do can be held accountable for his actions. One is forced instead to blame the causes, including ultimately the First Cause.

Much of human behavior is determined. In certain socio- or psychopathic states, it may be that all of an individual's actions may be so conditioned. But moral evaluation itself is called in question wherever such determination is conceived as absolute. Almost everything that religion and ethics ultimately stand for depends on the actuality of responsible personhood.

The chief difference between the "soul" and that of the older dualism is that the creative quality here delineated, man's freedom, does not exist in isolation from the total organism. It is affected and conditioned by the other dimensions of man's existence in very important ways, even though it cannot be completely reduced to them. Destroy the other dimensions and the "soul" is lost as well.

It may thus be fruitless to try to describe fully the psychochemical or other organic processes of the "soul." The two may involve qualitatively different conceptual realities; for example, "thing" realities as opposed to "function." Mind may not be a "thing" word in the way body and psychochemistry are. Wholism insists that one cannot ignore such factors as psychochemistry, even when dealing with such matters as willing and choosing. Man is a whole being. Central to his unity is a function in a sense transcending, but yet not isolated from, all other the other dimensions of his organic wholeness.

It is the recognition of the foregoing that has given new and serious impetus to a multidimensional approach to healing in our time. The true father of medicine came not only to make man whole, but to make the *whole* man whole.

Part V

Challenges

21
Freedom and Foreknowledge

Many young and some not so young people have wrestled with the logical difficulty presented by believing that God knows every person's ultimate destiny even before he or she is born. Can there be freedom of action under such circumstances?

The statement that God by foreknowing the future does not necessarily cause it is at least as old as St. Augustine and was repeated endlessly by the Augustinian theologians and philosophers. Augustine tried to solve the problem by relegating God to a category beyond all time-space considerations. To him, concepts such as sequence—past, present, future—were applicable only to our own finite world. Spirit knows no such limitations. Those who opposed the Augustinian viewpoint were always venturing to ask whether a conception of God outside of time and space did not reduce Him to an abstraction.

Augustine was worried about downgrading God's perfection that any limitations on His knowledge would suggest. If there were something that God did not know, He would be imperfect—a blasphemous allegation!

It should be recalled that the divine attributes were conceived by the theologians of the past as the ultimate and absolute projections of relative qualities in humans. That such a projection of God often robbed Him of His personality, causing Him to resemble more the Unmoved Mover of Aristotle than the active, creative person of the Bible, seemed not to have been to them a source of anxiety. A perfect God on this model would neither feel (the impassible God) nor act, since either would imply prior need and thus limitation and imperfection.

Let us consider God's power before we continue with God's knowledge. God cannot be omnipotent in an absolute sense as long as there is one individual in the universe who negates Him. To say that there is one person who is seriously saying "no" to God, and that God at the same time is all-powerful, is a contradiction. God might always, of course, eliminate the negator, or reduce him to a thing whose "no" is irrelevant, and thus regain His omnipotence, but both could not exist simultaneously without contradiction. Thus God's power included the capacity to limit His power by the creation of individuals who could deny His power. I see no reason why some such principle is not applicable as well to God's knowledge.

What might be known by God in an absolute sense, even in the presence of freedom? First, God would know Himself and His plans unequivocally. The total knowledge of His own nature, and thus of the nature of goodness would place the eventual outcome of things beyond question. Evil is death, deprivation, and non-being and could not ultimately gain the victory against God.

Second, God would have full awareness of all "things" in the universe, from the greatest to the minutest. He would be the Intelligence described by Laplace. He would know absolutely their course and destiny. God would be fully informed, for example, about the devil and all of his actions—past, present, and future. The same would be true of all other beings who by character fixation or death had passed beyond probation.

Moreover, if we remind ourselves that the free act is a relatively rare or non-existent experience in human life, we immediately conceive that there is very little which could not, in principle, be foreknown. Certainly foreknowledge would include the subject matter of the biblical prophecies, which for the most part are weighted by God's own continued actions. Nations follow nations, kings succeed kings but God is at work in the process as the prophet Daniel so clearly observes.[1] God is no absentee landlord.

Even Cyrus, who is named long before his birth, could function instrumentally without necessarily denying the moral freedom of creative acts; that is, those acts related to his ultimate salvation. Most of Cyrus' life could thus be predestined or determined without a violation of our principle. If there were a prediction in the Bible assuring Cyrus of a place in the kingdom of heaven the matter would be quite different. Might we change the metaphor of prophecy from that of an inexorable, universal clock, read off by the master horologist, to one more accurately depicting God's actions as the creation of history?

A study of the problem of freedom and foreknowledge requires us to review the Hellenization of Christianity in the early centuries of our era. There breathes a quite different spirit in the Scriptures. Label the picture of God anthropomorphic if you will, but it is that of a God who decides, acts and changes His mind, in the sense of changing His plan of operation, rather than changing His character, and He even appears to learn.

But does not the Bible also set up as evidence of God's priority over false gods His capacity to tell the end from the beginning? But from what beginning? Surely not God's beginning since He has none. And yet if there is a point in time short of eternity where He becomes able to foretell this end, the traditional argument is demolished. Might we not be able to say that God knows the end from the beginning insofar as the end is in or a consequence of a beginning? In one passage of the Bible, God outlines in great detail for the people of Israel the consequences of certain choices and then climaxes His pronouncements by saying:

[1]Daniel 4:17.

> I call heaven and earth to record this day against you, that I have set before you life and death, blessing and cursing: therefore choose life that both thou and thy seed may live.[2]

From beginning to end the Bible presents this appeal in one way or another. The predestinarian doctrine could only represent a special reading of a selected portion of Scripture out of the context of the whole Bible.

The position I am suggesting may be briefly summarized as follows: Freedom to choose as "creative act" is the *sine qua non* of *agape* love. The occasion for *agape* in the universe necessitated the risk involved in creating free agents and the distinct possibility that they would choose death instead of life. Freedom can be real only in the presence of genuine alternatives.

The creation of free, intelligent beings represents a self-limitation both on God's power and on His knowledge. These beings were in a limited sense granted the God-qualities of creativity. God assumed the risk this entailed and its concomitant responsibilities by doing all in His power, short of destroying freedom, to ensure that they would choose life.

He was not unprepared for the choice of death and, after it was made in heaven and on earth, God continued to act so as to restore freedom and thus to hold open the door of salvation. Freedom is a most tenuous quality and sin being what it is, freedom would now have been totally lost except for God's continued redemptive activity. The cross itself must be understood, at least partially, in this light. In some cases, however, it is virtually impossible even for God to restore the creative act without destroying other, perhaps greater, freedom in the process.

The creative moral act being what it is, in principle it could not be foreknown without logically turning it into something else. The problem is thus not one of God's causation—predestination—but of fatalism, or the pre-patterning of events, not by God, but in the nature of things. For the course of my life and ultimate destiny to totally exist in the mind of God prior to its existence, my actions

---

[2]Deut. 30:19.

would necessitate a kind of fatalistic perspective or a logical contradiction. There is another alternative, and this is to make the idea of "sequence" when applied to God meaningless, which is precisely what Augustine attempted.

The free act constitutes a novelty in the universe and does not exist anywhere before it comes into being in creative action. God is totally aware of all that exists, but it is a logical contradiction to have an entity that simultaneously exists and does not exist. There can be no contradiction in God according to the monotheistic premise. That God possesses full knowledge of what is, including that portion of the "is" that necessarily follows in the future, is as certain as God's existence. God would also be totally aware of the full consequences of each new "is" as it comes into existence by creative action.

Most of life is necessary and determined. When creative freedom is possible, all heaven waits anxiously for the outcome and rejoices when the choice is for life. For the one facing the moment of decision, eternity itself may hang in the balance.

This in no way disturbs the validity of divine prediction. Those prophecies having to do with nations and final events are predictable in terms of God's self-knowledge and His total knowledge of those beings that have lost their freedom to choose. For the most part, unpredictability would be confined to the soul-struggle within the individual human heart where personal eternal destiny is at stake. In such cases predictions are conditional. They are in effect descriptions of the present total state of the individual, the condition being that the present state of affairs persists.

Let us summarize some of the arguments against this view and some possible responses:

1. *It runs counter to the teachings of many of the great Christian thinkers of the past, including those of our own denomination.* Truth is not a function of age or prestige.

2. *It places in doubt the divine perfection by limiting God's knowledge.* To the contrary, this is a self-limitation and thus an evidence of God's power. Is it not limiting God to deny Him the ability to

create just such a state of affairs in order to bring into existence agape love? Rather, perfection becomes on this view dynamic instead of passive or static.

3. *Such a thesis is unwarranted speculation into the nature of God.* I recognize, of course, the danger of trying to look into mysteries that by their nature transcend my ability to comprehend. But to cry "mystery," "stop," too soon may be a way of preserving past error, excusing intellectual indolence, or even concealing obviously faulty logic. There are good reasons for believing that this is the kind of information which would be crucial to the life and vitality of the church, and thus most significant and essential to our own period of time.

4. *To deny God absolute foreknowledge may lessen our reverence and respect for Him.* Admittedly, Calvin and others with their predestinarian views gave enormous emphasis to the majesty and glory of God. But they did so at a price, as is evidenced by the puritanical moralism which everywhere accompanied this doctrine. Legalistic moralism is nearly always an over compensatory mechanism for feelings of insecurity, unworthiness, and unresolved guilt. Against this, is not our adoration for God truly awakened by knowledge of His having shared with us something of His own creative personality.

5. *Since God's foreknowledge of His own activity does not interfere with it, why should his foreknowledge of ours be construed as interference?* This is the old Augustinian argument. Two things must be noted. First, the present thesis is not aimed at predestination, which it denies out of hand. It does not say anything about God's interference except to admit that God is active in human affairs precisely for the purpose of setting up the occasion for the novel, creative act. Its chief concern is for the nature of the act itself and to avoid the fatalistic preposition. Secondly, God's choices are obviously not of the same quality as ours. God's alternatives are never between good and evil.

6. *The Scriptures and the Spirit of Prophecy appear to support the*

view that God foreknows even men and women's moral decisions. What, for example, of Peter's denial? Christ foretold to him the precise circumstances of his denial, including the sound of a crowing cock as background accompaniment. I hope that none would suggest that the cock possessed freedom of choice! Can it not equally be said, however, that Peter's actions were necessitated by his imperfect character and that Jesus, reading his heart, was in effect providing an accurate description of that character, and thus setting up the occasion wherein something new could enter Peter's life?

The suggested self-limitation of God's knowledge in no way extends to His awareness of the state of a person's character. Jesus' predictions regarding the actions of the Jewish leaders can be similarly understood. That persons necessarily act in keeping with their characters is unquestioned. But that they necessarily have to develop certain characters is what the position I am suggesting rejects. It is only during the process of character formation that the kind of freedom and principle of unpredictability we are discussing prevails.

God's prophecies regarding individuals are predicated on the basis of His full knowledge of their characters, and to the extent that character is as yet unfixed, they may be conditional. It is character which determines future behavior, not God. God's omniscience thus becomes the basis of what is called prescience. The forming of character involves the possibility of novelty.

It seems to me that all of the statements of the Bible and by Ellen White on this subject can be interpreted in this light. It must be so interpreted if consistency and coherence are to be achieved. There are only two serious problem statements by Ellen White that I know about.

One is in *Story of Redemption*:

> God knows the end from the beginning. He knew, before the birth of Jacob and Esau, just what characters they would both develop. He knew that Esau would not have a heart to obey Him. He answered the troubled prayer of Rebekah

> and informed her that she would have two children, and the elder should serve the younger. He presented the future history of her two sons before her, that they would be two nations, the one greater than the other, and the elder should serve the younger.[3]

I feel somewhat uncertain as to how this passage should be interpreted. Taken at its face value, it seems to imply a fatalistic determinism of the severest sort. On the other hand, if we remind ourselves of the individual genetically and environmentally conditioned differences in potential for freedom, and of the fact that God was here in the process of selecting a people who would play a certain historic role in providing the context for the promised Messiah, this passage can be interpreted to indicate that genetically there was a relative difference between these two boys in their potential to fulfill God's particular purposes. Esau, even genetically, lacked the characteristics which would allow him to cooperate fully with God in His plan. This need, of course, says nothing about Esau's ultimate destiny. It might say a great deal, however, about Esau's fitness for the task that God had in mind. The other passage is found in the *Seventh-day Adventist Bible Commentary*:

> I AM means an eternal presence; the past, present, and future are alike to God. He sees the most remote events of past history, and the far distant future with as clear a vision as we do those things that are transpiring daily. We know not what is before us, and if we did, it would not contribute to our eternal welfare. God gives us an opportunity to exercise faith and trust in the great I AM.[4]

There are several things that can be said about this passage which may aid in our understanding. In the first place, the last two

---

[3]Ellen G. White, *The Story of Redemption* (Tacoma Park, MD: Review and Herald Publishing Association, 1947), 87.

[4]Francis D. Nichol, ed., *The Seventh-day Adventist Bible Commentary*, Vol. 1, (Tacoma Park, MD: Review and Herald Publishing Association, 1953), 1099.

sentences seem to place the events of the future in the category of "things-that-happen-to-us." This is not what we have been indicating by the word freedom. Freedom, as we are using the term, refers not "to react" or to "be acted upon" but "to act." Things that happen to us might be entirely a part of a closed causal system.

Augustine used almost the identical words, "the past, present, and future are alike to God." But taken in total context it becomes apparent that Augustine and Ellen White do not mean precisely the same things. To Augustine this was the prerogative of Spirit totally other than and outside of space-time categories. In other words, this was the mind of a Platonic Greek at work. Ellen White, standing squarely within the context of biblical monotheism, saw reality as a whole. There was in her thought little of the enormous Hellenic conceptual gulf between supernatural and natural, between spirit and matter, mind and body. Time-space considerations were omnipresent in her conception of God. Some would even call her crassly anthropomorphic, as they would the writers of the Bible.

It is a fact of history that Augustine, steeped in the Greek *weltanschauung*, had difficulty accepting the Christianity of his mother until he could remodel the biblical picture of God in Hellenic—especially Platonic—categories. And what a flood that maneuver let in through the gates of Christian theology. Put this passage within the context of statements like:

> It is the privilege of every Christian not only to look for, but to hasten the coming of our Lord Jesus Christ. Were all who profess His name bearing fruit to His glory, how quickly the whole world would be sown with the seed of the gospel. Quickly the last harvest would be ripened and Christ would come to gather the precious grain.[5]

This is about as devoid of Augustinian determinism regarding the future as it can possibly be. Even the "great event" in Ellen White's mind possessed a certain open-endedness insofar as it was condi-

[5]Ellen G. White, *Christ's Object Lessons* (Mt. View, CA: Pacific Press, 1900), 69.

tioned by human freedom. Only God who is omniscient can know all of the complicated causal patterns which are involved in what truly *is*.

This brings us to some of the reasons for risking a new look at the problem of God's foreknowledge. There are several of these. First, it adds to the majesty of God the dimension of His active personality. Aristotle's Unmoved Mover and the God of Abraham and Jesus are poles apart. Second, it increases our sense of devotion to a God who not only is a person, but also has created us with the ability to share in some of His personal qualities—namely, creativity, *ex nihilo*, if you please. Third, by radically rejecting the ways of thinking that imply either the determinisms of predestination or fatalism, it is possible to bring new emphasis to human responsibility.

I do not intimate that human reason can encompass God. Far from it. Rather, I insist that the universe be seen as just that and not a multiverse. What I do know of God's revelation must be in harmony with what I now know. God seems to have revealed to us at least that. I believe my proposals provide a proper basis for a coherent view of reality, and in a world of increasing intellectual sophistication, a less rational view of God would seem to be selling Him short.

Beyond the question of ethics, there is the deadly serious picture of a church increasingly losing its sense of commitment to an unfinished task. The picture of an inexorable prophetic time clock must give way to a new sense of urgency derived from a rediscovery that God has placed the future to an important extent in our hands. We are to be responsible agents and not mere passive participants in the work of redemption. This is the real significance of freedom as creative act.

22
Pain, Prayer, and Miracles

Pain is good when it prevents or stops us from damaging ourselves or others. It is evil when its intensity or longevity outweighs its benefits. The problem with pain is not that it exists but that too much of the bad kind does. This calls for considerable reflection.[1]

The universe overflows with bad pain. Just as it does in our own bodies, this signals that something is wrong. Sin is what's wrong and this is indifference to or violation of the will of God which mandates that which is in harmony with each creature's true nature.

Knowing the truth about sin can help us banish it. Because knowing the truth is one thing and doing it is something else, this is not enough. Yet if we never discover for ourselves that its way of life is destructive, we will always play with it. Sin's outcomes must be given a chance to display its true nature.

---

[1]This is a synthesis of three shorter papers: (1) "Why Pain?" (2)"Teach Us to Pray" and (3) "The Nature of Miracle."

Part of the truth about sin is that its consequences hurt innocent people. Its destructive outcomes are not merely private, self-directed. Others get caught up in them too. This is especially true between generations because the sins of parents hurt their children who grow up and wound their own offspring with their own sins in what sometimes appears to be a never-ending process. This is not because God is punishing parents and children. Sin causes all this suffering on its own.

If God prevented every innocent person from suffering because of the wrongdoing of others, we might get only part of the picture. The truth is that good people do suffer from the sins of others and this must be made undoubtedly clear.

This is one part of a theological response to sin. It doesn't do much to encourage us when we are suffering or enable us to cope with it more successfully. Without the other part of it, this theological response might actually make things worse by tending to make us feel like hapless victims in a cosmic experiment that a cold and uncaring God is conducting.

Where, then, is God in this excruciating process? God is suffering with us because He has made Himself a part of the cosmic experiment. This is a major meaning of the cross. It shows us that God suffers in our suffering.

Because they believe this, many make suffering a matter of prayer. Unfortunately it is all too easy to doubt that there is really anything to prayer. Many of us give lip service to a belief in prayer and go through the motions without really building an active life around it. Even when we protest that we do believe, what we sometimes seem to be saying is that we believe in believing rather than actually believing. Or to be honest, we are often afraid of what will happen to us if we express our doubts. I suppose some of us feel guilty when we fail to pray, like feeling guilty for failing to write a letter home. Perhaps we are fearful of offending God by our neglect, or worse, making Him angry at us so that He will let bad things to happen to us.

Most of the time our neglect may be related to our overt or covert reservations about the value of prayer. Does it really make any difference? Does anyone really listen on the other end of that line? If so, how does it happen that we often fail to receive more obvious responses to our end of the conversation?

Like a number of other key issues in religious belief and practice, prayer cannot be isolated from the total framework of belief. Almost anything we say here will have implications all up and down the line, including the nature of God, the nature and destiny of man, and the whole range of relationships between the two.

We often misunderstand the nature and purpose of prayer. What ought we to expect? Ellen White tells us that "It is a part of God's plan to grant us, in answer to the prayer of faith, that which He would not bestow did we not thus ask."[2] On the other hand, God does not desire spineless, passive dependence. He created humans and not mere parasites. He wants ours to be a responsible dependence; and, therefore the prayer of faith is one in which man cooperates with God.

Does prayer actually change things? Not usually. More typically prayer changes people and people change things. Prayer, then, is not a means of maneuvering God, but the possibility of more adequately allying ourselves with God.

Not all of our prayers will be answered the way we wish. God not only *knows* better than that, He *is* better than that. Jesus asked whether good earthly parents would give their children stones when they asked for bread, or serpents when they requested fish? "How much more shall your father which is in heaven give good things to them that ask Him?"[3]

The opposite is also true. God sometimes gives us good things when we ask for bad, things like bread when we ask for stones and fish when we ask for serpents. God can surprise and perplex us either way, and often does.

There is one kind of prayer that God always answers precisely as we desire. This is the sincere prayer for forgiveness, for the grace of His acceptance, and renewal for a better life:

---

[2]Ellen G. White, *The Great Controversy: The Conflict of the Ages in the Christian Dispensation* (Mt. View, CA: Pacific Press, 1911), 525.
[3]Mathew 7:11.

> When we pray for earthly blessings, the answer to our prayer may be delayed, or God may give us something other than we ask; but not so when we ask for deliverance from sin. It is His will to cleanse us from sin, to make us His children, and to enable us to live a holy life.[4]

Prayer is not so much something we *say* or *do* as something we *are*. Once we've said the words of our prayers, the larger prayer begins. The words are, for the most part, the way one strengthens and reinforces that larger reality. Prayer is a way of life, one that is lived out not just in practicing the presence of God but also in realizing that presence and behaving appropriately.

The prayer of magic is essentially idolatrous. It assumes that man can make the almighty God conform to man's wishes. The prayer of faith, on the other hand, involves a life lived out according to the divine will, a life that takes hold of God's hand and employs those small whispered moments throughout a day for remembering that God cares very much and is very near to each one of us.

Sometimes prayer may send an expression of gratitude heavenward for the fact that we live in a moral universe, where other things are predictable, where you can depend on God because His universe is orderly, and because you can always trust Him to answer the true prayer of faith for cleansing, forgiveness, and strength.

Prayer is also the possibility of community. Groups of people as well as families who pray together stay together. This is the primary meaning of intercessory prayer. People who become concerned about each other and express that concern in praying for each other belong to each other in very special ways. Man who was made for community was also thus made for intercession. These are the real mountains that prayer moves, those that separate us from each other. In response to the disciples' entreaty "Teach us to pray," Jesus began, "*Our* Father which art in heaven." We cannot pray that prayer without discovering that we are a part of everyone for whom we pray because God is in fact *our* father.

We cannot discuss prayer, especially intercessory prayer, with-

[4]Ellen G. White, *The Ministry of Healing* (Mt. View, CA: Pacific Press, 1909), 70.

out thinking about miracles. What are they? Did they occur in biblical times? Do they happen in ours? Should we want more or fewer of them? Can we affect this either way?

Many thoughtful people turn away from traditional religion because what it often says about miracles and other things strikes them as irreparably irrational. They look elsewhere even though they respect the many practical benefits of being a member of a religious group.

Even though most theologians down through the centuries have believed that only God can create something from nothing, a popular picture of them as intellectual magicians or tricksters persists. This is because many have come to believe, with considerable justification, that they learn more from scientific laboratories than churches, synagogues and temples or even seminars in the humanities and social sciences.

Meanwhile, religion has its own internal problems. An acquaintance of mine, who had been a chaplain at a prestigious university, explained to me how things were where he once had worked. "On our campus," he said, "publish or perish is a fact of life which is not to be ignored." "God is dead," he added, "because He hasn't published anything for nearly two-thousand years."

Is this strictly so? Not if we consider as "publishing" the many different ways God is constantly revealing the truth about himself, scientific research being among them.

Many of the fathers of the scientific revolution, especially Isaac Newton, who did so much to establish the new way of thinking, were deeply religious men. They gave us a sense of the orderliness, dependability, and predictability of the universe as God's creation, and what a breath of fresh air that brought to the world!

The older world of myth and magic, where all kinds of things could happen without cause or reason, least of all with anticipation, was a frightening place to live. Multitudes of creepy, crawly things could generate out of nowhere and malevolent spirits hovered about every unknown place and activity ready to pounce upon one's improper employment of magical precautions. Even one's petitions to God could be overridden by the stronger prayers of another. In such a context, prayer to God degenerates into magic rather than an act and life of faith.

God's "publishing endeavors" in scientific publications should be viewed by all of us with gratitude. Adventists have had an additional advantage. This is seeing God publish again, in our time, in the somewhat old-fashioned biblical medium of the written word in the writings of Ellen White.

The biblical view of human nature which permeates her writings has implications that go far beyond what many of us have realized. To some extent it is derived from her biblical understanding of the nature of man. We call it "wholism."

In this view of things, there is no sharp disjunction between levels of reality in man as there is in the Platonic dualism of spirit and matter. In the language of Paul Tillich, man is a multidimensional unity in which every aspect of him interpenetrates and interdigitates with every other. What happens to him in any one dimension—physical, mental, environmental, spiritual, and so forth happens in some way to the whole of him.

From this point of view the term "supernatural" is probably a misnomer. Although some of God's activities might not conform to our statistical expectations, this does not mean that they are contrary to the "laws of nature." We might not yet understand how these events are thoroughly "natural," but they are and God knows how.

The proper distinction is not between "natural" and "supernatural." It is between God's *usual activities*, which we can now summarize in our own "laws of nature," and his *unusual activities,* which take us by surprise and arouse in us the feelings of awe and wonder. This is in keeping with the meaning of the ancient term from which we get our own world "miracle." This is "to stare at" with astonishment.

God is moral, dependable, trustworthy and orderly, and he has created such a universe. God is bound not by anything outside of him but by the laws of his own being. God is one in character as well as number. He is consistent with Himself. Nothing which is inherently self-contradictory can be in Him or by Him. This is why science is possible. This is why it is a meaningful enterprise, a sacred one.

All things which are inherently possible are possible to God. He cannot create square circles, four sided triangles, stones so big that he cannot move them, predict the future in complete detail or simultaneously give people freedom and force them always to do the right thing. This is because he is moral and consistent and each one of these involves an inner contradiction of one kind or another.

We must add one more thing. This is that God is also personal and thus creative. His creative acts are orderly. His equations are rational and in balance. But God is not simply another equation. He is in charge of His laws; therefore, He can act selectively and freely, albeit not chaotically. God can choose from a wide range of alternatives which are perfectly natural to Him and use them in ways that surprise us.

Christ's transformation of the water into wine at the wedding in Cana is an example. As many commentators over the centuries have noted, God turns water into wine every day of the year. That God accelerated this process in equally natural ways at the wedding at Cana is not surprising. How He did it this time is.

"How did God do it?" is not a meaningless or blasphemous question. I want to know how He turned water into wine on that occasion and I believe that someday He will tell us. How he will do this doesn't matter. It might even be through our own scientific research!

The God of the Bible is revealed to men in his routine activities of sustaining and guiding the universe; however, as the need indicates, He is not bound to continue his usual activity in the usual way. He can, and does, vary the routine to meet differing needs without contradicting himself. His unusual actions tell us something very important about God. This includes the fact that he is personal—unique, aware, intelligent, and active.

All that the monotheistic premise requires is that such actions not be essentially unnatural, that is, irrational and contradictory, even though to us they are extraordinary. They may not always conform to our expectations; however, they are always orderly and rational and we see this when we correctly observe and truly comprehended them. God who mainly acts in ordinary ways sometimes surprises us in extraordinary ways that fill us with wonder. A miracle is born!

23
The Creation/Evolution Debate in the Light of the Great Controversy Between Christ and Satan

My title clearly identifies the tradition within which I speak even though I suspect that some of the things I am about to say will hardly be considered traditional, at least by some. I make no apology for this. It is my conviction that the situation now facing the Adventist Church in regard to these matters is dangerous and calls for a high level of innovation and creativity on the part of all of us. How we handle these matters could spell the difference between disaster and progress for the life of the Church.

Certain fundamental beliefs of Adventism appear to be placed in jeopardy by this issue. For example, if we are forced to admit that living forms, including man, have existed on this planet for a very long time, what happens to the Adventist understanding of the Great Controversy? If we reject sudden, fiat creation in the first instance, can we anticipate with confidence a sudden, fiat creation of a new heaven and a new earth? Does not the imminence of the Second Coming seem inconsequential against a backdrop of millions years of human history? But Adventism was predicated on a belief in the "soon" coming. The Sabbath may not be as seriously threatened as some fear. After all, it was a creation of God and presumably He could create it at any time He wished.

Certainly church unity is in jeopardy. I recently heard one of our leaders in the field of creation-science say that we probably had come to a time in Adventist history for a "parting of the ways." I happen to think that this idea is dead wrong, and I will fight it with all of my strength. I see it as the special responsibility of the progressive intellectuals in the church to see that this does not happen.

It will not be easy. There are those among us whose beliefs are largely based on willpower rather than rational conviction. A bumper sticker I once saw read, "God said it, I believe it, and that settles it." There are those who say, "If the Bible says a whale swallowed Jonah, I believe it. In fact, if the Bible said Jonah swallowed the whale, I would believe it." The gulf between this attitude and the splendid, scientific integrity expressed in Sir Thomas Huxley's well-known admonition that we must have the courage to "face the facts though they slay us," is formidable.

But try to bridge this gulf we must, not only for the sake of church unity, but for reasons of integrity. God requires of us that we be persons of integrity, including intellectual integrity, even in the face of possible inaccuracy. We are not morally bound to be correct. We are bound to be honest while we endeavor to be as accurate as we can be. We shall discover that we were mistaken about many things when we get to the Kingdom of Heaven, but no one will be there who "maketh a lie."[1]

In these matters the trouble comes in trying to be as accurate

[1]Revelation 22:15.

as we can be. Those facts we are supposed to have the courage to face "though they slay us," are not all in yet, and those we have are often ambiguous. No earth-history model that I've yet seen fully provides that neat, coherent synthesis of ideas and experience that we generally indicate by the expression "the whole truth."

Whether we shall be able to come up with the whole truth regarding earth-history is open to serious question. We may have to live with unanswered questions and tentative perceptions throughout this life as "the way things are."

Being able to do this as a community engaged in a common quest for truth is going to involve the ability to distinguish what is essential to faith from what is inconsequential. The latter may be subject to revision and restatement. The former will require mainly a sharpening of focus.

I wish to approach these concerns from the standpoint of my special area of competence. I am a moralist by interest and special training and I take this approach because there broods over this scene, like the proverbial "Cheshire cat," moral issues that have not received sufficient attention. In our quest we ignore these at our peril. But first a few preliminary remarks.

The religious, biblically-oriented scientist will always carry out his work in a situation of balanced tension between inductive and deductive logic—observation and faith, reason and revelation. The "facts" must be derived from both.

As an example, something we shall be looking at in greater detail, there is the "fact" that there is personality at the heart of things, that ultimate reality is spelled "who" and not merely "what." Surely this belief is one of the "unrevisables" of Christian faith. It involves more than merely objective observation. "Things," "objects," on the one hand, just lie there waiting to be observed and manipulated. All that is required is that we "go after them" with single-minded persistence. Experience of personality, on the other hand, always depends to some extent on someone "coming after us," that is, upon initiative on the part of the person who is experienced.

Creativity, initiative, and autonomy are mainly the features we apply to personhood. In the realm of "person" lie actions that are unique, surprising, unexpected, unrepeatable, unpredictable, *Einmaligheiten.* These are things that happen only once. Personhood is thus, to some extent, beyond the methods of the ordinary, at least physical, science, although, of course, residual evidence of personal actions may be scientifically observed. This also means that uniformity in any absolute sense is "off" the moment personality is introduced into the equation. Adding the personal dimension to earth-history can introduce significant uncertainty both as to time and process.

A useful way of thinking about the synthesis of inductive and deductive logic in the service of the "whole truth" is in terms of a two-dimensional model—a model with both horizontal and vertical qualities. The horizontal dimension corresponds to the world available to ordinary scientific investigation, what "just lies there," is repeatable, testable, predictable, and objectively observable. The vertical corresponds to the surprising, the unexpected, and the personal. To Christian believers these two dimensions repeat themselves throughout the whole of reality wherever personality is present.

They are present, for example, in man, who, while a multidimensional unity, shares many qualities with all men as man, and this makes it possible for us to write textbooks on anatomy, physiology, biochemistry, etc. Yet each is also *this* particular man, unique, irreplaceable, who decides, who acts, who creates, who chooses. The former is the horizontal dimension of human science; the latter, the vertical dimension of personality, sometimes cuts across the ordinary, the uniform, in surprising and unpredictable ways.

In this, man is a microcosm of the divine, for God, too, is a bidimensional being, insofar as He is personal. This is the basis for the inclusion of deductive factors in the belief-system of Christians who are involved in the scientific enterprise. *Person*, is a general "given" belief from which one deduces certain particulars.

Another unrevisable "given" from which we deduce essential elements in our belief system is the *goodness* of that eternal Person at the heart of things. The elemental goodness of God is not always easy simply to read off the record of man's historical encounters with Him. This is so mainly because it is man who has done the recording. But in the normative disclosure, the incarnation of our Lord, it becomes indelibly clear for all to see if they but have the eyes and the will to see it.

From this "given" we deduce another. God is not alone as a power in the universe. If God is "One" (another "given"), and He is good (still another "given"), He cannot be omnipotent, at least not now. This is because there is also evil in the world along with goodness. The fact of *evil* is another "given," both through our individual and corporate experience and by divine disclosure.

But as soon as we posit evil in the universe, that is, evil in the sense of "sin," evil for which someone is guilty, we have also posited evil personified. By definition, there cannot be "sin" without a person who sins. Impersonal forces in the universe, even enormously destructive ones—exploding suns, hurricanes, earthquakes, volcanoes—are not evil in the sense of "sin." They simply "are." They are amoral in and of themselves.

Destructive actions of subhuman animals are likewise amoral. Were the wolves to eat the lambs, they would not be "bad "wolves. That's what wolves as we know them are supposed to do. Only persons commit evil in the sense of "sin," for only they can be responsible through choosing. Immoral persons can employ amoral means to achieve their evil ends, of course, but that does not thereby invest the amoral means themselves with moral value.

What we are talking about, of course, is the Satan side of the Great Controversy to which we referred in the title. To engage in serious warfare with God requires that the contenders for the throne be at least somewhere near the same league. I once heard Krister Stendahl, then dean of Harvard Divinity School, and not an unsophisticated primitive, by the way, say that it is impossible to deal rationally with the problem of evil without positing a personal devil. He immediately went on to note that to him the devil was not a simple notion and almost as difficult to define as God Himself.

A central issue in all of this, indeed, perhaps, the central issue, has to do with the characters of the protagonists in the conflict. Here is where the issue takes on the moral quality to which we referred at the outset. What we face is not a battle of Titans for power, for territory, for material possessions, and for the other usual things that set *men* against each other. It is a spiritual conflict. Satan, the destroyer, is not merely attempting to undo what God has done. His aim is not merely to destroy. Rather, what is being set forth, I believe, is an alternative ordering of reality.

The clearest expression of the demonic side of the conflict that I know of is set forth in the writings of a German philosopher who, in terms of his devastating impact on the world, may have been one of the most influential thinkers the world has ever known. Born in the latter half of the 19th century, Friedrich Nietzsche was reared in a somewhat straight-laced religious home mainly by aunts and sisters. When he was 18 years of age he gave up his Christian faith. Later he was to say that it was the easiest thing he ever did. He seems, however, to have spent the rest of his life, trying to prove that it was the easiest thing he ever did.

The book expressing this most clearly was named appropriately, *Der Antichrist*, a title chosen with care, because Nietzsche had come to hold Judaism and Christianity responsible for most of the world's social ills. Jews and Christians, he said, had "transvalued the values." They had veritably turned morality on its head in the service of their own decadence. But let him tell you in his own words,

> What is good? Everything that heightens the feelings of power in man, the will to power, power itself. What is bad? Everything that is born of weakness. What is happiness? The feeling that power is growing, that resistance is overcome. Not contentedness but more power; not peace but war; not virtue but fitness.
>
> What is more harmful than any vice? Active pity for all the failures and all the weak: Christianity.
>
> What type of man shall be bred, shall be willed, for being higher in value, worthier of life, more certain of a future. Even in the past this higher type has appeared often—but

as a fortunate accident, as an exception, never as something willed. In fact, this has been the type most dreaded—almost the dreadful—and from dread the opposite type was willed, bred and attained: the domestic animal, the herd animal, the sick human animal—the Christian.

Christianity should not be beautified and embellished; it has waged deadly war against this higher type of man; it has placed all the basic instincts of this type under the ban and out of these instincts it has distilled evil and the Evil One: the strong man as the typically reprehensible man, the "reprobate." Christianity has sided with all that is weak and base, with all failure; it has made an ideal of whatever contradicts the instinct of the strong life to preserve itself; it has corrupted the reason even of those strongest in spirit by teaching men to consider the supreme values of the spirit as something sinful, something that leads to error—as temptation.

Christianity is called the religion of pity. Pity stands opposed to the tonic emotions which heighten our vitality; it has a depressing effect. We are deprived of strength when we feel pity.

Quite in general, pity crosses the law of development, which is the law of selection. It preserves what is ripe for destruction; it defends those who have been disinherited and condemned by life; and by the abundance of the failures of all kinds which it keeps alive it gives life a gloomy and questionable aspect.

Wherever the theologian's instinct extends, value judgments have been stood on their heads and the concepts of "true" and "false" are of necessity reversed: whatever, is most harmful to life is called "true;" whatever elevates it, enhance, affirms, justifies it, and makes it triumphant, is called "false."[2]

---

[2]Friedrich Nietzsche, "Der Antichrist," in Walter Kaufman, ed., *The Portable Nietzsche* (New York: The Viking Press, 1954), 570, 571, 572, 576.

And where did Friedrich Nietzsche get this? Expressions like "will to power," "self preservation," and "the law of selection," come straight out of Charles Darwin's *The Origin of the Species*.[3] The name of the survival game is power, power of the strong over the weak and the will to use it. That is the way it is in nature. The fittest survive. The big fishes eat the little fishes and the little fishes eat the littler fishes. The fit survive by possessing more wit, greater agility, stronger muscles, and sharper claws.

On these terms, man as a part of nature, when he is true to his origins, participates in the general behavioral configurations of the rest of nature. The truly noble men of the earth are thus like the ancient Romans whose legions marched through the world conquering and displacing its weak and decadent inhabitants such as the Jews and Christians who had perverted the very meaning of morality by transmitting weakness and decadence into virtue.

Ideas have consequences. It would be naïve to attribute to ideas even as forceful as these more credit than they deserve. Although the causes of Two Great World Wars were vastly more complex than anything Friedrich Nietzsche had to say, there is strong evidence that Nietzsche furnished much of the philosophic undergirding of those two major human catastrophes.

All of which stands in sharpest contrast with the way of life proposed by our Master when He was here among men. "Blessed are the meek," He said. "They shall inherit the earth."[4] And in His familiar contrasting of the worldlings with His own followers He admonished them:

> But Jesus called them *unto him*, and said, Ye know that the princes of the Gentiles exercise dominion over them, and they that are great exercise authority upon them. But it shall not be so among you: but whosoever will be great among you, let him be your minister; And whosoever will be chief among you, let him be your servant: Even as the

---

[3]Charles Darwin, *The Origin of the Species: A Facsimilie of the First Edition* (Cambridge, MA: Harvard University Press, 1964).
[4]Matthew 5:5.

> Son of man came not to be ministered unto, but to minister, and to give his life a ransom for many.[5]

Constantly, He urged them by word and example to show compassion and pity for the weak, to extend kindness even to the enemy, to nurture and care for the unfortunate, to become as innocent as little children. He condemned the leaders, the haughty priests, scribes, and Pharisees for their shameless, arrogant, and self-seeking pursuit of power. Nietzsche knew well his true enemy!

It wasn't just a matter of contrasting human lifestyles. In Christ versus Antichrist, two opposing conceptions of reality itself were displayed. These were the terms of the great, universal controversy between Christ and Satan. Two different ways of ordering the universe were placed in opposition.

This extended even to the natural order. The Old Testament's depictions of the ideal natural world, especially Isaiah's prophecies of the new heaven and the new earth, are consistent with the way Christ taught men to deal with one another. Isaiah declared,

> The wolf also shall dwell with the lamb, and the leopard shall lie down with the kid; and the calf and the young lion and the fatling together; and a little child shall lead them. And the cow and the bear shall feed; their young ones shall lie down together: and the lion shall eat straw like the ox. And the sucking child shall play on the hole of the asp, and the weaned child shall put his hand on the cockatrice' den. They shall not hurt nor destroy in all my holy mountain: for the earth shall be full of the knowledge of the LORD, as the waters cover the sea.[6]
>
> The wolf and the lamb shall feed together, and the lion shall eat straw like the bullock: and dust shall be the serpent's meat. They shall not hurt nor destroy in all my holy

[5]Matthew 20:25-28.

[6]Isaiah 11:6-9.

> mountain, saith the LORD.[7]

I know that these are examples of sublime Hebrew poetry and intended as artistic description of the state of God's people after their restoration from their Exile in Babylon. He may not have intended literally to portray a natural ecosystem differing markedly from anything we can imagine as actually functioning.

It is of no great importance to my point in any case. When the ideal state is depicted by the prophetic artist, the tubes of paint have colors that are harmonious with Christ's portrayal of reality! This state for man is illustrated by an idyllic animal scene, and it is hard to imagine that that scene bears no resemblance whatever to reality, especially since it is so consonant with the ideal picture of man Christ gives us in word and deed.

The trouble with that vision of nature is that it does not clearly resemble anything we can observe now or anything that has ever been as far as we can tell by the paleontological record. The record of the long past seems very much like the present, and Nietzsche's picture of reality seems vindicated rather than Christ's. As near as we can discover, the big fishes have always eaten the little fishes and the little fishes have always eaten the littler fishes, both in man's ecosystems and in the ecosystems around us.

This is not totally true, of course. If we are attuned we can hear the strains of both worlds commingled. This is true in the natural world where there are moments of beauty, even in the midst of nature's tragedies, when notes from that other land seem wafted in on the air. It is also true in the human.

The Bible accounts for this by the Fall. What was created by God as "very good" becomes changed by man's sin. In ways that are not entirely clear, the whole of nature is involved in man's sin and looks forward to redemptive deliverance. Paul writes,

> For the earnest expectation of the creature waiteth for the manifestation of the sons of God. For the creature was made subject to vanity, not willingly, but by reason of him

---

[7]Isaiah 65:25

> who hath subjected *the same* in hope, because the creature itself also shall be delivered from the bondage of corruption into the glorious liberty of the children of God. For we know that the whole creation groaneth and travaileth in pain together until now. And not only *they*, but ourselves also, which have the firstfruits of the Spirit, even we ourselves groan within ourselves, waiting for the adoption, *to wit*, the redemption of our body.[8]

In this present world it may not be possible to separate the commingled realities either conceptually or in practice. I am not aware that it is possible, as things now stand, to run a business, or a railroad, or an institution, or a country, or a denomination on a pattern of strict, literal adherence to the admonition contained in the Sermon on the Mount. In this life, businessmen who respond to the theft of their coats by giving up their cloaks too, usually lose their shirts, pants, shoes, and socks. Countries that do not look to their defenses soon cease to exist as free states. In this life we may seek to be as harmless as doves, but we had better keep a sharp eye peeled. Perhaps it is like the wheat and the tares. They are truly separable only at the harvest. What is required of us, however, even now, is that we know the difference. While living in this world we must keep our eyes on that better land. Otherwise we are in danger of committing the Nietzschian error of normalizing the imperfect.

I certainly do not have the answers to the questions confronting us, but I am going to make a suggestion developed over many years of pondering the matter and talking with many esteemed friends, both inside and outside of the scientific community. It is based on the above notion of the Great Controversy.

If we grant the conflict the awesome, cosmic and temporal proportions I have suggested, and if the protagonists have the qualities I have outlined, it becomes plain that this battle of the Titans is finally a struggle between two competing orderings of reality. The victory of one over the other at the end comes with a demonstration that one, even though giving the appearance of success for

[8]Romans 8:20-23.

a time, has within it the seeds of its own eventual destruction.

Since Satan is a genuine contender and time is not a limitation, could it be that the working out of his principles could look very much like what we see in the natural record, which is attributed by the secular scientist to the autonomous working in its process of evolution? Such intelligent guidance of the process of evolution is precisely the link that is missing in the ordinary secular version. The idea of a totally random evolutionary process is utterly incredible on the face of it. It would take an *almost* divine, personal intelligence to make it work. I am proposing that this almost divine personal intelligence which has influenced the process of evolution is Satan.

Suppose that at some point of relatively recent time, after Satan's principles have become clear to the hosts of heaven, God stepped in to demonstrate His alternative to the devil's method, and this is the Genesis story. With the options before them, there is a choosing of loyalties and there is war in heaven to be continued here on earth until the end of time.

Fantastic? Of course. Is this the way it happened? I have no idea even though the above conjecture is not inconsistent with the record. The record certainly shows signs of the demonic kingdom at work, if our characterization of the two kingdoms is anywhere near accurate. The evolutionist's picture looks more like a painting of the devil than it does a portrait of God. Indeed, the record shows elements of both kingdoms even though the imprint of God's kingdom was so quickly obscured by the Fall.

The advantage of a model like this is mainly that it can take the "heat" off while we carefully examine the evidence. It is one with which I, for one, can live until we have more facts to go on. It leaves the Genesis story largely intact. It also allows us to take seriously the messages of the rocks and fossils. Both accounts of origins could contain truth. They could just be addressing themselves to different aspects of reality, the one a record of the kingdom of darkness, the other the story of God's kingdom, but neither, by itself, a complete history.

One final word. In the light of the Great Controversy, the

one thing we cannot allow is confusion regarding God's character, which results from attempts to make God the author of the evolutionary process. This is also the implication of spreading our creation week over vast periods of time. Nietzsche's god is not the God of Jesus Christ. Of that there must be no doubt.

24
Was Ellen White a Fraud?

Ellen White's literary dependency is now fairly well known. Most informed Adventists have at least some awareness of her extensive use of the writings of others without giving them credit. Although a few individuals must have always had some understanding of the extent of the problem, only in recent years has this information become generally available through the efforts of such persons as Ronald Numbers, Don McAdams and Walter Rea.

The few who have had this information have apparently been reluctant to share it with rank and file church members, presumably out of concern that doing this might weaken Ellen White's position of authority in the church. This reluctance continues to be expressed as an attempt to minimize the quantity of dependency.

This effort to keep her literary dependence largely unknown is understandable but misplaced. It may also prove to be counter-productive in the end. If the issue had been dealt with candidly from the beginning, we might now be spared what is and will continue to be a wrenching experience for many sincere church members.

The discovery should not be all that disturbing. It mainly puts in jeopardy a concept of verbal inspiration that has always been logically untenable. This is why it was officially rejected by the denomination from the beginning. We would have benefited from its thorough demise throughout the entire membership a long time ago.

The *amount* of "borrowing" is not of great moment. The figure could be 100%. providing only that the prophet retained essential control over the selecting, combining and interpreting editorial process as he or she used the words of others to express his or her inspired thoughts.

An interesting analogy is provided from the world of art. Some of the great works of the masters were designed by the credited artists who maintained quality control over the painting but actually employed assistants to carry much of it out. Guzton Borglum conceived the massive sculpture at Mt. Rushmore in South Dakota. He designed it, supervised it, and maintained control over its artistry. However, he, himself, did very little of the actual "jackhammer" work on its face. He did not even survive to see it completed. Yet no one denies that it is *his* work of art.

What has been going on of late with regards to the writings of Ellen White has long been going on with the Bible with similar conclusions. Diminished religious certainty is the chief danger some face upon discovering how the Bible came in to being and this is why they resist learning this. Persons who have felt secure in their beliefs "because the Bible tells me so," are likely to feel uneasy over the possibility that others besides those to whom God spoke directly may have had a hand in the process of creating it.

I shall leave it to our biblical scholars who are familiar with the historical-critical approach and have the courage and faith to apply it, to deal with this. I am writing as a Christian moralist about the charge that Ellen White was a fraud because she did not reference her sources and seems at times even to have denied that she used them.

Quite a number, including me, have been troubled by this. I write for them and to clarify my own thoughts and feelings. It is a serious charge which, if not faced fairly and openly, has potential for threatening the faith of many honest souls in the Seventh-day Adventist Church.

If Ellen White were completely to disappear from the scene, our major doctrines would remain largely intact because they are biblically based. Yet the admission that we have been fraudulently misled by the founder and founders of this movement could produce enough moral outrage to endanger what they brought into existence.

Let us face the issue in its worst possible terms. In this scenario, the prophet sits down in her study with a number of books by different authors spread out before her and as she wrote her "inspired books" she simply lifted the material out of these authors, usually paraphrasing, but sometimes using the same words, and often following their sequence of ideas. And then she deliberately denies dependence upon these authors, claiming rather guidance from God.

This sounds very much like conscious, deliberate deception. Suppose we accept this as intentional deception for the purposes of discussion. Is it possible to have something like this happen but there be an honest denial of human dependence? Is that too tall an order? Let us see.

I must confess at the outset that I find the idea of Ellen G. White being a fraud both logically and emotionally repugnant. I do not believe it for admittedly biased reasons. I have always believed, respected and loved her. Some, I realize, because of an authoritarian misuse of her writings in their lives, have experienced her as a restrictive, inhibitive, and oppressive force. Her writings have frequently been misused in this way. But it was different for me.

My early life involved much insecurity and uncertainty. The important people in my life were perhaps too permissive and uninvolved in its direction. Not that they did not care. They did. However, they didn't understand my anxious search for meaning and purpose.

I discovered Ellen White largely for myself and I found purpose and direction in that discovery. No books of any kind have been as important to my spiritual life as have her *Desire of Ages*[1] and *Christ's Object Lessons.*[2] They were even more important to me than the Bible in my early years. At least I could understand her words and I eagerly read them again and again. Take these away from me now and something central to the core of my being will have died.

This is not merely a question of emotional bias. I have difficulty believing that so manifestly a godly woman was internally capable of so crass a falsehood over so long a lifetime. I think it externally unlikely too. Sooner or later, what was going on would have surely slipped out. The worst of the charges against her seem to me to be as farfetched as the claim that the Christian movement began because a small group of people stole the dead body of Jesus and then proclaimed that He had been resurrected. How long could that have been kept a secret?

Before we proceed, let me interject a word about what I consider to be the correct relation of truth to authority. A thing is so because it is so and not because someone, be he biblical or modern priest or prophet, says so. It is not so even because God "says" it is so. He says it is so *because it is so,* even if His speech may bring it into being in a creative sense. *Truth is related to reality not to authority.*

It is on this basis that I quote Ellen White. The paragraphs that I select from her writings are not philosophically and psychologically true because she wrote them. It is actually the other way around. Insofar as what is published under her name is true, it is so on its own merits, and her writings recognize this and conform to it.

The statements by her that I quote are philosophically consistent with the logic of human freedom. If there is such a thing as freedom to choose, to *act* and not merely to *react* or be *acted* upon, then something like what she wrote on this subject is a necessary corollary.

---

[1]Ellen G. White, *The Desire of Ages* (Mt. View, CA: Pacific Press, 1940).
[2]Ellen G. White, *Christ's Object Lessons* (Mt. View, CA: Pacific Press, 1940).

Although we might want to modify her language, the psychological truth of what she wrote on this subject is attested to by psychological observation and experiment. Consider this:

> The brain nerves which communicate with the entire system are the only medium through which Heaven can communicate to man, and affect his inmost life.[3]

"Brain nerves" is not modern, technical language. We would now speak of the central and peripheral nervous system. The point is that human neuroanatomy and neurophysiology are very much involved in the process of knowing. Even prophetic revelations and inspiration are properly studied with the resources of psychological learning theory and other scholarly disciplines.

We learn something from her writings which we learn from scientific research and philosophical reflection as well. This is that all of our perceptions of reality are conditioned by previous experience. To greater and lesser degrees, everything which has ever happened within and without us creates a "filter" through which all new experience must pass.

The new experience comes to be seen in terms of that "filter" just as light shining through colored glass takes on the color of the glass. None of us is ever able to perceive reality exactly as it really is. Only God can do that. We can only perceive reality from our perspective, as we see it. *We see things not as they are but as we are.*

The prophet's own understanding of the process of inspiration before accepting the prophetic role is a major factor in how he "sees" it. How did Ellen White perceive what took place as God spoke to her?

There is no single answer to this, obviously, since the communication took a number of forms. One of her statements, which is a creative copying and reworking of a portion of a nineteenth century book by Professor C.E. Stowe,[4] is pertinent.

---

[3]Ellen G. White, *Testimonies for the Church*, vol. 2 (Mt. View, CA: Pacific Press, 1948), 347.

[4]C. E. Stowe, *The Origin and History of the Books of the Bible* (Hartford: Hartford

> It is not the words of the Bible that are inspired, but the men that were inspired. Inspiration acts not on the man's words or his expression but on the man himself, who, under the influence of the Holy Ghost, is imbued with thoughts. But the words receive the impress of the individual mind.[5]

She appears to be distinguishing the revealed *concept* from the *wording*, which is the vehicle of its expression. Only the former is attributed to the Holy Spirit. It is important that we recall this distinction when we consider her claim that what she wrote she received from the Holy Spirit.

How does this differ from the "inspiration" each of us may feel as we read moving or especially enlightening passages in books by a variety of authors, including some we would think of as quite secular? Are all men "inspired" in this manner?

All men can be inspired in this way. The Holy Spirit is not the private property of prophets. There is no absolute difference between prophets and other men and women at the level of humanness and process. The difference, if any, is at the level of the divine activity.

The prophet is chosen by God. The prophet does not decide to become a prophet like someone chooses to become an engineer, a doctor, or a tradesman. "Prophecy came not in old time by the will of man."[6] God selects the prophet and the selection is not random or purely arbitrary.

Because all men perceive reality in a more or less distorted way, it is appropriate that God would choose someone in specific situations who would distort reality the least. God selects the prophet, not because he is able to perceive things "as they really are," but because he is the least distorting available vehicle at the moment of need. Let us remember that in Adventist lore Ellen White was the third person to be invited to have a prophetic role and, only

---

Publishing Company, 1867).

[5]Ellen G. White, *Selected Messages*, vol. 1 (Tacoma Park, MD: Review and Herald Publishing Association, 1958), 81.

[6]2 Peter 1:21.

after the first two rejected it, did the invitation fall on her who was thought to be "the weakest of the weak."

God also provides the ongoing experiences by which the more or less distorted view of the prophet increasingly approximates reality as God sees. Truth is progressive, or better, the perception of truth is progressive, even for prophets. Ellen White's observation that she was "no longer the child she once was," is consistent with this notion.

The prophet differs also in being given a role in his community. The prophet is chosen for leadership and communicative purposes. Therefore he must be given a hearing. When the prophet speaks people must listen. God's word must carry authority and one way to make this happen is to invest the vehicle of His work with authority.

What provides this ring of authority differs according to time, place, and custom. For John the Baptist it was the account of his birth, early training, diet, wilderness habitat and dress. For Ellen White, the times seem to have been suited to paranormal bodily manifestations.

The prophetic role would also have an undoubted effect on the self–concept of the prophet. The physician looks at the world through physician's eyes, the minister perceives as a minister, a housewife as a housewife, a church administrator as an administrator. The prophet, having accepted and lived with the prophetic call, would experience the world through a prophet's eyes.

Another difference would again derive from the divine action. Having chosen a prophet and set him or her apart in a way that insured his or her being listened to as one speaking with authority, God then reveals Himself in special ways. "If there be a prophet among you, I the Lord will make myself known unto him in a vision and I will speak unto him in a dream."[7]

Now let us put all of this together and see if it has anything to say to the situation at hand. All of us have had the experience, while reading, of feeling that God has spoken to our hearts in a special way. When this happens, do we say, "Ah, C. S. Lewis, or

[7]Numbers 12:6.

Francis Schaeffer, or Karl Barth, or even Ellen White really spoke to my heart today?" Or in reading the Bible do we say, "Moses, or Isaiah, or John really spoke to me in my reading today." Or do we say that God did?

When we read expressions by Ellen White like "The word of the Lord came unto me" or "I was shown" or "I saw," we must remember that those expressions come out of a prophet's intensive self-consciousness and not ours.

I suspect that a prophet who felt the enlightenment of the Holy Spirit while reading in his or her library would be even less inclined to give the credit to the human author. The sense of the divine presence—the "light" behind those words—would seem so intense that it would seem inaccurate, indeed almost blasphemous, certainly demeaning, to attribute it to a human source.

Could this be a factor in why Ellen White frequently used the writings of others without giving them credit? The distinctively prophetic distorted view of reality would tend to transport the prophet back to those times before modern copyright ethics where the gifts of the Muses were nobody's private property. They came from the *Muses* and people gave them credit. It is only in the relatively modern period that one assumed that creative effort was a personal possession.

The charge of plagiarism or fraud could be appropriate if one of us did what the prophets did, whereas the intent to deceive might be utterly absent from their perceptual point of view. If Ellen White sensed that God were speaking to her through the vehicle of these written words, she would probably not feel dependent on the human author of them.

In summary, was Ellen White a fraud? No. I think the more likely possibility is that this godly woman was so sensitive to the influences of God in what she read, and responded to them so intensely, that she tended to overlook customary amenities like saying thanks to the ordinary writers who provided the occasion. A woman, who as a "born again" child could "hear" workmen "praising God" while they were probably saying and doing rather ordinary things, would very likely in her adulthood be attuned to things that most of the rest of us might never hear.

This doesn't mean that everyone involved gets "off the hook" this easily. I feel justifiable resentment toward those well-intentioned people who concealed these facts from us all of those years out of a mistaken impression that we couldn't handle them. Those leaders who spoke so freely at the 1919 Bible conference and then went home with their lips sealed showed, at the very least, a lack of courage.

Having the spirit of the prophets is to have one's eyes open to the future. The prophet is given to open doors and not to close them, to give guidance to growth not to give final authoritarian answers to our questions.

It may be good for the church to go through this period of crisis, a period characterized by the shaking of our certainties. Perhaps it may be a new occasion for discovering that certainty never lies in having all the right answers, but in knowing and trusting our Lord and thus being free to face up to the questions. The finding will ever be in the questing, not in final solutions. The spirit of the prophets is a spirit of eternal openness and expectancy.

Part VI

Reflections

25
The Way We Were

My life has spanned an interesting period in the life of the church, and in the life of man, for that matter. When it began, missionaries were still reaching their "far-flung" fields by uncertain vintage automobiles, trains, steamships, and finally ox-carts and the like. It took months to receive letters from home, and you went out with the intention of remaining "forever," and it sometimes seemed like it too. You learned the language, became separated from your children when they became old enough to attend secondary school, not seeing them again for years. Finally, if you didn't succumb to one of those dreadful, untreatable tropical diseases, you returned home in old age to a world that had largely passed you by, a world of new ideas, habits, and dress styles, and where the home Church seemed very worldly and uncaring about its world mission. Later you would call it culture shock. You also felt a great emptiness for the friends you had left behind forever in the mission field and you banded together for comfort with others who had similarly spent their lives.

Workers who remained in the homeland, particularly evangelists, prepared for their campaigns by flooding the community with often lurid handbills, setting up the Conference's tent in a vacant lot as close to the center of town as possible, putting up their eye-catching billboards, and waiting for the crowds that they were usually assured of drawing since theirs was often the only show in town.

The audience was almost certainly church-going, and Bible-believing. They may have been ignorant of what the Bible actually contained except for the usual familiar stories; however, if you could prove what you had to say from the Bible, it carried conviction. Local ministers might be more or less successful at warning their flocks on Sunday morning against being taken in by these Adventists, even providing alternative interpretations of troublesome proof texts. Some of them might even be foolish enough to engage the evangelist in open debate.

Ah, those were heady days! They were sometimes filled with unbelievable hardship, especially for the ministerial intern and his new bride attached to the seasoned evangelist whom we were. But they were also days filled with adventure, excitement and meaning. These were the "people of God," "the Remnant," the "True Church," out to "Finish God's work."

I recently finished reading a delightful book by Miriam Wood depicting that period in our history entitled *Those Happy Golden Years.*[1] If you haven't read it, I recommend that you do so just to get a feel for the way we were then.

Her book is obviously a compilation of anecdotes she picked up by talking to prominent, old-time evangelists. It is pretty authentic, even if a bit overblown by its concentration on the unusual and spectacular. Some of her informants later went on to do other things. Her husband became editor of the *Adventist Review.*

I first began my ministry toward the end of that period. As a boy I had helped the evangelist when he came to our town, spreading the sawdust that formed the floor of the tent, helping set up

[1]Miriam Wood, *Those Happy Golden Years* (Tacoma Park, MD: Review and Herald, 1980).

the benches or folding chairs as the case might be, operating the slide projector, and getting barked at by the neighborhood dogs as I passed out the weekly handbills in the territory assigned to me.

Because we had no seminary in those days, after completing the basic ministerial course in college, I joined the team as a singing evangelist, if you can believe that! My young wife was the pianist and we made quite a team, even singing gospel duets on occasion!

Our first "effort," as we called them in those days, was held in Salt Lake City, Utah. We didn't have access to a tent so we rented an empty store on a busy street in the center of the city. Those were the war years and we capitalized on the spirit of the times by using motion-picture newsreels, along with vigorous gospel singing, both as a way of stimulating attendance and setting the mood for our sermons on Bible prophecies concerning the "last days."

Armageddon was not hard to imagine in those days. I constructed a three-dimensional display of it in the storefront window. I cut out and painted huge clouds in it with lots of bombers in the sky and tanks and cannons on the ground, all in garish reds and blacks and khaki greens, and soldiers all over the place with guns at ready. In the foreground lay a Bible, open to the appropriate scripture passages and lighted with a spotlight from above. It was all rather eye-catching, if I do say so myself.

There were other "efforts" afterwards but none that stand out so vividly in my memory. I especially remember the drunk who kept coming in off the street to keep warm. He sat in a prominent place in the back near the door where he smelled of booze and snored loudly in the warmth of the lecture hall. I also remember a prominent leader of the Latter-day Saints Church who seated himself nightly in a highly visible place near the door as a reminder that the Church was interested in what meeting the "saints" were attending.

If you were not an Adventist, they must have struck you as a peculiar lot. Often not mixing well with their neighbors, they were clannish, hard to have over for a cup of coffee or tea, or to a meal because you couldn't be sure what they could eat or drink. Almost none of them would eat pork or oysters and things like that. Some of them would eat other meat and some wouldn't.

They wouldn't say it to your face usually, but if you read the magazines they wrote for themselves or attended their meetings on Sabbath or Wednesday nights, you would occasionally hear expressions that were a little puzzling, to say the least, if not downright arrogant. These were expressions like "People of God," "Church of God," "Remnant Church," "True Church," and they spoke of "The Truth," as if it were their private property.

They did an awful lot of quoting from one Sister White in their meetings. If you pressed them about who she was, they would admit that she was a modern prophet, their prophet. Mormons understood this but almost everybody else found it a little hard to take. They surely seemed to know their Bibles, though, and given half an opening, they would be handing you religious tracts or inviting you to take what they called "Bible studies."

They seemed sincere, maybe a little too much so. They never ppeared to do any of the things that seemed like fun to the rest of the crowd. They had their own elementary schools, which usually didn't look like much. If some of them went to the local high school, they were usually left out of almost all of the extracurricular activities like football, and especially basketball, which was usually played on Friday nights, which they considered part of their Sabbath.

And the dances? You would almost never find an Adventist young person at the Senior Prom. They didn't take part in the school plays. They didn't go to the movies. Ask one of them out on a date, and even if you received an affirmative response, it wasn't worth the hassle. There were so many restrictions. And you always sensed that the girl's parents didn't approve.

They dressed plainly and didn't wear jewelry, even a class ring. Sometimes you almost felt sorry for them. Strangely, most of them didn't seem to feel very sorry for themselves. Some of them seemed embarrassed if someone asked them why they didn't do these things. Often the answer would be a kind of evasive, "because I am an Adventist," as if that explained anything. Some of them acted as if they knew something others didn't but couldn't explain. You wondered whether their "Sister White" had anything to do with it.

There were good things and bad things about having one for an employee. They were usually honest and dependable. Their strict requirements for membership apparently tended to weed out those who weren't. You didn't find them wasting time lighting up or stinking up the place with tobacco smoke. They were never suffering from Monday morning hangovers and generally spent less time on sick leave. The bad thing was that you had better never have a rush order that called for overtime on Friday afternoon. You would be left completely in a lurch.

We wore the "Adventist" part of our name more prominently in bygone days too, in our sermons and publications and even in our private conversations. We spoke often of "the signs" of the last days. World War I was leading up to Armageddon. Surely World War II was. We watched with great interest whenever we heard that some locality had passed an ordinance requiring that places of business be closed on Sunday.

The Pope didn't figure in the news nearly as prominently in those days, but we watched each account of his activities with fascination. Myron Taylor's being sent as a U.S. representative to the Vatican was about it. We knew what the labor unions were up to also. What with "men running to and fro and knowledge being increased," in science and industry, the growing disparity between the rich and the poor, the gathering storm of violence and crime in our cities, the "wild" behavior of our young and not so young, the new dances, and all, the conclusion was obvious. The Day was at hand, at least so the preachers, evangelists, *Signs of the Times*, and *Review* reminded us. Apparently, we didn't know enough yet about geography and demographics to be overwhelmed by the task remaining.

In retrospect, some of this may have been "style" rather than substance. This was Adventist "vocabulary." It was the way a couple of generations before us had taught us to talk. It was as though some Adventists had come to "believe in believing."

I once heard my elders discussing whether it was appropriate for Adventists to plant trees that wouldn't bear fruit for four years.

Didn't that give evidence of a lack of faith in the nearness of our Lord's return? They said similar things when it came to building church buildings while they went about their private affairs as if the "Parousia" were still a "far off divine event."

I myself know that there were many teenagers in my day who surely hoped so. We held that it was all right for the Lord to return, but not until we had had our fun, at least not until we had a chance to experience the "joys of marriage," as we called it in those days.

Style or not, it pretty much kept us out of politics and other "worldly" activities, including professions that were not directly associated with "finishing the work." There were only three or four legitimate vocations for which we prepared in college in those days. They were: (1) Ministry, (2) Medicine and (3) Teaching.

If you didn't make it in the ministry, or were not accepted at Loma Linda because of your poor grades, you ended up in the last category. There were always those, of course, for whom teaching was a first choice. For those who cared about such things, there were business courses designed to prepare young people to become accountants, secretaries, stenographers, and the like for positions in conference offices, school industries, publishing houses, hospitals, and other institutions.

If you didn't fit into any of these authorized categories, you were doomed to spending the rest of your life as a layman, or worse, a mere housewife, thereby disappointing your parents by not being "in the work." In those "happy golden days," there were almost no Adventist lawyers, engineers, financiers, architects, and so on who add so much to the richness, and I also mean affluence, of contemporary Adventist life. There were faithful laymen who tried to uphold the hands of the workers who themselves wanted "a piece of the action," including wanting to hold their leaders accountable; however, there weren't many, as compared with now.

Those of you who remember those days will recall a much greater sense of community than we enjoy today. Some would call it a "ghetto mentality." There were fewer of us, for one thing. If you had been to one of our colleges you were "in" all over the world. You could always count on seeing someone with whom you either went to school or knew someone else who had. There was also a greater similarity of life style and socio-economic status so that you felt comfortable with other Adventists even though you had never seen them before.

You could nearly always tell the "insiders" from the "outsiders." Our "tribal marks," as Dr. John Peterson likes to call them, or perhaps better, our lack of them, made it possible to recognize each other even if, in fact, we were complete strangers. Add to this our peculiar Adventist jargon and you have the stuff of which strongly cohesive in-groups are made. All you had to do was look at the fingers, the ear lobes and the lips, and what hung around the neck, and then smell and listen for a moment and you could usually know whether you had found a brother or sister in "The Truth." That, too, was pretty heady stuff even though some of us, especially our teenagers, didn't appreciate it very much.

Then came radio, television, electronic satellites, computers, jet transportation and, for Adventists, higher education. Suddenly everything was different. That comfortable little world of "the way we were" all too quickly became that world of "the way we are."

The pressures created by the technological revolution have created a profound longing in the hearts of many Adventists, particularly those in my age bracket, for those "good old days." I know because I have sometimes experienced the feeling myself. Some are even attempting to turn the clock back to that more secure period when we all knew who we were and why we were here.

I read another book during the past couple of weeks that epitomizes this longing. It is a Jeremiad entitled *Creeping Compromise*.[2] Some of you may have read it. I understand fully, out of my own past, what the author is trying to say, even though I know that the effort is largely misplaced. Had he begun the book with a clear presentation of the "Good News," and put his concerns in that frame of reference, he would not have had as much to say but he would have said it better. He also would have been able to eliminate the weak defense against the charges of legalism that he tacked on at the end.

---

[2]Joe Crews, *Creeping Compromise* (Rocklin, CA: Amazing Facts, 1990).

Unfortunately, the effort is misplaced because it really can't be done. There is no going back to "the way we were." In the words of Thomas Wolfe, "You can't go home again."[3] We really can't. We shall have to come to grips with the way things are and plan for the road ahead.

---

[3]Thomas Wolfe, *You Can't Go Home Again* (New York: Harper and Row, 1940).

26
The Way We Are

As my family's history attests, Seventh-day Adventism changed much between its official organization as a denomination in 1863 and my birth in 1920. I sensed this anew as I took another look at a sermon my great-grandfather preached in an Adventist church in 1890. It was his last sermon. My aunt had saved it for me. What he said and how he said it seemed strange and far away to me at this time in my life; however, they did not seem as strange to me in my early years. Obviously, I have changed.

I have the same feeling now when I read the early publications of the church: *Review and Herald,* the early *Present Truth,* even the *Early Writings* of Ellen White. The early changes were apparently gradual, mainly changes of style rather than substance, which probably represented literary and intellectual maturation on the part of the writers. Writers improve with practice, as do persons in other disciplines, and writing styles change.

There were watersheds of theological change, such as that following the Minneapolis General Conference in 1888, which we remember today for its discussion of Righteousness by Faith. My great-grandfather apparently was too old to catch the new wave. He was still thinking of the Three Angel's Messages in terms of the "wrath of God" and "the Cup of His indignation" while Ellen White was speaking of Righteousness by Faith as the Third Angel's Message "in verity."

The difference between that earlier gradualism and what has taken place during the last half of this century is due largely to the revolution in technology, mainly in communications and transportation, based on an improved management of information. Social and conceptual ghettos are no longer possible. A former generation could protect its children form Hollywood's dangerous influence by warning them against going to places where their guardian angels would leave them at the door. This caution has a different ring when television brings Hollywood into the living room or den. If you refuse to invest in a television set, can you lock your children up so they don't visit the neighbors? The Adventist ghetto is gone.

The same can be said for almost all of the other means we once used to isolate our children from the "world." If you keep your child in the Adventist school system all the way from kindergarten through college or professional school, what then? Some will want to go on to graduate school or residency programs. Can you isolate them there too? Our own universities are staffed by teachers who earned their degrees "out there."

The bigger question is whether we should try to isolate our children perpetually? The answer is that we can't, but, even if we could, we shouldn't. We must face it. The world has changed, we have changed along with it, and it was inevitable.

Not that change is necessarily a bad thing. Indeed, change is the order of things. That's the way God made them. Throughout God's creation, from the minutest atom to the most distant quasar, everything is in motion. Loosely paraphrasing Heraclitus, "The only thing that does not change is change itself."

Heraclitus was wrong. There is something else that does not change in God's universe and this makes it a universe. Total change would be chaos. What does not change is the character of God.

He is dynamic and active, as the Bible clearly attests, but He never steps out of character. His character, always loving, always gracious, ever consistent and dependable, provides the continuity and order that prevents motion and change from being other words for chaos.

Orderly change, which is what growth is all about, has always been an Adventist ideal. When we spoke of "The Truth" we called it "Present Truth." In the words of Ellen White, "The word of God presents special truths for every age.... God is leading our His people step by step. Truth is progressive."[1] What she meant by this, of course, is that our perception of truth is progressive." This, too, is by her:

> Whenever the people of God are growing in grace, they will be constantly obtaining a clearer understanding of His word. They will discern new light and beauty in its sacred truths. This has been true in the history of the church in all ages, and thus it will continue to the end. [Note the expression "the church in all ages," as it forms an important base for what we shall be saying later.] But as real spiritual life declines, it has ever been the tendency to cease to advance in the knowledge of the truth. Men rest satisfied with the light already received from God's word, and discourage any further investigation of the Scriptures. They become conservative and seek to avoid discussion.[2]

Ellen White once wrote of a "superficial conservative class whose influence has retarded the work," who will one day take "their stand with its avowed enemies."[3]

Even in eternity, the process will continue. Ellen White wrote

---

[1]Francis D. Nichol, *The Seventh-Day Adventist Bible Commentary; the Holy Bible with Exegetical and Expository Comment*, vol. 2 (Washington: Review and Herald Pub. Association, 1953), 1000.

[2]Ellen G. White, *Counsels to Writers and Editors; a Grouping of Messages of Counsel Addressed to Writers and Editors* (Nashville: Southern Publishing Association, 1946), 38-39.

[3]Ellen G. White, *Testimonies for the Church*, vol. 5 (Mountain View, CA: Pacific Press, 1948), 463.

of "new heights to surmount, new truths to comprehend." She said that, "The years of eternity, as they roll will bring richer and still more glorious revelations of God and of Christ. As knowledge is progressive, so will love, reverence, and happiness increase. The more men learn of God, the greater will be their admiration of His character."[4]

When they are true to their roots, Adventists are committed to change. It is a commitment to orderly change, to growth and not chaos. The very name "Adventist" implies this. The word suggests expectance, anticipation. Adventists are those who expect something new, who look forward to the coming of the Lord. There is a way of life in that anticipation, an eternal way of life. This life is an expectant school for the future.

Because change is the nature of things, ordinarily we handle it rather well by adapting to it and synthesizing the past with the present and future in an unbroken stream of identity. But there can be times when change is so rapid and so total that we are overwhelmed by it. The world is in such a time now. This is the reason for the almost universal crisis of identity mankind is now experiencing. No segment of society can totally escape what happens to the larger whole of which it is a part, not even a church with a history of isolation from the "world."

Social movements have a history that is somewhat analogous to the life history of individual persons. It begins with the innocence of childhood with its exuberance, enthusiasm, and limited horizons of experience. The world is the family, the neighborhood and the people in it, the children with whom we play and attend school, and their values. This is followed by a time of rapid change and identity crisis. This is adolescence with all of its confusing new feelings and relationships, its rapidly expanding world of experience, its uncertainty about the self. We are caught between the comforting familiarity of childhood and the demands of adulthood, often feeling pulled in both directions, oscillating between them, no longer the child, and yet not quite the man. Finally there

---

[4]Ellen G. White, *The Great Controversy* (Mountain View, CA: Pacific Press, 1950) 678.

are the stages of adulthood: young-adult, middle-age, old-age, and senescence.

Adventism is experiencing something analogous to the discomfort and anxiety of adolescence in many ways. This is not intended to be a disparaging remark. Adolescence, despite its uncertainties, is an exciting time to be alive because it is filled with hope. This is about the only time in life when we don't know too much about the challenges of life to dream. Perhaps in no other time in life does what happens make so much difference. So many roads stretch out ahead, there are so many choices to make and so many changes that can still be made. Wouldn't we all rather be adolescents than old? It is also a troublesome, even painful, time; however, at no other time can we make choices that are so pivotal for the future.

There are some obvious differences, like size. There just are many more of us now. We are also no longer a North American church. We are truly a world church with only a small percentage of us living in North America. The centers of power, largely for reasons of money, still reside here, but that's changing rapidly. The traditional American hold on administrative power is increasingly tenuous. Sooner or later someone from a different culture, probably from the Third World, is going to garner enough votes to assume general leadership of the Church. This change has made us a multinational, multi-cultural church.

We are also more affluent. Not all of us have shared individually in the upward socioeconomic mobility brought about by our fathers' work ethic and our emphasis upon professional education; there are a few Adventist millionaires around – not many, but a few – and the whole church has benefited in economic ways. There are many middle and upper middle class Adventists, especially in North America. Even in economically deprived parts of the world, Adventists are likely to be better off than their compatriots.

The institutional benefits gained from this increased wealth are obvious. Adventist health care, and all that it represents, for example, is the envy of other denominations. On the other hand, wealth has also brought its share of tensions. Let's face it, the rich do not live the same as the poor. There are those who will say that the rich have less reason to dream about mansions in heaven. Whether or not that is true, they surely have opportunities open to them here and now that are denied to others. I suppose it will always be an open question as to whether it is worse to have an unseemly amount of possessions or to envy those who do.

Closely associated with affluence is another change that probably has been more fateful for the future of Adventism than anything else. This has to do with education. Adventism's emphasis on education, stimulated by Ellen White and motivated by our mildly paranoid minority need to excel, has paid off well, with us having a disproportionate number of higher degrees when compared with the national average.

There is no overestimating the importance of this development for several reasons. Not the least of these is that things do not look the same to one after one has come to know "those people," read "those books" and come to grips with "those great ideas." You can never go back to the way things were.

One of the major consequences of this is a loss of a sense that God is our private property. In other words, terms like "Remnant," "People of God," "True Church," and having a kind of corner on "The Truth," can never again have quite the same ring. There are too many marvelous Christian people out there who do not belong to my church for me to continue to believe what some of my spiritual ancestors believed about the superiority of Adventist Church. And that discovery must surely be a plus.

Unfortunately, it can also be a minus. The educational process has not been even across the whole church body, creating problems in internal understanding. We no longer all speak the same language. If that discovery also means that being an Adventist doesn't make a difference to too many Adventists, the Adventist Church as a power in the world does not have much of a future.

Adventism isn't going to simply disappear. We are too well organized and institutionalized for that. Elder Reuben Figuhr, who was once our General Conference President, used to say, "The machinery runs good." And indeed it does. The Adventist Church could perpetuate itself merely by its own inertia.

But it could fade into the woodwork as just another denomination with no real justification for its separate existence. At that point Adventism will have lost one of its major points of identity. My great grandfather differed from Ellen White after 1888 somewhat in emphasis, but they were united, and all Adventists were united, in the conviction that being an Adventist made a difference! This movement represented a "called" people with a special message for a special time in earth's history. And that belief united and motivated the entire Church. This is one of the convictions, I submit, that is slipping through our fingers today, resulting in a fairly widespread confusion of Adventist identity.

Adventists have always known that God's true church is bigger than any particular institution, even one with a label such as Seventh-day Adventist. How else is one to interpret the following: "From the beginning, faithful souls have borne a faithful testimony to the generation in which they lived . . . God brought these witnesses into covenant relation with Himself, uniting the church on earth with the church in heaven."[5] "The church of God below is one with the church of God above. Believers on the earth and beings in heaven who have never fallen constitute one church."[6]

The theologians of the past called this the "Church Invisible," invisible to us, that is, not invisible to God. The Church Invisible is made up of individuals who, in whatever age, were faithful to the light they had. They are the "honest in heart." They are characterized not by their labels but by their integrity as God counts integrity. When we finally enter the Kingdom of Heaven, where the invisible becomes visible, we shall be astonished by the variety of labels that the true church of God formerly wore.

The theologians also spoke of the "Church Visible." These were those who consciously wore the label institutionally and were thought by others to be members of God's church though in actual fact they might or might not also be members of the "Church

[5]Ellen G. White, *The Acts of the Apostles* (Mountain View, CA: Pacific Press, 1911), 11.

[6]Ellen G. White, *Testimonies for the Church*, vol. 6 (Mountain View, CA: Pacific Press, 1948), 366.

Invisible." The category seems to be what we would speak of as Christendom.

There is a third category that I have chosen to call a "prophetic movement." I have selected the word "movement" over "church" to suggest an entity less institutionalized than a church tends to be. The word "prophetic" is used in the sense in which Isaiah or Jeremiah were called to take messages to God's people Israel. They did not become "His people" by being called. They were prophets to "His people." Their primary reason for their existence was to convey the messages that God had for His people.

Sometimes groups or even a whole people have functioned as a "collective prophet." Israel was called to be such a people for the whole world. "A kingdom of priests and a holy nation." The book of Jonah clearly tells us of the universal fatherhood of God. God loves the whole world. A people may be called to speak for Him to the people He loves. Such is a "prophetic movement." It is my conviction that Adventists were called to be such a movement.

Notice what such a notion can do for our sense of identity. It preserves the sense of vocation, of calling, so crucial to the past and continued vitality of our movement. We were called to give a message to the world God loves. While it does this, it also eliminates the arrogance that goes with the claim to be the people of God, as though He belonged to our church. It also shifts our sense of identity from institutional labels, always a shaky foundation on which to build a sense of self, to discovering our identity in our message. It is the message we carry that gives us a reason for being, not our institutional structures.

The road ahead will become clear and certain for us Adventists only to the extent that we can discover why we are here. Why we are here, on the terms which I have outlined, has to do with the message which we have been called to carry, in all of the different ways that we have been called, individually and institutionally, to carry it.

27
The Road Ahead

As a Seventh-day Adventist who comes from a family that has been active in this movement for generations, I have reflected out loud about "The Way We Were" and "The Way We Are." In the second of these, I commented on the identity confusion in the Church as a part of the larger confusion brought about by too-rapid change. The changes in Adventism have included an increase in numbers, affluence, higher education, loss of defenses against the "world," and the painful discovery that God is not our "private property." Add the diminished confidence in Church leadership, the reduction of Ellen White's authority, and the theological confusion experienced by many and the summation is a denominational existential crisis.

I am sure that the World Council would welcome us with open arms if we want to enter into the general ecumenical spirit of things. The other pastors in our localities with whom we have been establishing good relations at ministerial association meetings will be glad to have us quit trying to steal their sheep. Becoming fully involved in the ecumenical movement would be a little difficult in some respects, mainly because of our different day of worship; however, this shouldn't be too big a deterrence.

If we Adventists slip back into the denominational woodwork as one more facet of the larger "Church Visible," we will have lost something essential. My preacher great-grandfather never did catch on to what Ellen White was promulgating after the Minneapolis General Conference in 1888; however, they agreed that this movement was a "called people," something special, and this united them, and it united the whole church, even as they argued.

As I suggested earlier, one way to describe this sense of specialness is to speak of Adventism as a "prophetic movement." The prophets of old, even a prophetic people, Israel, were called not because God plays favorites, or because they were necessarily superior to everyone else, but because they were in the right place at the right time to be used by God to say something to His larger people. A prophetic movement, such as ours, gains its reason for being from its message. God has something important to say to the world before the end of time and He has called a people to say it.

It should be obvious from this that the continued viability of the Adventist Church depends on it being clear about what it has to say. Its future depends upon this. Our present task, then, is not to roll back the curtains on the road ahead, for which I have no talent in any case, but to examine the present as it determines tomorrow. How we perceive the task of this movement will deeply condition how well we carry it out. We seek those qualities of Adventist teaching that are unique, that are the special Adventist contribution to Christian thought and practice. What are they?

I recently spoke in a little church on the Olympic Peninsula in the state of Washington. As I was waiting for my part on the program, I looked over the church bulletin. As is the case in many Adventist church bulletins, the back page listed our major beliefs. As I read them one by one, it occurred to me that there wasn't a single one that clearly sets us apart from everybody else. Although they might express it in other words and metaphors, conservative Christians everywhere would say "amen" to virtually everything on that list. They would perceive even our hallowed notions of the "Heavenly Sanctuary and Investigative Judgment," when stripped to their essentials, as just other ways of synthesizing the "process" and "crisis" elements in Christian theology.

I thought to myself, "Given this list, why are we here?" Should we not be candid about it and work to break down the institutional barriers that fragment the Christian Church as a whole? Is there really any justification for all of this wasteful duplication of effort and bickering?

This observation is disturbing many Adventists. "The other churches are stealing our best lines," they say. "Stealing" them? I don't know. But they are surely "speaking" them. What remains for the prophetic movement to do?

Actually, this should be a cause for rejoicing. Unless, he is working for his own or an institution's goals rather than God's goals, the primary function of a prophet is to work himself out of a job. As John the Baptist said, "He must increase and I must decrease."

Perhaps we are looking for the wrong thing. If what we said about the Adventist commitment to "present truth" is correct, our ideas may come not by innovation but by gradual progression. On such terms, ideas are never immaculately conceived. They always have a past that continues to linger with them. The fact is that all of our Adventist teachings have roots in what others have said before us.

According to a book by Howard Snyder, titled *The Radical Wesley,* some say that the founder of Methodism,

> Never had an original idea in his life. He just borrowed from others. Even if true, this would hardly solve the riddle of Wesley. His genius and originality lay precisely in his borrowing, adapting and combining diverse elements into a synthesis more dynamic than the sum of its parts.[1]

Besides being an apt description of the work of Ellen White,

---

[1]Howard A. Snyder, *The Radical Wesley and Patterns for Church Renewal* (Downer's Grove, IL: Intervarsity Press, 1980), 143.

who had deep Wesleyan roots, this is as good a definition of a movement with a commitment to progressive truth that I know of. Our movement's Truth is not based on its novelty but upon the way it brings together in a powerful synthesis of ideas the wisdom and insights of the ages.

This synthesis is the Three Angel's message of Revelation 14. God, who has over the centuries been gradually unfolding the truth about Himself, His Kingdom, and the nature of evil, finally brings it all together just before the return of Jesus Christ to this world. This is a disclosure that both vindicates God and brings the world into final judgment.

I would like to illustrate how this synthesis works in a few cases and suggest that you continue to push what I'm saying still further. The *synthesis* is the Adventist message, not the individual doctrines, almost all of which we share with others.

Let us begin with a couple of general observations. First, Ellen White in several places says that though there are Three Angels, their messages should be treated as one. Second, according to her, this message is essentially the Gospel, Righteousness by Faith, "in verity." This latter observation leads to the third. The message has a positive and a negative aspect and the essential message is in the positive. The "smoke of their torment" and "the wine of the wrath of God" portions describe what happens to those who reject so great a salvation. The essence of the message, then, is in the proclamation of the first angel.

The call to Worship the Creator of everything that is, "the heavens, the earth, the sea and the springs of water," is central to the whole. If there is any concept where Adventists will always be at the growing edge of truth, it will be the notion of God as Creator. At least this is so as long as they remember to keep the Sabbath. Worshipping the Creator comes as close to being a unique feature of this prophetic witness as anything can be. The Sabbath will always be a symbolic reinforcement to such worship and this provides a definite doctrinal advantage.

Several additional truths flow from this radically monotheistic statement, truths that shine with peculiar luster in the Adventist treasure house of belief. It is the basis for a wholistic understanding of reality.

This wholistic monotheism is in sharp contrast to that ancient two or three story universe where God operates in the realm of the "spiritual" or "supernatural," while the "natural" pretty well runs itself.

In this wholistic view of things, God is at work in the natural order as well as in the supernatural and thus there is no real gulf between them. Nature's laws are God's laws. One is called to obedience to these laws as one is called to obedience to moral law. If one worships the Creator, one must respect the creation, and especially man, who was the consummation of God's creative activity.

Think of the power that this notion brings to concern for physical, mental, and spiritual health. Those who worship the Creator will always have a higher level of health consciousness than others who do not. This extends also to the creation around us.

Worship of the Creator also stimulates respect and nurture for the living environment. It is God's sky; these are God's streams and lakes; it is God's soil. Adventists haven't done nearly as well on this score as their teaching demands.

Those who worship the Creator come to perceive the Creator's holiness pervading the whole of existence. Observe this in the following:

> God desires that His workers in every line shall look to Him as the giver of all they possess. All right inventions and improvements have their source in Him who is wonderful in counsel and excellent in working. The skillful touch of the physician's hand, his power over nerve and muscle, his knowledge of the delicate organism of the body, is the wisdom of divine power to be used in behalf of the suffering. The skill with which the carpenter uses the hammer, the strength with which the blacksmith makes the anvil ring, comes from God. He has entrusted men with talents, and He expects them to look to Him for counsel. Whatever we do, in whatever department of the work we are placed,

> He desires to control our minds, that we may do perfect work. Religion and business are not two separate things; they are one . . . Divine and human agencies are to combine in temporal as well as in spiritual achievements. They are to be united in all human pursuits, in mechanical and agricultural labors, in mercantile and scientific enterprises.[2]

To those who worship the Creator, all of man's vocations, providing that they are in harmony with the Creator's intentions, are sacred. The laboratory is as holy as the chancel, the market place as holy as sanctuary, and there is holiness in housework, being a mother, or the construction of a fine piece of furniture or a home. There are no intrinsically sacred or profane professions. There are only sacred or profane people in them. There are, of course, callings and places and times and people set apart to remind us of that fact.

A wholistic conception of reality is also reflected in the way that man is understood as a microcosm of that larger whole. Man is a multidimensional unity. There is no separation of mind, or spirit and body. In death his spirit has no independent existence from the body. He sleeps until the resurrection when as a whole being he is restored to life. Meanwhile he exists only in the memory of God.

Let's take another example. If one combines the doctrine of Creation with the Gospel, what does that give us? First and foremost, it confirms the Pauline statement that man becomes a "new creature." The Gospel message of freedom from guilt and condemnation is a reality based not on clever transactions with the devil or legal legerdemain designed to outwit the law in pursuit of the satisfaction of justice, as in those old atonement theories. It depends upon a creative act of God. There is no other basis for our freedom from sin.

God has to preserve His moral universe by demonstrating that He did not commit the injustice of imposing forgiveness on unrepentant hearts. He also has to provide the assurance, without which we are unable to accept that freedom. But we are free simply because He says so. "He spoke and it was so." God can so speak

[2]Ellen G. White, *Christ's Object Lessons* (Mt. View, CA: Pacific Press, 1900), 349.

because He is the Creator. God can and will forgive sins! This is the Good News.

One of the elements of this synthesis that interests me as an ethicist is how it bases ethics on Creation. This means that the ethical rules are not mere accidents of social history. Nor are they arbitrary impositions. They are based on the nature of things as they came from the hand of the Creator. The commandments are descriptive of the way things were made. Obedience, then, is a question of self-interest and self-fulfillment; that is, of the self God intended. Violation of the ethical rules is not just an offense against God; it is a violation of one's own being.

This notion is most helpful when we are dealing with some of the bioethical issues that the newer technology thrusts upon us, such as genetic engineering, in vitro fertilization, embryo transfer, artificial insemination, and surrogate parenting.

Some of these have no precedents in the history of morals. But Creation has a "history." For example, the principle of living in harmony with the Creator's intentions can be useful when we are considering the reproductive family, providing one can discover what these intentions are. Those who are persistent can usually discern them from revealed sources.

A synthesis of the gospel, worship, obedience, and faith provides an interesting counter to the legalism that has always been near the surface in Adventism. The Good News is that our burden of guilt and self-loathing for past failure has been taken away forever. This should result in enormous relief, if we but have the faith to believe it.

Worship is an appropriate response to this Good News. The highest expression of worship is obedience. Our obedience is the thank offering we place on the altar of God's grace. It is our way of celebrating the New Creation, just as the Sabbath was in the Genesis story. Seventh-day Adventists should understand this like no one else.

I'm afraid that most Adventists have little understanding of appreciation for the great treasure that has been placed in their hands. Many have been become preoccupied, even resentful, as they have contemplated the church, which is the "earthen vessel" in which the treasure is contained, and they have undervalued their divinely given privilege. Yet a religious human institution is not too different from all other human institutions. They are all led by human beings just like you and me, no better, no worse.

We can deal with the questions and uncertainties that the road ahead forces upon us only with a new emphasis on the "treasure" rather than the earthen "container" that it is in. This can make the difference. It is the reason for our being.

After the Revolutionary War had been won, the founders of our nation met in the First Constitutional Convention to decide whether the thirteen colonies which had fought for freedom shoulder to shoulder would separate or become the United States of America. The verbal battle waged long and hard. Some days it went one way and some days the other. Finally the Union was assured.

Benjamin Franklin, who was something of an elder statesman by then, said when the battle was over. "Gentlemen, for the past several days I have been looking at the back of that chair over there." It was a high-backed wooden chair with a carving on the back of it depicting the sun hovering over the horizon. "I have been trying to decide," he went on, "whether that sun is rising or setting. Today, with this good news, I have decided that it is rising." A movement in a crisis of identity would do well to look to its treasure. Only then will the sun rise for sure on the road ahead.

Index